The New History of Cumnock

The Ne

Contents

Illustrations

Cumnock from the South (based on engraving dated 1861) *Title page*
Cumnock Square, projected reconstruction

LINE DIAGRAMS
(Devised by author, drawn by Thomas Kirkwood, D.A.)

PLATES

Foreword

It was a happy decision by the Council when they agreed to sponsor a new History of Cumnock to mark the centenary of the town becoming a police burgh. We were fortunate in being able to engage a writer of the quality and experience of Dr. John Strawhorn, author of several works on Ayrshire history and Principal Teacher of History at Cumnock Academy.

After two years' intensive research Dr. Strawhorn has produced a book that combines at once the broad sweep of our long history with the local minutiae proper to such a work. Within its pages the bare bones of historical fact are cleverly clothed with a fine web of authentic anecdotes, traditional tales and apposite quotations from local writers. To me the most absorbing part of the whole book is that dealing with the last hundred years—its triumphs and tribulations, its clashes and concords; the influence of Keir Hardie; the advent of that stormy petrel Emrys Hughes; the post-war developments, with the engaging of the eminent architect Professor Sir Robert H. Matthew; industrial growth, the plans and hopes for the future.

I commend this book to all who are interested in the story of a town's struggle for growth, for expansion, for industry, for a better way of life. It should appeal most strongly to those, both at home and abroad, whose roots are in this area. For the exile it will be like a vision of home, not only evoking nostalgic memories, but also giving an up-to-date picture of Cumnock of 1966. For us, at home, it is a timely reminder of the strenuous efforts of our forefathers. They set the course and weathered the early storms. To-day the wind is fair and a bright and prosperous future is in sight.

Provost THOMAS FINN, M.A.
Cumnock, December 1966

Chapter 1

The Background

Cumnock is a community of over eleven thousand people, half of them living within the bounds of Cumnock burgh, the others in Logan, Netherthird, Craigens, and elsewhere in the landward part of Old Cumnock parish. Cumnock's modern history started just one hundred years ago when it was established as a police burgh and it is now one of Scotland's 175 small burghs. Before that Cumnock was a burgh in barony, created by royal charter in 1509. Even earlier, Cumnock was the site of a parish kirk, the centre of a wide area now Old and New Cumnock Parishes. When human settlement was first made here is not known. The name itself bears witness to an early origin. It would seem to be of Gaelic derivation, though opinion varies whether Cumnock means the hollow in the hills, the sloping hill, the meeting of the waters—or something quite different.

Cumnock is certainly situated in a hollow of the hills of eastern Ayrshire, where the moors slope down, and the Glaisnock Water meets the Lugar. The enlarged river finds its westerly way by Ochiltree and joins the parent River Ayr near Mauchline, and thence flows onwards into the Firth of Clyde at Ayr, sixteen miles due west of Cumnock. Cumnock's situation has contributed to its growth. From early times traffic has come from Ayr and the west through Cumnock to the Muirkirk gap and on towards Edinburgh in the east. Other travellers from the north have found their way via Cumnock towards Nithsdale and the south. At the junction of the Glaisnock and the Lugar, where these two routes met, Cumnock grew up.

The centre of modern Cumnock is on that little plateau between the Lugar and the Glaisnock. It is sheltered by high land which sweeps round from north and east to the south. The Glaisnock Water comes down from the south through a little valley, but from the north east the Lugar has had to cut a twisting way for itself through a deep gorge.

The way the land lies dates back many thousands of years before there was life. Here on the bed of shallow warm seas were laid down layers of limestone and sandstone. Here in conditions of tropical swamp were formed the extensive beds of coal which were to be exploited so long after. Here earth movements pushed up the hills and twisted the strata, with innumerable cracks creating valleys above ground level and breaking up the seams by faults underground. Long ages after, during the Ice Ages, the surface was planed by glaciers, rock was crushed into boulder clay and was brought down from the high lands to provide a covering of soil.

As the glaciers melted the streams began to flow over their present courses. Grasses and plants and trees began to move north and seed themselves on the rich boulder clay until the land was covered with forest. So, some six thousand years ago, the first human visitors came to a prehistoric Ayrshire that must have resembled in climate and landscape the Alaska of today.

EARLY TIMES

These first explorers were Mesolithic people, primitive fur-clad food gatherers. Shell mounds and flint relics found near the shore at Ballantrae, Shewalton and Ardeer bear witness to their presence. Some may have found their way into the forests of the interior. Over a period of two thousand years impoverished little family groups may from time to time have passed this way, searching for nuts, berries, and game. But if so, no traces have survived.

Sometime before 2000 B.C., Neolithic peoples moved up the west coast and some established themselves on the open uplands, to hunt and herd animals. Half a dozen sites in west Ayrshire and miscellaneous stone axe finds throughout the area confirm that a few small settlements were being made. Some centuries later, perhaps about 1800 B.C., came the first to colonise the Cumnock area. The coming of three waves of Bronze Age immigrants can be traced by archaeologists in the great and

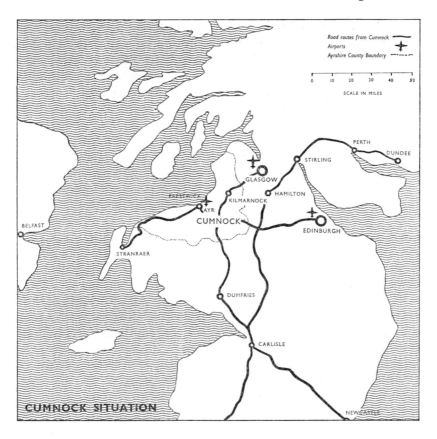

Road routes from Cumnock
Airports
Ayrshire County Boundary

SCALE IN MILES
0   10   20   30   40   50

PERTH
DUNDEE
STIRLING
GLASGOW
PRESTWICK
KILMARNOCK
HAMILTON
AYR
CUMNOCK
EDINBURGH
BELFAST
STRANRAER
DUMFRIES
CARLISLE
NEWCASTLE

CUMNOCK SITUATION

varied collection of relics of these people—pottery, bronze and stone implements and weapons, and burial sites. Bronze Age burial urns have been found throughout the district, in the neighbouring parishes of Ochiltree, Sorn, Auchinleck, Muirkirk, and New Cumnock, and at Boreland farm in Old Cumnock parish. At Wellwood near Muirkirk the remains of two Early Bronze Age huts have been discovered. At Wallacetown in Auchinleck parish, near the junction of the Bello and Glenmuir waters, standing stones from this period indicate that a highly organised social system with religious rites had been established.

This sparse population, living in open spaces in the forest, herding cattle and cultivating small patches of land, was brought under the control of a warrior aristocracy by a series of Iron Age invasions in the last few centuries before Christ. When the Romans came to north Britain they found the people between the Solway and the Clyde belonging to a tribe they called the Damnonii.

Two expeditions by the Romans, about A.D. 81 and again in A.D., 142 brought the southern part of Caledonia under temporary military occupation. Great forts like that near Loudoun Hill were established as garrison points. It is guessed that legionary forces marched up Nithsdale and may well have constructed a military road crossing the Lugar near Cumnock on their way north. But despite claims, for example, that there was a Roman camp at Avisyard, no definite traces of the Romans have as yet been substantiated in the area.

The first thousand years of the Christian era in north Britain is a Dark Age. We know it was an era of conflict. All over Ayrshire there are remains of Iron Age fortified hill forts. At Lochlea near Tarbolton there was a crannog—a lake dwelling sited for protection in time of stress. There must have been rivalry among local Celtic British groups as well as fighting with new waves of incomers—the Scots coming from Ireland, the Anglo-Saxon English from the south and east, and latterly the Viking raids on the coasts. In 681, it is said, invading Scots were defeated at Mauchline; and in 702 others were defeated at Coilsfield by Coilus, a British king. In 750 Eadbert of the English kingdom of Northumbria came up Nithsdale and seized Kyle.

There was however peaceful progress. During the Bronze and Iron Ages were established the farm settlements which continue in the upland areas, still bearing their old Celtic names, like Changue, Horsecleugh, Taiglim, Auchengibbert, Garleffan, Clockclownie. Anglo-Saxon immigrants bringing with them improved ploughs and superior implements began clearing the forests and cultivating the lowlands. The farms they created bore Anglo-Saxon names like Longhouse, Ryderston, Boylston, Thomarston, Skerrington, Boreland. The augmented population was governed by kings who ruled over little areas, like Coilus who defeated the Scots and is by tradition regarded as the original Old King Cole, and whose kingdom became known as Kyle. Many small kingdoms were united into a greater one, and the whole of the south west became part of the Kingdom of Strathclyde, with its capital at Dunbarton.

Christianity came to this part of the world when Ninian set up his church at Whithorn in Galloway in 397. A century later Mungo was preaching in the Glasgow area. One of his disciples was Conval, the son of an Irish prince, who was teaching on Clydeside at the end of the sixth and the beginning of the seventh centuries, and by tradition brought the message of Christ to the Cumnock area and upper Nithsdale.

By A.D. 1000 the area was settled by a mixture of people, finding subsistence from cultivation and cattle on the upper slopes and in forest clearings. The population was small, but they maintained a tribal aristocracy who enjoyed considerable wealth, and there were signs that civilisation was advancing.

THE MIDDLE AGES

In 1034 Duncan, king of Strathclyde, became the first ruler of the whole of Scotland. He was overthrown by Macbeth, and it was a long time before royal authority was effective throughout the entire kingdom. The Scottish kings were assisted by Norman warriors and in the twelfth and early thirteenth century we can see royal power being established in south west Scotland. First of all David I took over the area north of the River Irvine, which was made the bailliery of Cuninghame. Then he annexed the area between the Irvine and the Doon and split it into two parts. The northern part was granted to one of his Norman friends whom he had made Steward of Scotland, and this area became Stewart Kyle. The southern part, on the south west frontier of his kingdom, he held in his own hands as King's Kyle. The boundary between the two parts of Kyle was formed by the River Ayr and its tributaries, the Lugar and Glenmuir and Guelt Waters. Finally, William the Lion detached from the semi-independent state of Galloway the area south of the Doon called Carrick, joined it with King's Kyle, Stewart Kyle, and Cuninghame to form the Sheriffdom of Ayr, and established his castle and royal burgh at Ayr in the early years of the thirteenth century.

The Norman friends of the king were granted lands in return for their help, and set up castles as centres from which they controlled their baronies. The original castles were wooden towers built on the top of natural hillocks or great artificial mounds of earth. Cumnock Castle was of this type, established at the Castle, New Cumnock. A similar motte-and-bailey castle was at Boreland farm. The Mote Hill near Cumnock, overlooking the Lugar Water, may have been such a castle or an earlier hill fort.

It is not known to whom the king originally granted the extensive Barony of Cumnock, extending south from the Lugar to the southern boundary of Ayrshire. By the early fourteenth century it was in the hands of the Earls of March, and later in the century it passed to a junior branch of that family—the Dunbars—who held it till the seventeenth century. The old wooden castle of Cumnock was eventually replaced by a more modern stone castle, occupied until the late seventeenth century at least.

Boreland Castle, of which only the site remains, may have been held by a local representative of the baron of Cumnock. About 1400 it came into the possession of a branch of the Hamilton family, and afterwards by marriage to the Montgomeries. The Dunbars must have feued out other parts of their barony, for two separate small estates were formed in the north west on the banks of the Lugar. Leifnoreis is first recorded in 1440 and was held by the Craufuirds who erected a strong stone tower house and held it till the mid-seventeenth century. A mile to the east stood

Terrinzean Castle, earlier known as Craufurdstoun. This too belonged to a branch of the Craufuirds before 1467, when it passed to the Earl of Arran and eventually to the Earl of Loudoun (one of whose titles is Baron Terrinzean). The ruins of Leifnoreis and Terrinzean were excavated by the third Marquess of Bute and the latter partially restored.

The Normans who came in the twelfth century and became a feudal aristocracy brought with them churchmen who established places of worship and transformed the loosely-knit Celtic church into a highly organised ecclesiastical system. Generous grants of land were made to the regular orders. In north Ayrshire the Tyronensians, a reformed Benedictine order, came from Kelso to institute Kilwinning Abbey; to south Ayrshire from Paisley came Cluniac monks to found Crosaguel Abbey; in Kyle a house was set up at Fail of the Red Friars of the Order of the Holy Trinity for the Redemption of Captives; while to Melrose Abbey were granted the wide lands of Mauchline extending through Sorn beyond Muirkirk. At the same time chapels were instituted, those associated with the major baronies developing into parish churches, so that the place of worship built at some unknown date near the meeting of Lugar and Glaisnock came to serve the people throughout the wide parish of Cumnock. A glebe was provided to maintain the parish priest. This was the two merk lands of old extent upon and around which the burgh of Cumnock grew. The patronage of the parish church was in the hands of the baron of Cumnock, and in the fifteenth century this rectory of Cumnock was allocated to Glasgow Cathedral, which provided a vicar and derived revenue from the parish. Also in the parish was a chapel, associated with Boreland Castle, on the land called Chapelhouse.

During the Middle Ages the population was small, depending entirely on the produce of the land. Each farm unit was a group of cottages, each with its kailyard, and with fields nearby which the folk of the ferm toun cultivated together. These fields were unenclosed by fence or dyke and were set in a wide area of rough pasture which extended to the marches of the next ferm toun. The fields grew the staple crop of oats, with some barley, peas and beans. Cattle and sheep were pastured in the care of herds, their number limited by the dearth of hay and lack of winter fodder. Oatmeal formed the basis of the diet, supplemented by a few vegetables, some cheese, and salted meat in the winter. The land also provided wool for clothmaking, hides for leather, wood and peat for fuel, and materials for building. Each tenant farmer produced a subsistence for his family, plus a meagre surplus to pay rent to the feudal landlord, dues to the church, with perhaps a little to buy the few necessities which could not be home-produced. Throughout the middle ages the only places in Ayrshire where trading was conducted were on the coast, the royal burghs of Ayr and Irvine, and the baronial burghs of Prestwick and Newton-upon-Ayr.

For the peasantry life was short and restricted. Only the upper classes were concerned with politics. In the Middle Ages during the Wars of Scottish Independence, Ayrshire became an arena. William Wallace, the younger son of a baron who held lands both in Kyle and Renfrewshire, came into conflict with the English occupying forces. Taking refuge at Auchincruive on the banks of the Ayr, and involved in incidents in the royal burgh, he gathered support, mustered his forces on Mauchline Muir, and set off on his campaign to liberate Scotland. His unsuccessful efforts were continued by Robert Bruce, Earl of Carrick. Coming back from exile and landing at Turnberry in 1306 he began to harry the English; and the castle of Cumnock formed a strategic point in the contest until with success he moved on to the final victory.

Chapter 2

The Origins of Cumnock

In the year 1509 Cumnock's history makes a real beginning with a royal charter establishing a burgh in barony.

Round about 1500 great changes were beginning to affect the whole of western Europe. The voyages of discovery and the crossing of the Atlantic by Columbus in 1492 were followed by an extension of world trade, and a quickening of economic life. Inflation brought difficulties to the feudal landlords, quarrels, feuds, and rivalries. In Scotland as elsewhere the monarchs were seeking to suppress these disorders and enhance royal power and prestige. All this and the spread of new ideas contributed to the undermining of the old Church and the creation of the new Protestant churches of the sixteenth century. It was in these circumstances that the burgh in barony of Cumnock was created.

In Scotland the accession of James IV in 1488 marked the beginning of a new period of royal power and development of commerce. In Ayrshire new burghs were created at Newmilns (1491), Auchinleck (1507), Cumnock (1509), Mauchline (1510), and in the reigns of James's successors at Maybole (1516), Kilmaurs (1527), Saltcoats (1529), Ballantrae (1541), and Kilmarnock (1592). In some cases local barons obtained burgh charters for reasons only of social prestige. There is no evidence, for example, that Thomas Boswell's charter for a burgh at Auchinleck was ever put into operation. But in many cases a burgh charter was followed by the establishment of a market and a community of craftsmen, fulfilling—as in the case of Cumnock—a useful function as a trading centre in an expanding economy.

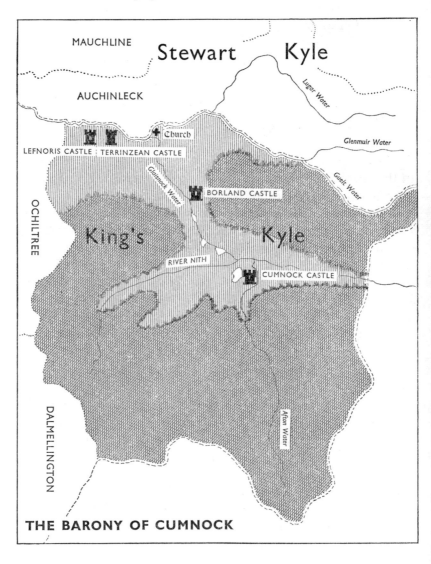

THE BARONY OF CUMNOCK

CHARTER OF JAMES IV
CREATING CUMNOCK AS A BURGH
IN BARONY 1509

James, by the grace of God, King of the Scots, to all honourable persons throughout his realm, both among the clergy and laity, greeting.

Know that for the special favour which we bear towards our beloved James Dunbar of Cumnock, for the growth and good government of the barony of Cumnock, especially in the neighbourhood of the parish church of Cumnock, and also for the well-being and civil freedom of our lieges gathered there, we have made and created, and by this our present charter do make and create, the ecclesiastical lands and glebe of the said church of Cumnock, extending to two merk lands of old extent, with the adjoining grounds in the said barony of Cumnock within the county of Ayr, a free burgh in barony to be called the Burgh of Cumnock in perpetuity.

We have likewise granted to the inhabitants of the said burgh, present and future, full power and absolute right to buy and sell in the said burgh wine, wax, pitch and bitumen, woollen and linen cloth, both broad and narrow, wool, skins, oxhides, salt, butter, cheese, and all other kinds of merchandise, together with power and liberty to possess and keep in the said burgh bakers, braziers, tanners, butchers, sellers of flesh and fish, and all other tradesmen belonging to the liberty of a burgh in barony.

We have also granted that in the said burgh there shall be free burgesses, and that the same shall have power in all future time to elect annually bailies and other officers, needful for the government of the said burgh, and that the said bailies and officers shall be elected with the consent of the baron of Cumnock for the time being, and that no officers shall be elected without the approval of the baron, and that the persons chosen as bailies of the said burgh shall reside within the same.

With power to the burgesses and inhabitants within the said burgh to have and maintain within the same, perpetually, a market cross and a market on the Saturday of each week, as well as an annual public fair on the day of St. Matthew the apostle and evangelist, and for eight days thereafter, with right to uplift dues, along with all other privileges which belong to public fairs or may justly be regarded as belonging to them at any time hereafter;

And with power and liberty to our beloved clergyman, Master Thomas Campbell, canon of Glasgow and prebendary of the said church of Cumnock, and to his successors, to feu the aforesaid glebe lands, in whole or in

*part, in burgh roods for building purposes, in such a way as shall be for
the profit of the said church and its prebendaries, or at least without loss
to the church, provided the consent of the said baron for the time being is
obtained;*

*The lands of the said church to be held and possessed, as is here set
forth, for ever, with all the privileges, liberties, and advantages written
above, together with all other benefits, titles, and rights which pertain to
a free burgh in barony or may justly be regarded as pertaining thereto in
the future, and that as freely as any burgh in barony is given in fief within
our kingdom by ourselves or our predecessors without any impediment or
revocation whatever;*

*Saving, however, and reserving to the said James and his heirs, the
barons of Cumnock, their own liberty and their right to hold a court
within the barony of Cumnock, together with the privilege of blood and
bloodwite in the same court over the inhabitants of the said glebe, to be
enjoyed, used, and exercised by them and their bailies in the future according
to the tenor of their infeofment, ancient usage, and general custom;*

*In testimony whereof we have ordered to be affixed to our present charter
our great seal in the presence of the following witnesses:*

> *Alexander, Archbishop of St. Andrews, Chancellor;*
> *William, Bishop of Aberdeen, Keeper of Privy Seal;*
> *Andrew, Bishop of Caithness, Treasurer;*
> *Archibald, Earl of Argyll;*
> *Matthew, Earl of Lennox;*
> *Andrew, Lord Gray;*
> *Master Gavin Dunbar, Archdeacon of St. Andrews;*
> *Master Patrick Pauntere, Secretary;*
> *Richard Colville of Ochiltree.*

*At Edinburgh, the 27th September 1509,
and the twenty-second of our reign.*

It is clear from the charter that its purpose was to establish at
this convenient centre—marked by a market cross—an opportunity for buying and selling local produce at the small weekly
market, and on a larger scale at the great annual fair to which
merchants might come from far and near. Arrangements were
made for feuing ground so that craftsmen might set themselves
up to practise useful trades and develop small-scale rural manufactures.   The evidence is sufficient to conclude that such a small

community, of perhaps a few dozen families, did in fact grow up around the parish church.

Nowadays when the principal function of a burgh council is to provide and administer various local public services it is important to realise that the purpose of the early elected body was quite different. To organise and operate the markets and fairs was the main duty, and other matters they might deal with relating to the common good were incidental. Again, it is well to understand that while the ' bailies and other officers ' were elected, they were not chosen by all the inhabitants but only by a select few who could afford to be admitted as burgesses. And it is obvious that a close supervision was maintained by James Dunbar and his successors as burgh-superiors. Not only did they retain their rights of justice over the burgh as over all other parts of the barony, but they might exclude undesirable persons from office. Indeed, though this old type of burgh continued till the nineteenth century, Cumnock was in fact being administered by a baron-bailie appointed by the superior.

SIXTEENTH CENTURY—REFORMATION TROUBLES

Cumnock's early years were punctuated by the civil and religious disorders that convulsed sixteenth century Scotland. The failure of the crown to maintain effective continuous government left the local lairds free to engage in the notorious Ayrshire feuds. The old Church, attacked by Protestant critics, became involved in the political conflicts and was overthrown in the Reformation of 1560.

The strong government of James IV came to an end with his death in 1513 at the battle of Flodden. There were killed with him many Ayrshire men, including Robert Colville of Ochiltree, Thomas Boswell of Auchinleck, and Sir David Dunbar of Cumnock. Even before this, trouble had broken out in Ayrshire. In 1512 Patrick Dunbar of Corsincon was murdered when attending mass in Cumnock church. One of his assailants, Andrew Campbell, was taken and hanged, while the others escaped punishment—Duncan Campbell, John Stillie, Robert Campbell of Schankstoune, his brothers George and John Campbell, and

James Campbell of Clewis. Thirteen years later, as part of the great feud between the Kennedys of Carrick on the one hand and the Craufurds and Campbells of Loudoun, in 1526 the Earl of Cassillis was ambushed and killed at Prestwick by a party fourteen hundred strong under Hugh Campbell of Loudoun, Sheriff of Ayr, among whom were Craufurds from Kerse, Drongan, and Leifnoreis. Then signs of the spread of Protestant ideas followed. In 1533 Andrew Stewart of Ochiltree was accused before the Bishop of Glasgow of casting down images in the Kirk of Ayr. In 1544 George Wishart visited Mauchline on a preaching tour. In 1551 Alexander Dunbar of Cumnock was denounced as rebel for assisting one of the assassins of Cardinal Beaton. In 1556 John Knox passed through Ayrshire preaching at Galston, Kinzeancleuch, Carnell, Ochiltree, Gadgirth, and Ayr. Finally in 1559 came the prelude to the Reformation when the Lords of the Congregation marched on Perth, and the Ayrshire contingent of two thousand included Lord Ochiltree and Matthew Campbell of Terrinzean.

In 1560 when the Reformation was carried through, the great abbeys and monasteries were abandoned and the extensive church properties passed into lay hands. It seems certain that many of the old parish churches like Cumnock would survive, their interiors converted to Protestant purposes. In some cases the priests went over to the new church, and took with them their stipends. In Cumnock, however, this seems not to have happened. John Dunbar, parish priest, though prohibited from continuing to celebrate the old rites, retained possession of the glebe and parochial revenues for the rest of his life. Without a stipend to maintain a new protestant minister, Cumnock was served by John Inglis, minister of Ochiltree, till 1572 when John Rynd came as Cumnock's first protestant parish minister.

The establishment of protestantism was accompanied by ambitious proposals for establishing a school in every parish. It took two centuries before this aim was near realisation, but locally before 1642 schools had been established in Mauchline, Ochiltree and Cumnock. The first reference to a school in Cumnock is in 1625, when ' Helen Lockhart, Spouse to Charles Campbell of Glaisnock maid his testament . . . I geve and leif to be wairit and bestowit upone the school of Cumnock, twentie punds money.' The site of Cumnock's first school is unknown but it was certainly somewhere near the parish kirk. We first find it mentioned in presbytery records for 1642 when ' Mr. Andro Bryane, schoolmaster and reader ' complains of non-payment of his stipends by some of the heritors (i.e., landowners). Three years later Bryane was dismissed for unsatisfactory conduct in the school and unseemly behaviour outside. But the school continued. Later in the century the schoolmaster was Hugh Campbell, promoted to Maybole in 1695, but called back several times by the Cumnock Kirk Session to answer for his ' vagrant way of living.' He was succeeded by Mr. William Muir, whose morals were found equally deficient, and by 1703 Cumnock was again without a schoolmaster.

Despite the staffing difficulties, and the problem of persuading some of the landowners to contribute their quota towards the upkeep of the school, there was now opportunity for those parents who cared and could afford it to give their children an education. A rare few might be given sufficient training to prepare them for university in their early teens—the fact that two of the early schoolmasters were designated Mr. signifies that they were graduates. For most there was a simple training in reading, with sometimes practice in writing as well. For all who attended there was careful attention to religious instruction, so that there grew up succeeding generations well acquainted with the Bible, able and many of them anxious to argue points of religious dogma. Each Sunday in the parish kirk they could listen critically to sermons expounded by protestant pastors, John Rynd (1572-1576), George Campbell (1576-1578), William Hamiltoun (1578-1595), George Dunbar (1599-1608), James Cunningham (1608-1644), and John Halkeid (1644-1646).

SEVENTEENTH CENTURY — COVENANTING TROUBLES

Religion had become every man's concern and many common folk were ready to participate in the disputes regarding the organisation of the kirk. Hamiltoun, Dunbar, and Cunningham were staunch presbyterians who resented royal claims to supremacy over the kirk. Cunningham indeed played quite a prominent part in the events leading to the signing of the National Covenant of 1638 and in the subsequent Glasgow Assembly which abolished episcopacy. Presumably some local zealots took part in the battle of Mauchline Muir, 1647, when the extremists defeated those who sought a compromise with King Charles I. One special cause for complaint was that until 1649 and again after 1662 parish ministers were appointed by the chief local landowner, who was not always sympathetic to presbyterian opinion.

In the case of Cumnock the barony changed hands in the early part of the seventeenth century. From the 1570's, the Dunbars had begun to sell off their Cumnock lands, and the barony and patronage of the church passed through several hands. Eventually the family of Crichton of Sanquhar became established as superior of the barony and principal landowners. William, ninth Lord Crichton of Sanquhar, having befriended King James VI and I, was in 1622 created Viscount of Ayr. Eleven years later in 1633 King Charles I elevated him to the peerage with the title of Earl of Dumfries. In 1629 he purchased the lands of Cumnock from Cunynghame of Caprington, acquiring also Glenmuir (1630), Barshare (1631), Leifnoreis (1635), and building up an extensive estate before his death in 1642. His son William, the second Earl, as a privy councillor to Charles II, enjoyed considerable prestige. His son Charles, Lord Crichton, was in 1680 created a lord of regality, and Cumnock as a burgh in barony acquired as a consequence the distinctive title of burgh of regality thenceforth.

The Earls of Dumfries came to dominate the district in succeeding generations. But though they controlled the major part of the parish, in the course of the various land transactions of the seventeenth century several smaller estates remained separate. Glaisnock had been in possession of a branch of the Campbell family since before 1586. Another family of Campbells had held Skerrington since the fourteenth century. Campbells also held Garrallan till 1676 when it passed from Margaret Campbell to her son Hugh Douglas. Logan was acquired and named by a person of that family in the seventeenth century or earlier. Boreland passed in 1673 out of the hands of the Hamiltons when Hugh Hamilton resigned it in favour of his grand-daughter and her husband Hugh Montgomerie. But Terrinzean in 1696 and Schankston after 1700 followed Leifnoreis to become part of the great estate of the Earl of Dumfries.

One further alteration in the local situation occurred in the seventeenth century. Many large parishes were divided into smaller units. So from the great parish of Mauchline in 1631 was detached the Muir Kirk of Kyle, and in 1652 Dalgain or Sorn. In 1653 a corner of Ochiltree parish was cut off to form the new parish of Stair. In 1650 the parish of Cumnock, previously comprising the whole of the Barony of Cumnock, was bisected. In 1667 the Earl of Dumfries had this decision annulled, but in 1691 separation was confirmed and thereafter the two parishes of Old Cumnock and New Cumnock retained their separate identities.

The restoration of Charles II to the throne in 1660 and his reintroduction of episcopacy roused the opposition of those who had subscribed to the Covenants, and plunged the south west of Scotland into a generation of strife and bloodshed. The parish minister of Cumnock, John Cunningham, who had been ordained in 1647, refused to submit to bishops and conform to the new episcopal rule, and from 1662 till his death in 1668 was deprived of his charge. He was superseded by ministers appointed by the Earl of Dumfries, Samuel Nimmo, followed by Francis Fordyce in 1686, who accepted episcopacy, to the disgust of many of their parishioners. In 1662 Patrick Crawford of Cumnock was fined £2,000 Scots and John Campbell of Glaisnock £480 Scots for refusing to accept the new arrangements. In 1666 an insurrection broke out in Dumfries and the rebels came up Nithsdale to be joined at Mauchline by an assembly of Ayrshire Covenanters. Under the command of Colonel James Wallace of Dundonald and Auchans this little army of nine hundred men marched from Mauchline through Ochiltree to Cumnock. On 23rd November ' They broke up from Ochiltree about eleven of the clock in the morning and marched to Cumnock.' Thereafter they 'marched the same night to the Moorkirk in a most violent rainy night.' They continued via Lanark towards Edinburgh, and were scattered by General Thomas Hamilton of Dalziel at Rullion Green. The collapse of this Pentland Rising was followed by repression. Among those local rebels taken were George Crawford, a weaver from Cumnock, executed in Edinburgh on 14th December 1666, and Patrick McNaught, indicted in 1667.

After a period of leniency there was renewed repression. In 1678 all heritors (landowners) were required to take a bond that ' neither they, their wives, bairns, tenants, cottars, and servants . . . shall go to field conventicles, or harbour or commune with rebels.' To enforce this, the Highland Host was brought into Ayrshire and the south west as an army of occupation. Two hundred and fifty Caithness men were quartered for fifteen nights in the parishes of Old and New Cumnock. There followed in 1679 a second rebellion commencing with the rout of John Graham of Claverhouse at Drumclog and concluding disastrously in the defeat at Bothwell Brig. A year later a group of extremists who had evaded capture published the Sanquhar Declaration and commenced a last desperate insurrection. It ended with Richard Cameron and his little party of sixty men being taken at Airdsmoss near Muirkirk.

The severities of the Killing Times followed. John Gemill and James Mirrie, two Cumnock men, were captured at Bothwell Brig. After months of suffering confinement in Greyfriars kirkyard, Edinburgh, they were sentenced to be transported to America. Their prison ship was wrecked off the Orkney coast and Gemill and Mirrie were among the drowned. Rebels were hunted and renewed efforts made to enforce conformity. In 1682 the Earl of Dumfries examined all persons in the parishes of Auchinleck and Cumnock and fined those who had had children baptised by any but the legally-appointed minister. In 1683 a court was held in Cumnock to enforce attendance at church regularly— which meant at least every third Sunday. Groups of armed rebels had to be dispersed. In 1680 Captain Creichton, an Irish kinsman of the Earl of Dumfries with a commission against the rebels, was ambushed at Bello Path. In 1684 Graham of Claverhouse was authorised to scour the country and take arbitrary action against those who would not take the test and renounce rebellion. In the proclamation for the apprehension of outlaws nineteen local names appear—in the parishes of Old and New Cumnock: Mr. John Halbert in Cumnock; James Mitchell, cordiner there; – Crichton in Craigman; Patrick Gemill in the old Castle of Cumnock; William Stillie there; John Reid; Alexander Stillie in Townhead of Cumnock; John Tenant at the old Castle of Cumnock; James Dalziel near the kirk of

Cumnock; John Wood, son to Hugh Wood in Lowis; William Lambie in Polquhays; James Steel, tenant to Carleton; George Gemmil in Minaucht; – Greig there; Robert Murdoch in Knockmarnock; John Mackechan in Auchingibbat; James Wilson at the old castle of Cumnock; William Skilling in Pablow; John Campbell in Townhead of Cumnock. Under other parishes three Cumnock names are included: Robert McGavin in Cumnock; William Campbell in Townhead of Cumnock; and John Weir, tailor in Cumnock.

1685 was the year of killings. In that year Robert Mitchell, a native of Cumnock, was shot at Ingliston. Thomas Richard, eighty-year-old tenant of Greenock Mains farm by Muirkirk, was brought to Cumnock and executed. Two Covenanters from the Borders, David Dun and Simon Paterson, were captured on Corsegellioch Hill, executed in Cumnock, and also buried at the Gallows Hill. A year later the celebrated Covenanting preacher, Rev. Alexander Peden, was buried beside them. Peden, born at Auchencloigh in the parish of Sorn in 1626, studied at university, and served as schoolmaster in Tarbolton before being ordained to the ministry in New Luce, Galloway, in 1660. Two years later he was deprived of his charge and began his career as a field preacher, punctuated by periods of exile in Ireland. A fanatical and enigmatic character credited with gifts of prophecy he enthused his followers, organised incidents like a raid on the Earl of Dumfries's house in 1685, and eluded arrest always. He died peacefully in 1686 at the home of his brother, the farm of Ten-shillingside in the parish of Mauchline. Buried in Auchinleck, his body was exhumed by troopers from the garrison at Sorn Castle and taken to Cumnock to be hanged on the gibbet. This seems to have been averted, but he was buried at the foot of the gallows on Barrhill. Sometime afterwards an inscribed slab was laid over his grave; a plain tombstone was later erected; and in 1892 a granite monument was added; all under the shadow of a tree known as Peden's Thorn.

The last of the local Covenanting martyrs was John McGeachan, a farmer in Meikle Auchingibbert, who lost his life when a group of Covenanters in 1688 organised the rescue of Rev. David Houston. On the evening of 19th June Houston was under custody in the Blue Tower in Cumnock, being taken by dragoons to Edinburgh.

The following day the party was ambushed at Bello Path. Houston escaped, wounded; McGeachan lost his life in the affray.

Late in 1688 relief came unexpectedly with the Glorious Revolution in England, the expulsion of King James and the accession of William and Mary. Presbyterianism in Scotland was recognised. Episcopalian ministers were ' rabbled ' and ejected. In Cumnock a band of ninety armed men forced Rev. Francis Fordyce into the churchyard, tore his gown, and forbade him to preach further. The congregation could now proceed to select a minister of their own choice, and following a unanimous call, Hugh Kilpatrick became parish minister in 1692.

THE TOWN BEFORE 1750

For two and a half centuries after its creation in 1509 we have only occasional glimpses of life in the little market burgh of Cumnock. Of public buildings there was a kirk and a school. Of professional people there were, besides the minister and the schoolmaster, one or two notaries who provided legal and secretarial services. Most of the small community were small merchants and craftsmen—woollen and linen weavers, cordiners (shoemakers) and other workers in leather, and wrights working with wood. Each had his cottage and an adjacent patch of land which augmented his family's living. In the seventeenth century there was at least one inn, the Blue Tower, catering for wayfarers. About 1600 it is related that two travelling merchants who had been denied entrance into Ayr because of the threat of plague came to Cumnock and there sold what was in their packs. There followed such a plague in Cumnock that, it is said, ' the living were hardly able to bury the dead.' Many victims are reported to have been buried at Greenbraehead overlooking the Glaisnock. Records tend to mention the exceptional and ignore the everyday, so that the sole reference to Cumnock market over a long period is in 1606 when ' George and Andrew McCubene, servitors to George Crawfurd in Lefnoreis, complain that while they were attending the market in the town of Cumnock on – October last, Johnne Hervie, of Skellingtoun Mill, and his eldest son George, pursued them for their lives.' The absence of further references suggests that through the difficult times of civil and religious dispute, the ordinary people of Cumnock continued their daily tasks with little alteration in the character of the community.

Some interesting glimpses of old Cumnock occur in the Dumfries House papers. In the late seventeenth and early eighteenth centuries there was a Regality Court which seems to have been responsible not only for the burgh but for the whole estate area. The bailie of the regality was the estate factor, James Riddock, succeeded by John Fergusson sometime between 1707 and 1710. In 1707 there is mention of a town's officer and burgesses of the 'Brough of Cumnock'—but if there was any special burgh organisation, no records have survived. There was never, as far as is known, a tolbooth. After the abolition of the Regality Court and other heritable jurisdictions in 1747 (and until the nineteenth century) the bailie was apparently simply a nominee of the superior.

Some details of the 'toune of Cumnock' can also be found. The Glebe extended to the high road crossing the Lugar at Stepends, with a small patch to the west in what later became the Tanyard. Rev. John Steel found even this considerable area insufficient, and had rented also land to the east—the Bank and Fauld. These fields with 'the Writers Aiker Lying betwixt the ffauld, the Bank, The entry to the moat and alongst the waterside' had with Templands across the 'water of Luggar' been acquired by William Gemmill, notary in Cumnock, and latterly by Sir Thomas Wallace of Craigie. About 1700 coals were being worked at the Bank and Templands. From the latter there was 'no good road but . . . horses with coalls pass that way.' Near the manse beside the water was Sand Bed Miln, occupied by Alexander Duncan till 1692 and thereafter by George McGawn, then his son John McGawn. All persons in the regality of Cumnock were required to bring their corn to this mill, and their barley for malting. Those that brewed for sale 'alwise payed Intouns,' those who brewed for private use paid 'outentouns.' Alexander Duncan, the miller, also possessed Barshare and a piece of land called Waterside. This, later known as Duncan's Holm and Houses, was on the banks of the Lugar west of the Stepends ford, and later part of the Tanyard was built on it. It was owned by Sir Thomas Wallace of Craigie who in 1738 claimed that this and his other lands in Cumnock parish were outwith the authority of the Regality of Cumnock and of Lady Dumfries. About 1690, it was mentioned as evidence, ' There was a plea fell out amongst some Tinkers, and the Magistrate of the Regality of Cumnock sent in search of them and the Tinkers to get off, came about by the back of the Toune to Duncans Houses and the officers finding them there offered them Drink and would have them up to the Toune because the party said they could not attack them there.' But it was agreed that Alexander Duncan, his son who succeeded him, and later still Isobell Moor, had each—though tenants of Wallace—' performed all services to the miln conform to other Brewers in the Toune of Cumnock'; they paid their share for ' keeping the Drum and Clock'; soldiers were quartered upon them ' as upon other Inhabitants of Cumnock'; they had, from time to time, been summoned to the Regality Court of Cumnock; Duncan had been a Birlyman and indeed ' the only ordinary Birlyman to pryze poinded goods brought to the Cross of Cumnock'; and, most telling argument of all, ' The Martinmas fair in Cumnock was alwise keept upon part of the Gleib and Duncan's Holm.'

The inquiry was held in Cumnock in 1738 before Charles Cochran of Ochiltree and John Dick of Glaisnock, with John Hamilton, writer in Cumnock, as clerk. Those called as witnesses were Hugh Logan of Logan, Rev. John Steel, and a group of knowledgeable residents. These included three farmers—John Johnston in Underwood, Robert Dalziel in Dykes, George Richmond in Barlannochan. There were four merchants from Cumnock—Robert Douglas, Alexander Drummond, James Campbell, and Charles Wilson. And two other men from Cumnock were called because of their long local knowledge—John Hunter (aged 86) and John Brown (aged 88).

Perhaps the most interesting sidelight from the evidence are the remarks about the site of Cumnock Fair. It had always been held near the Stepends ford, on the open land belonging to Duncan's Holm, the Glebe, and extending into Charles Wilson's Holm on the east side of the high road. The market cross, however, was not there. The weekly markets may always have been held in the Townhead area. By the middle of the eighteenth century, with the building of the Stepends Bridge, the establishment of the Tanyard, and the erection of a kiln on Charles

Wilson's Holm, it would become necessary to find a new site for the great fairs—at the market cross in the Townhead and later in the Square.

From the Dumfries House papers a miscellaneous collection of leases and other documents provides further material for piecing together a picture of early Cumnock. The parish kirk was surrounded by the kirkyard. The highway or ' common streit' coming from the Stepends ford passed down the 'back vennall' (now Bank Lane) along what became Tower Street, towards the 'Townheid' where the 'high street' led to the 'old croce.' Other thoroughfares were Manse Lane, variously described as ' the causeway that leads from the said burgh to the manse of Cumnock' and ' the highway leading from the church-yard and ministers mans.' It connected with ' the highway that leads from the Barhil to the said burgh.' In the same area (possibly the later Black Bull Close?) must have been ' the passage to the churchyard and cross of Cumnock.' Perhaps coming from the Dubb ford was ' the calsay head that leedeth from the toun end to the Church styll.'

Various properties around the kirkyard and in the Townhead were occupied by merchants. On the south side of the kirkyard were several buildings described as ' merchant shops.' To the east was one called the Craigheid, and this lease is worth quoting as typical, with rent paid partly in money, partly in kind. ' 20th March 1722. To Alexander Johnstoune, eldest son to James Johnstoune merchant in Cumnock, of that tenement of houses etc formerly possessed by the deceased James Stillie, officer in Cumnock, and now by Margaret Limmont, his relict, and by the said James Johnstoune and William Blackwood, his sub-tenant, together with the merchant shop presently possessed by the said Alexander Johnstoune himself, within the town and burgh of Cumnock in that place thereof called the Craigheid, for 21 years for the yearly payment of £21 together with 2 hens in January or February and to the house of Leifnoreis two loads of coal yearly. At Leifnoreis, witnesses John ffergusson bailie of the regality of Cumnock, and James ffergusson writer there.'

All the merchants mentioned in the several documents may be listed, giving for each appropriate dates: Andrew Dalzell (before 1699), Daniel Sutherland (1699, 1703), John Allan (1699),

Alex. Drummond (1701, aged 74 in 1737), William Wilson (1701, 1707), Hugh Wallace (1701, 1720), James Begg (1701, died before 1713), James Campbell (1701, aged 60 in 1737 and 40 years' resident), William Aikin (1703), Robert Douglas (1707, aged 64 in 1737 and 33 years' resident), William Kissock (1712, 1731), his son George Kissock (1712, died before 1720), Andrew Crawford (1731).

There was a group of craftsmen. Weavers mentioned were John Murdoch (1701, 1720), William Hodge (1709), James Rankin (1730), William Murray (1738). Tailors were Hugh Campbell (1699), Robert Todd (1712), David Murdoch (1720), John Martin (before 1731), John Halbertson (1731). John King (1707) and James Kissock (1720) were dysters. Matthew Reid (1699) was a litster, John Hodg (1701) a cooper, George Thomson (1703) a baxter, Robert Tutor (1721) a mason. Shoemaking was carried on by cordiners: Robert Mirrie (1701), Malcolm Nicoll (1704), Robert McGoun (1704, 1709)—the last having a tannpit and lime-pit beside his house on the south side of Townhead. There was a smithy in what is now Lugar Street—George Patersoune and later Gabriel Johnstoune were smiths there (before 1702). There was a Glover's house on the west side of the kirkyard. At the mill was Alexander Duncan (till 1692) followed by George McGawn, then his son John (who was 40 in 1737).

Professional services were supplied by the parish minister; the parish schoolmaster—Hugh Campbell (1701), Robert Trotter (1710); writers and notaries—Robert Lochhead (before 1699), John Fergusson (1699, 1731), his son James Fergusson (1701, 1720), James Hamilton (1730, 1735); George Campbell, apothecary (1704), and James Campbell, chirurgeon-apothecary (1720, died before 1735). There were several officials. James Riddock was bailie (1699, 1707), followed by John Fergusson the writer (1710, 1731). Presumably also involved in the burghal administration were James Stillie (1710) and John Wilson (before 1731), described as officers. Edward Creichton (1701, 1707) and John Crichton (1731) were messengers. The bellman was John Hunter (aged 86 in 1737, resident since 1685). Some of these are familiar local surnames, several presumably kinsmen of persons who played an active part in the religious conflicts of the sixteenth and seventeenth centuries.

Chapter 3

Cumnock begins to grow

The eighteenth century saw the beginnings of an age of rapid and revolutionary progress. The Act of Union in 1707 brought not only the union of the Scots and English Parliaments but new prospects for Scots merchants of trade with England and overseas. The end of the Jacobite rebellions at Culloden in 1746 was followed by conditions of civil peace in which the development of agriculture, manufactures, and trade became possible. Economic progress ensued and with it came social and political advances.

EIGHTEENTH CENTURY LAIRDS

In the eighteenth century the landowners still dominated society. William, third Earl of Dumfries, died unmarried in 1694 and was succeeded by his sister Penelope, Countess in her own right. By her marriage in 1698 to Colonel Hon. William Dalrymple, second son of the first Earl of Stair, the family fortunes were enhanced. Her eldest son William succeeded as fifth Earl of Dumfries in 1742 and as fourth Earl of Stair in 1760. He engaged the Adam brothers as architects and built Dumfries House in the years 1754-60—with James Armour, later Robert Burns's father-in-law, reputedly employed in the work. Earl William began laying out the extensive policies—and Dettingen Wood commemorated the great battle of 1743 in which he fought. He began the work of agricultural improvement, realising the profits to be gained from selling Scots cattle in England and from supplying wool, flax and leather to the merchants who were exporting manufactured goods from the Clyde to America. For enriching the land, he opened up the limestone quarry at Benston, and to provide fuel for lime-burning initiated coal mining at Garlaff in 1767.

Twice married, he died childless in 1768. His cousin succeeded him as fifth Earl of Stair, while the sixth Earl of Dumfries was his nephew Patrick Macdowall.

Also an army officer, the sixth Earl served as a Scots peer in the House of Lords from 1790 till his death in 1803. He continued the improvements on the Dumfries House estate initiated by his uncle, and was actively assisted by his wife, the Countess Margaret. A knowledgeable observer wrote that ' Lady Dumfries is the best assistant that ever blessed a man who delights in improvements. She is the very soul of husbandry and manufactures in that part of the country.' Together they improved the land by liming and draining. The Lugar was widened and its banks raised to prevent flooding. New crops like turnips and potatoes were raised. Grassland was much improved and was in great demand by farmers who wished to increase their herds of cattle. Experiments in sheep breeding were made. By 1793 the parish supported a thousand cattle, a hundred score of sheep, and 220 horses. The landscape was enhanced by the extensive woodlands, the more productive fields, and by the enclosures. It was estimated that in less than thirty years he had planted 40 miles of hedges and made half that length again of stone dykes. The Earl and Countess were both deeply concerned with the prosperity of Cumnock. Lady Dumfries encouraged the weaving of woollens and linen and erected the ' Jeannie House ' in Lugar Street. The Earl continued his uncle's work in exploiting the estate's mineral resources, but his more ambitious proposals were unrealised, and progress was limited. The Earl was superior of the burgh, and through his baron-bailie organised the markets and fairs. Since the reintroduction of patronage in 1712 the Earls of Dumfries had been responsible for the appointment of the parish ministers in both Old and New Cumnock, and indeed they played an active role in the Kirk. Along with the other five heritors and the kirk session he was responsible not only for the kirk and kirkyard, but also for the school and for poor relief. In a wider capacity he served as one of the Commissioners of Supply who since the late seventeenth century had been responsible for land tax and various duties relating to the county as a whole.

The other five heritors were also involved in improving their estates as far as their more restricted resources allowed. Garrallan remained in the hands of the Douglases, the most notable member being Patrick Douglas, one of Robert Burns's associates, who suffered losses in the Ayr Bank crash of 1772. Financial difficulties also affected the Logan estate, which passed eventually into other hands. Glaisnock had been acquired from the Campbells by John Dick before 1730; in 1776 the owner was a Mr. Stevenson; about 1797 it was purchased by Alexander Allason. Skerrington still belonged to the Campbells. Of the smaller estates Avisyard belonged for a time to Rev. Dr. Andrew Mitchell of Muirkirk and later Monkton; Whitehill was acquired about 1760 by James Rankin and continued in that family; Boreland was sold off and broken up in 1751.

One of these heritors was a character long after remembered throughout the county—Hugh Logan, the ' Laird of Logan ' and celebrated wit. His biographer describes him: ' The personal appearance of our Laird was extremely prepossessing. His stature was tall, and his form extremely handsome; while his frank and open countenance was lighted up by eyes, black, full of penetration, and highly expressive of the character we have given of him. In youth his hair was light, but as he advanced in life he became bald, and in his latter years he wore a wig assimilating to the colour of his eyes. His weight varied from eighteen to twenty stones. Though not fastidious about his clothes he was always appropriately dressed, wearing generally a blue or brown coat, with light-coloured shorts, having buckles at the knees. In respect to morals, the conduct of Logan may, by many be regarded in a great measure unexceptionable; and what is perhaps not a little singular, considering his associates and the scenes of dissipation in which he but too frequently mingled, only one instance of an illicit amour has been laid to his charge—the offspring of which is, we believe, at present living in Cumnock and is remarked for the striking resemblance she bears to her distinguished parents.' The laird's hospitality, and the lively share he took in the social round among the Ayrshire gentry made sad inroads upon his fortune and he was forced to sell the greater part of Logan in 1798 and remove to Wellwood where he died in 1802 at the age of sixty-three. His memory survives in numerous anecdotes attributed to him, of which two examples may be quoted.

At a meeting of the Cumnock Heritors, the repair of the wall round the graveyard was being considered. Logan declared it was unnecessary, remarking: ' It's time enough to repair the dykes when the tenants start complaining.' Another time, dining near Ayr with a family called Shaw, new potatoes were on the menu. Asked how they tasted he complained: ' I can hardly tell. There was nae getting at them for the Shaws.'

THE TOWN, 1750-1800

By the middle of the eighteenth century we discover Cumnock as a well-established village of some five hundred people. On Roy's Map is shown a cluster of houses around the kirk and stretching up Townhead, with the four converging roads—from Auchinleck and across the Lugar by a ford at Stepends; from Ayr and Ochiltree past Greenmill and over the Glaisnock by ford; from Muirkirk by Logan and down the Barrhill where the gallows once stood; from New Cumnock past Craigens and Barshare into Townhead.

The second half of the eighteenth century saw the beginning of many changes. As a result of the Ayrshire Turnpike Acts of 1766 and 1774 new main highways, from Kilmarnock towards Dumfries, and from Ayr towards Edinburgh, were constructed by the Turnpike Trustees, while local parish roads were made by the Earl of Dumfries. As early as 1753 a bridge was constructed to cross the Lugar at Stepends—with four men and four boys killed in the building. Growing traffic necessitated an alteration of the main thoroughfare. Until this time traffic seems to have passed by way of what is now Bank Lane and Tower Street into Townhead. About the middle of the eighteenth century it was decided to cut a main street through the kirkyard. A new burying ground was chosen beside Peden's place of interment on the Barrhill—the oldest burial seems to have been in 1756, of a Frenchman killed at the building of Dumfries House. About 1768 burials ceased in the old graveyard around the kirk; the gravestones were removed; and the whole area opened up for general traffic. The road from Auchinleck now took the present route north and east of the kirk, and after an awkward exit from the new Square, passed up Townhead. Thereafter, traffic turned towards Barshare and Craigens for New Cumnock, or by Drumbrochan for Muirkirk. Possibly because it obstructed the new wheeled traffic, the Market Cross was removed from its site in Townhead. It bears the inscription ' 1703, repaired in 1778 ' and the arms and motto of the Earls of Dumfries. Presumably this market cross, replacing an earlier one, was erected in the Townhead in 1703; before 1769 it was moved to a site on the north-east corner of the Square. Later the road to Muirkirk by Drumbrochan, and the alternative route leaving the Square by the lane behind the Black Bull Hotel, were abandoned in favour of more direct access from the Square to Barrhill. This required a further transportation of the market cross from the north-east corner of the Square to its present site on the south side of the church, outside the main entrance. The old road to New Cumnock by the Townhead had also been abandoned, before 1775, by a new way leaving the Square and crossing the water by a bridge to Glaisnock Street. The main route headed south, with Ayr Road branching off west to join a new road west through Dumfries policies towards Ochiltree and Ayr.

Stage coaches started travelling through Cumnock on the way from Glasgow through Kilmarnock to Carlisle in 1787, and already for the convenience of travellers there was the New Inn in Glaisnock Street (later the Dumfries Arms). By 1793 there were in the parish itself five wheel carriages as well as one hundred and fifty carts, whereas only a generation before conditions were so difficult that wheeled vehicles were virtually unknown in Ayrshire and farmers had to use sledges.

The construction and upkeep of the roads was financed by tolls levied at turnpike gates. In Cumnock parish, besides the main roads from Auchinleck to New Cumnock and Ochiltree to Muirkirk the following roads were turnpiked—the road past Skares towards Knockshinnoch in New Cumnock parish; the road from beyond Boreland intersecting it and leading towards Craigman in New Cumnock parish; and the road from Boreland to Logan which by-passed Cumnock. Traffic through the town had to pass through the tollgate at the corner of Ayr Road and Glaisnock Street, replaced later by one down Ayr Road at Bridgend and another up Glaisnock Street at Pottery Row. For traffic avoiding the town (and perhaps seeking to evade payment of tolls) four gates were strategically placed on the Skares road at Garlaff (2), Mossback, and Shieldburn; another nearby on the Craigman road at Shield; and one on the Boreland-Logan road by Loganhill.

The increase in goods and passenger traffic is a fair indication of economic expansion. The establishment in 1787 of Catrine Cotton Works and Muirkirk Iron Works not very far away shows how industry was developing. Farm produce was being exported from the parish to feed the workers in Catrine and Muirkirk, and local people were leaving to seek work there and even further afield at the new cotton weaving in Kilmarnock, Paisley, and Glasgow.

Even so, the village population was growing, and its trades were thriving. Numbers may have declined a little between 1755 and 1765, but between 1765 and 1792 the village grew in numbers from 580 to 787, while the entire parish enjoyed an increase from 1305 to 1632. In the latter year it was estimated there were 282 dwelling-houses in the parish, of which 80 were either new or rebuilt within the previous ten years.

Rev. Dr. Miller in 1793 described the manufacture in the villages as ‘ weaving, shoemaking, tanning, dyeing, etc.’ The making of textiles had expanded to become the principal craft. Not only were there thirty-five handlooms employed weaving the traditional woollens and coarse linen, but thirty-nine new handlooms were working with the new cotton and producing muslins. There were twenty-eight weavers as well as their apprentices. There were also seven stocking weavers; other textile workers were three lint dressers and two waukers, who helped finish the cloth; and fifteen tailors. Shoemaking had also expanded. Six thousand pairs of shoes and 100 pairs of boots were made annually—there was one tanner who prepared the leather (presumably in the Tanyard) and 33 shoemakers. There were two skin and wool dealers.

In the town and throughout the parish there were typical tradesmen—nine carpenters, three cart and mill wrights, three coopers, twelve masons, and nine smiths. On the farms princi-pally were forty-four male servants, seventy-two female servants, and thirty-five day labourers. There were three millers, five carriers, and eight carters, plus miscellaneous people like one gardener, four Chelsea Pensioners, and twenty-three paupers. In 1753 there had been a wigmaker (called John Good).

Dr. Miller noted that there was no regular market. While fairs continued to be held periodically, the old weekly markets were no longer adequate for all the buying and selling that was necessary. Ten shopkeepers were now established as well as three butchers and two bakers. There were also four innkeepers and stablers. And for other needs of the people, besides the parish minister and the schoolmaster there were now two surgeons.

EARLY MINING VENTURES

By the eighteenth century the value of the underground resources of the parish was becoming recognised. Dr. Miller noted that coal was plentiful, remarking that ' a considerable part of the parish is supposed to stand upon it.' Outcrops were being quarried by land-owners, principally to provide fuel to burn lime for enriching the fields—hence the various lime-kilns dating from this period.

The Dumfries House papers include a mass of documents relating to the exploitation of the minerals, initiated by the fifth Earl just before his death in 1768, and continued by his successors. On the high ground to the south-west of the parish easily-accessible seams had been proved, and from there coals could be transported downhill to the various parts of the Dumfries estate in creels on horseback. Working at Garlaff was begun on 4th April 1767 and coal was supplied to the house and lime-works at Leifnoreis; to the Earl's tenants for lime-burning; large quantities to the lime-kilns at Benston; and some was sold to other local customers at 3d. per load or 3/- per ton. It was a small-scale enterprise with three men employed as miners to begin with (William Boile, William Hanna, and William Johnston). Costs were small. The highest paid miner received just over 1/- a day, and the weekly wage bill for the face-workers amounted to about 14/-. Others were employed in ' riding below ' (presumably carrying coals from the face to the pit bottom) and in bringing up coals to the surface. These were almost certainly women and children—there are occasional payments for 'criles wanes,' the children who handled the creels. Other expenses were regular purchases of candles, and other items like riddles. The miners must have provided their own tools, for these are never listed. A sample week's accounts may be quoted.

14*th May* 1768	£	s.	d.
William Hanna—6 days . . .	0	4	0
James Cowan—6 days. . . .	0	3	6
William Johnston—6 days . . .	0	6	3
for raising 144 loads Coals . .	0	12	0
for Candle	0	0	7
for Riding Below	0	1	0
for Criles wanes	0	0	6
the Week's oncost	1	7	10
Adam Ralston—12 loads daily			
John Johnston—12 loads daily			
144 loads . . .	1	16	0

The new large-scale demands for lime for agricultural improvements made coalmining a promising venture. In 1770 the Earl opened another pit at Coalburn in New Cumnock parish. By 1771 he had installed at Garlaff a steam engine for pumping water and so permitting deeper working. In the same year there was being sold 'lime to Air with 2 horses.' In 1773 the Earl negotiated with the Duke of Queensberry a contract to supply to Sanquhar 2,000 tons of lime yearly for 19 years. The Garlaff coal works and Benston Lime Quarry had been leased since 1768 to William Moore. Despite rising prices (in 1775 Benston used 2,500 loads of coal at 6d. a load) and profits at Garlaff and Benston estimated at £150 a year, Moore got into difficulties. The Guelt lime quarry opened before 1774 was losing money. Between 1771 and 1776 there was heavy expense in making a road between Benston and Garlaff, even though Patrick Douglas of Garrallan shared the costs. Moore was also spending heavily on farm improvements. In 1778 he went bankrupt; but by 1781 he had paid up his debts, £500 to the Earl, £200 to other creditors. The coal and lime-works were sub-let and trade flourished. In the year 1779-80 Garlaff produced 19,323 loads of coal at a cost of £154, selling for £282, yielding a profit of £128. By 1784 it was pointed out that ' many of Lord Dumfries's Tennants burn Coal who formerly burnt peats . . . there is an increase from the village of Cumnock as for some time Lord Auchinleck's Coal did not go regularly . . . increased sale towards parishes of Ochiltree and Caltown as the price is lower than Drongan Coal . . . increase by the burning of the lime nearly double.' Between 1780 and 1786 the possibilities of Glengyron were investigated, and for a short time there were some shallow workings. Further west, coal was also worked above the smithy at Pluckburn. At Auchingilsie outcrops were worked for a few summers. Near Grimgrew an outcrop of blind or culm coal was also exploited. Burning without smoke, it was used in the hothouses at Dumfries House and sold to millers for drying grain. Earl Patrick conceived the idea of transporting this coal to Ayr and exporting it to Ireland. A sloop was sent, but the enterprise proved unprofitable. The road to Ayr was still so inadequate that the soft and brittle coal was reduced to powder in transit. Indeed, the successful sale of coal outwith the immediate vicinity remained impossible till the construction of the railway in 1850.

Despite the failure of his scheme for exporting coal, the Earl persisted in his hopes of development. He was prepared to make heavy investments, even if returns proved to be slow in coming. A new phase began when in 1790 he engaged James Taylor to make a report on the mineralogical prospects of the Dumfries estate. Taylor was born at Leadhills in 1758. After a medical education, he was engaged as a tutor by Patrick Miller of Dalswinton in 1785. Miller was at this time experimenting with paddle-driven boats powered by hand. Taylor suggested the use of a steam-engine, and with the technical assistance of William Symington, another native of Leadhills, a steam-driven paddle-boat was constructed and driven at five miles an hour on Dalswinton Loch in Dumfriesshire on 14th October 1788—the first successful venture in steam-navigation. Among those present was possibly Robert Burns, who tenanted Miller's farm at Ellisland. In 1789 a speed of 7 miles an hour was attained with a larger vessel on the Forth and Clyde Canal. The credit for inventing steam navigation goes to William Symington—and to Henry Bell and Robert Fulton who both inspected the 1789 vessel. Taylor had a hand — his family were later awarded a government pension in belated recognition of his contribution. But Taylor had left Symington in complete charge and abandoned his experiments to come to superintend the mineral workings on the Dumfries estate.

Taylor reported to Earl Patrick in November 1790, listing the resources of the Dumfries estate in coal, lime, and ironstone. Aware of the establishment of an ironworks at Muirkirk three years before, he suggested the erection of four blast furnaces at Pennyfadzeoch near Dumfries House, with a water supply brought from the Loch of the Lowes. He anticipated £10,000 annual profit and envisaged the possibility of a second ironworks at Coalburn. These grandiose proposals were not implemented. Though not forgotten, they were laid aside in favour of a smaller and quite different project. In 1770 the Earl had initiated the working of a wodd (or blacklead) mine at Craigman in New Cumnock parish. He and Lady Dumfries had the idea of using the graphite to make crucibles for foundries, and from 1778 onwards made repeated efforts to keep the Craigman mine open and establish a crucible pottery. When William Moore's lease of Benston and Garlaff ended in 1791 a forty-year contract with Taylor was arranged to take over all the mineral undertakings (signed in 1792); and a second contract was drawn up by which Taylor with the assistance of James and John Henderson, two Glasgow potters, would set up a crucible manufactory. Three acres at Greenbraehead were leased and a pottery works set up in 1791. There were various difficulties. Supplies from Craigman were inadequate, and it proved impossible to make graphite pots. The thirteen men employed had to limit themselves to making earthenware pots from local clay. Expenses were high; by the time of his death in 1803 the Earl had lost nearly £1,000 in the pottery; indeed it was not till 1812 that it began to make money. Meanwhile, the mineral undertakings also under Taylor's management were not making the anticipated progress.

A new quarry was opened at Benston and the lime made £160 a year, and at Guelt earlier losses were converted into a small profit. But the three coal mines were less successful. Coalburn made only £40 a year, Auchingilsie £15, and Garlaff's annual profits dropped to £70. Garlaff workings were proving difficult, and its sales were faced with competition. Until 1792 Douglas of Garrallan was paid an annual premium for not working coal on his estate, but thereafter he leased his minerals, and the sale of Garrallan coal forced down the price of Garlaff coal to 2/6 a ton. Altogether from 1791 till 1801 the total mineral profits were only £679, and this was all swallowed up in paying Taylor his annual fee of £100 plus commission. Earl Patrick's hopes had not materialised. Despite heavy capital investment, business failed to expand. In 1792 there were still only eighteen colliers in the parish, and coal remained a minor feature of the local economy.

EIGHTEENTH CENTURY SOCIAL LIFE

Throughout the eighteenth century the kirk occupied a central position in the life of the community. There were two services each Sunday, forenoon and afternoon; periodic celebrations of Communion, which brought in visitors from all the surrounding parishes; and from time to time Fast Days were ordained. The kirk session concerned itself not only with these matters, but with the well-being of the people generally, exercising severe discipline on those who transgressed. Those who broke the observance of the Sabbath or were guilty of misconduct at any time might be fined, or set before the congregation in the place of repentance to receive public rebuke. Only after 1800 did this practice die out, the last instance in Cumnock being 1808. The early volumes of Kirk Session records are almost entirely filled with lists of transgressors compeared for immoral conduct.

As late as 1793 Dr. Miller recorded of the local people: ' Next to the occupations peculiar to their several lines of life, their leading object is to converse and dispute about religious subjects and church government, concerning which there is considerable diversity of opinion among them.' Rev. John Steel (1701-1746) had been elected by the congregation and was a noted Auld Licht and proponent of the traditional Calvinist doctrines, which had a widespread appeal. After 1712 patronage was restored, and Rev. Adam Thomson (1748-1751) and Rev. George Muir (1752-1766) were nominated by the Earl of Dumfries. Thomson's stay was brief, and Muir, a great evangelist influenced by White-field, had an enthusiastic following. The appointment of Thomas Miller in 1767 however was followed by difficulties. He was a scholar—graduating Doctor of Divinity at Edinburgh University in 1788—and a worthy man. But he was a poor preacher, and of moderate New Licht views which did not commend him to those who held firm to the Covenants and the strict Calvinist dogma. He continued as parish minister till his death in 1819, at the age of 80, after 52 years of service. But he left a divided church whose reunion had to await the twentieth century.

In 1689 when presbyterianism was recognised, some of the extreme Covenanters were still so dissatisfied that they stayed outwith the established church and worshipped separately. A group of such local dissidents conducted a praying society, meeting at Wallacetown farm in Auchinleck parish. Following a dispute in the established church nationally in 1733, the Secession, and the formation of the Associate Presbytery, the Wallacetown Preaching Society became attached to this Seceders' Kirk and came under the care of Rev. David Smyton of Kilmaurs. Dissension among the Seceders as to the legality of taking the burgess oath led to a schism. The Anti-Burghers continued in Auchinleck parish, building in 1765 a kirk of their own at Rigg, and having Robert Smith as their minister (1763-1809). In Cumnock there was a group of Burghers, with John Rankin, a watchmaker who had come from Glasgow about 1755, as their spokesman. Their numbers were augmented by those who disapproved of the new parish minister after 1767. Open air services were started in 1773. A petition for a preacher was signed by Alex. Vallance, James Whyte, Colin McDougall, John Young, James Mitchell, John Rankin, and thirty heads of families. From John Murdoch a piece of ground was acquired near the Tanyard, by the junction of the Lugar and Glaisnock waters; though the Earl of Dumfries's factor refused to sell sand, a flood provided a good supply, which was esteemed a miracle. The church was

erected and ministers called—James Hall (1777-1786); David
Wilson (1788-1822). In 1757 Rev. George Muir had estimated
the number of seceders in the parish at fifty-one, of whom four
lived in the town; by 1793 Dr. Miller said there were about 300;
around 1800 there were 800 members and adherents who contributed to providing a manse.

The parish kirk however was in an advantageous position as
legally established. About 1750 the heritors built a new parish
manse and in 1754 the old kirk was itself replaced by a new
building. It was a low building with a squat spire containing the
old Dutch bell. To cater for the growing population, it could
accommodate 700 worshippers. To one of the outside walls
were fitted the jougs, where offenders were exposed to public
shame.

The kirk session in association with the heritors was also
responsible for the parish school. Though there is doubt about
where exactly Cumnock's first school was sited, according to
J. W. Crawford it was at the corner of Lugar Street and the
Square, beside Bank Lane. This old school was left for a time
without a master in 1703 after the time of William Muir, but
before 1710 Mr. Robert Trotter had been appointed and served
till 1724. Thereafter follows a regular succession: James Wilson
(1724-1727); William Rae (1727-1764); William Hogsyard
(1764); David Vallance (1764-1768); George Swinton (1768-
1785); Archibald White (1785-1787); William Clogston (1787-
1788); William Simson (1788-1815). In 1793 there were about
forty pupils, all being taught reading, some writing and arithmetic, and eleven taking Latin. The master received a basic
stipend from the heritors, supplemented by fees from the pupils
for reading, writing, arithmetic, and Latin, making a total income
of about £12 per annum. Though Dr. Miller reported that
'education is little valued,' in a few years' time when an Act
of 1803 authorised a long-needed increase to within the range
from 300 to 400 merks, Cumnock awarded Simson the maximum
salary of 400 merks—£22 4s. 5d. per annum. Then in 1804
the heritors authorised the construction of a new parish school
on the site now occupied by the Clydesdale Bank.

The changes of the eighteenth century were many and varied—
a growing population; new ways of work for many; an extended

diet with potatoes, bread, sugar, and tea being added to the traditional oatmeal staple, and with meat becoming more commonly used; changing fashions, women in particular finding cotton an attractive alternative to hodden grey woollens and coarse harn linen; and new ways of life were emerging.

The changes brought social stresses. It was a period when wages and prices were both advancing. Prices, said Dr. Miller, had almost all doubled, with the exception of oatmeal, in fifteen or twenty years. In 1793 meal was 11d. or 11½d. a peck; beef, 4½d. to 6d. a pound of 24 oz.; mutton, 4d. to 5d. a pound; veal, 4d. a pound; lamb, 5d. a pound; pork, 5s. a stone; a fowl, from 8d. to 1s.; eggs, from 3d. to 4½d. a dozen; butter and cheese, 1s. a stone; common cheese, 3s. 6d. to 5s. a stone; sweet milk cheese, 6s. to 8s. a stone. Wages for skilled workers had advanced at a reasonable rate: a mason, 1s. 10d. a day; a carpenter, 1s. 2d.; a tailor with maintenance, 6d. a day. Wages for servants had also risen; men farm servants £7-£10 a year; women servants, £2-£4. Day labourers were poorly off, getting only 10d.-1s. 3d. a day without meat. People with fixed incomes were badly off, like the schoolmaster with £12 per annum. So were small tenant farmers without capital to improve their farms—like Burns at Mossgiel. The parish minister, however, was well-off with an income (including the glebe rent) of £100 a year.

Summing up, Dr. Miller described the people as 'moderate in their expenses, strangers to luxury, but with the country in general acquiring a taste for dress, which with other slight symptoms of progress in civilisation, will probably in time be an incitement to their becoming more industrious. At present the great body that make up the inhabitants of the parish may be said to enjoy freedom to work or to be idle; strangers in general to intemperance, their living is chiefly supplied by the dairy; the manufacturers excepted, who with a few others, may be said to be better acquainted with a meat diet and with the use of beer; which it were to be wished, could be substituted for the prevalent use of spirituous liquors.'

In 1793 there were twenty-three people on the poors roll. These were provided for by the heritors committee out of church collections, supplemented by a levy on all landowners, and

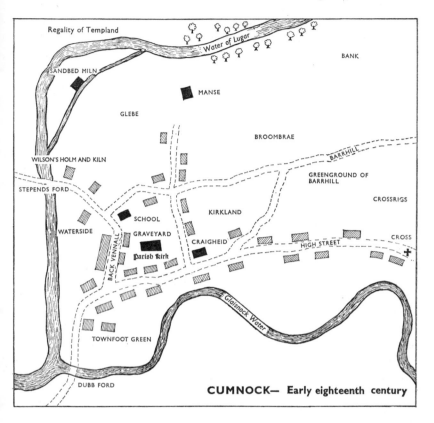

A reconstruction based on Roy's Military Survey and Dumfries House papers. Numbers and location of houses and some thoroughfares are uncertain.

charitable gifts—for which the Earl of Dumfries and his family were noted. Stringent measures were adopted to deal with a difficult problem. In times of emergency, as in the bad harvests of 1799 and 1800 when meal prices soared, a public subscription was inaugurated to supply foodstuffs at reduced rates to those who needed it. An interesting example of co-operation for mutual insurance was the Cumnock Social Depository, set up about 1790, for the assistance of members in distress.

Life was not all dull. For children there were ' the spinning of the peerie, the lashing of the top, the rolling of the hoop, the flying of the kite, and the skipping of the rope, the agility shewn in the exercise of leap-frog, with the playing at ball, and the pitching of the quoit . . . shinty, in which two parties contended in closed encounter which should drive a ball by clubs or bats beyond a certain limit, skating and curling when the thickness of the ice permitted.' Handball was played in the Square against the walls and shuttered windows of the kirk. For older folk, there were opportunities at the fairs for sports and games of chance. Weddings—and funerals—were occasions for revelry. There were old festivals like Hallowe'en. And there were informal gatherings called rockings, and kirns at harvest time.

Only brief glimpses of these social activities are possible, as when the Kirk Session minutes report with disapproval in 1724 that ' a dancing master and a musician having come to the town without any testimonials were cited before them.' In 1752 John French was born in Cumnock, and the environment was sufficiently musical to enable him to leave his trade of shoemaking to devote himself wholly to music. A self-taught violinist, he enabled the Earl of Dumfries to win a wager that a Cumnock man could play a hundred different tunes without a pause and without a score. After his death in 1803 a collection of sixty-four of his compositions was published.

The late eighteenth century also brought Cumnock some reflected fame through the association of some of its folk with Robert Burns. First of all was William Simson, born in 1758 at Ten Pound Land, Ochiltree, educated at Glasgow University, and schoolmaster at Ochiltree from 1780 till 1788, when he transferred to Cumnock as its schoolmaster till his death in 1815. A contemporary of the poet, he is immortalised as

'Winsome Willie' in one of Burns's Epistles. Another correspondent was John Kennedy, factor to the Earl of Dumfries from 1783 till 1793; and Burns is also supposed to have known Rev. James Hall, the Secession minister. Patrick Douglas of Garrallan and sometime surgeon in Ayr, is reputed to have arranged Burns's proposed emigration to Jamaica. He had purchased an estate in the neighbourhood of Port Antonio in Jamaica, and his brother Charles was made its manager. It was there that Burns was to go as a book-keeper. But as we know, the plan fell through. Another Cumnock resident known to Burns was Annie Rankine of Adamhill near Tarbolton, who inspired *Corn Rigs*, later married a Cumnock man, and as Mrs. Merry lived here till her death in 1843. Two other local people have a link through his poems. Rev. Dr. Mitchell, owner of Avisyard and minister of Monkton, is satirised in *The Kirk's Alarm* as ' Andro Gowk.' And in *Passion's Cry* there is supposed to be a reference to Eleanora Campbell, Mrs. Maxwell, of Skerrington, who was in 1787 involved in a Court of Session case—in which it was decided that her husband could take legal action against a third party, Captain Montgomery, without requiring to divorce her for her misconduct.

Chapter 4

Early Nineteenth Century

In the nineteenth century Cumnock continued to grow. For the first four decades there was a steady increase in parish numbers —from 1,798 (1801) to 1,991 (1811), 2,343 (1821), 2,763 (1831), 2,836 (1841). In the forties population rose rapidly to 3,777 (1851), then was halted at 3,721 (1861) before continuing to grow thereafter. This growth was mainly the result of the expansion of the town. In 1792 it had 787 inhabitants; by 1831 it had more than doubled, with 1,600; by the 1860's it had probably about 2,600 inhabitants.

ECONOMIC DEVELOPMENTS

This growth was the result of the expansion of the local trades. Weaving continued to be the main occupation. The handloom weaving of cotton, begun in the 1780's, had rapidly become the principal line of business. In 1811 there were seventy muslin weavers in Cumnock, and by the 1830's there were more than 120 looms at work. Associated with the cotton trade, Ayrshire embroidery was made and many women and girls were engaged in this hand-sewing. As a consequence of the expansion of cotton manufacture the traditional textiles suffered a decline. Linen weaving became a thing of the past, and wool dealt with only at a carding mill and dye works. Shoemaking, too, died away, as farmers began to specialise in dairy cattle and the local supply of hides for tanning diminished.

The cotton weaving was centred in the Townhead. Almost every house had its loom. Three had six looms each, six had four looms. Several agents lived in the town, representing Glasgow firms, who secured the webs from the weavers after they were completed. During the early decades of the nineteenth century the industry flourished, till in the forties and fifties handloom weaving began to decay. Power looms were introduced elsewhere, the American Civil War cut off the supplies of raw cotton, and the Scottish manufacture of cotton goods survived in only a few places such as Catrine. The handloom weavers suffered severely from distress. In November 1861, for example, the Cumnock heritors agreed to give £50 if the inhabitants of the town subscribed £20 more ' for the purpose of providing webs for the weavers out of work.' Only a few weavers continued in the latter part of the century. In 1899 three were still working in Cumnock—one in Townhead, one in Ayr Road, and a third on the way to Glaisnock.

New trades, however, emerged to supersede the old decaying ones. Principal among these was the manufacture of snuff boxes. There is some doubt as to the origins of this skilled local manufacture. It appears however that sometime about 1800, while repairing a snuffbox, a local man called William (or John) Crawford hit upon the idea of an ' invisible wooden hinge ' and started a vogue for such snuff boxes. According to one version, he was working at the time with Mr. Wyllie, a gunsmith and watchmaker in Auchinleck, and after a number of years Crawford fell out with him and set up business on his own in Cumnock. Certainly the secret spread and eventually wooden snuff boxes were being manufactured in Cumnock, Auchinleck, Catrine and Mauchline. Its greatest prosperity was between 1820 and 1830. About sixty were employed in Mauchline, as many in Auchinleck, and for a time over a hundred in Cumnock.

The boxes were made from plane or sycamore wood, thoroughly seasoned for five or six months before use. One set of workers made the boxes. A second set decorated them. A third group, mainly women and children, varnished them—thirty coats of spirit varnish or fifteen coats of copal varnish—and polished them, working eleven hours a day. In the early 1820's, boxes to the value of £6,000 Sterling were being produced annually— individual boxes without painting or varnishing being sold for 30/- each. As much as £6 or £7 could be obtained for the best executed boxes with highly-finished designs. Box-makers could earn a guinea a week, scene-painters twice that, and varnishers 12/-. The high wages attracted young artists and three who afterwards rose to some fame worked as miniature painters in Cumnock—Daniel Macnee, later knighted and President of the Royal Scottish Academy; Horatio McCulloch, noted for his Highland landscapes; and William Leighton Leitch, the water-colourist. The leading Cumnock box-making firms were Peter Crichton, Alexander Lammie, James Drummond, Adam Crichton, George Crawford, and George Buchanan. But by the 1830's difficulties were developing. Single unfinished boxes which previously fetched 30/- were by 1837 being sold at seven for 12/-; and the yearly value of Cumnock-made boxes had dropped to £1,600. Box-makers were making only from 10/- to 12/-, painters 15/-, and varnishers 5/- to 6/- a week. Machines worked by boys were decorating the boxes with elaborate chequering, and superseding the fine artistic work. At the same time snuff-taking was dying out, and the demand for boxes declining. Efforts were made to manufacture fancy wooden boxes for other purposes, but these could not compete with mass-produced alternatives manufactured elsewhere. By 1843 only the first three of the six firms noted above were still manufacturing. After 1850, when the railway came and stage-coach traffic through Cumnock ceased, the sale of fancy boxes to passing coach-travellers ended. Thereafter the trade dwindled and by the 1880's was wholly extinct in Cumnock—though it survived in Mauchline till the twentieth century.

In the 1830's when cotton weaving and box-making were the principal trades of the town, they were supported by two other recently-established and diverse businesses—the making of pottery and threshing machines. The first, established in 1791 by the Earl of Dumfries in association with James Taylor, began to make money in 1812. Using local clay, brown ware was manufactured, including plain and glazed flower pots. These ' Scotch Motto Ware ' items found in the later nineteenth century a wide sale throughout Britain and even abroad, and the firm continued in operation into the twentieth century. The manufacture of threshing machines commenced in 1812. A young engineer, George McCartney, on completing his apprenticeship started working for himself at Clockclownie farm. His first threshing machine was so successful that in 1832 he moved into Cumnock and set up production at Burnside with six men and a blacksmith. Eventually a hundred machines a year were being turned out and sold at an average cost of £80 to farmers at home and

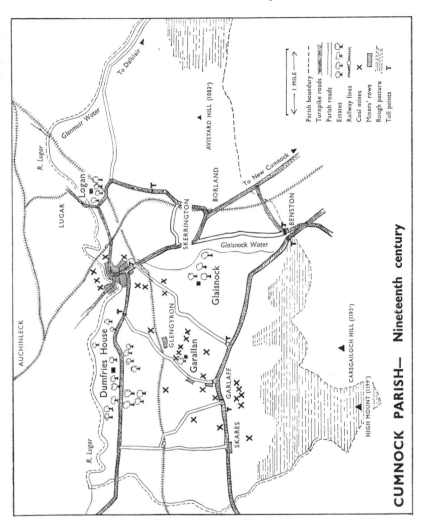

CUMNOCK PARISH— Nineteenth century

abroad. McCartney died a bachelor at the age of 78 in 1868, and was buried in Ochiltree. He had never patented his improvements and died a comparatively poor man. His business continued into the twentieth century.

The early nineteenth century saw only small developments in mineral working in the parish. Under the management of James Taylor since 1790, the Dumfries estate undertakings comprised the lime quarries at Benston and Guelt, coal pits at Garlaff, Auchengilsie, and Coalburn, and the graphite mine at Craigman in New Cumnock parish. In 1803 Earl Patrick died and was succeeded by his nine-year-old grandson as the seventh Earl. A year later Taylor reported to the curators of the young Earl. He noted that while coal was sold locally at 4/- a ton, it could fetch from 11/- to 13/- at Ayr. Soon after the Muirkirk ironworks had been set up, Admiral Stewart had suggested a canal to Ayr, and Taylor renewed this proposal: a canal from Glenbuck via Auchinleck to Ayr, with aqueducts crossing the Lugar and Coyl waters, and branches north to Sorn and south to Cumnock, Guelt, and Glenmuir. He remarked that ' Cumnock very happily situated might become a large manufacturing town.' Like his earlier proposal in 1790 for establishing an ironworks, the canal project was never taken up. Indeed, the pottery and mineral undertakings, small as they were, had proved costly to develop. In 1812 Taylor's contract was broken. Apparently he gave up control of the pottery, and there was a court settlement in 1817. He seems to have continued as manager of the coal and lime works, at an annual salary of £280, till his death in September 1825 at the age of 67. He was survived by a widow and four daughters, who continued to live at his house in Ayr Road, Cumnock.

A mineralogical report by Dr. John Barker in 1824 indicated that Garlaff was still the main coal working. The competition from Garrallan had been stopped by an annual premium of £20 to the proprietor. Some blind coal was being worked for local use; smithy coal was obtained from Craigman; Coalburn was supplying fuel for Benston; and there was a small unprofitable working at Woodside. At Garlaff in 1837 (according to the New Statistical Account) output per man was two tons per day, for which they earned from 3/- to 4/-. Coal could be had at the pit for 5/- a ton, or delivered in the town at 8/- a ton. The Dumfries

House papers include a ' Statement of Coal put out at Garlaff from a book kept by Geo. McTurk ' revealing for the years 1840-1841 and 1841-1842 an output of 15,641 and 13,696 loads. The costs were 4½d. a load and the sale price was 11½d., assuring comfortable profits after all expenses were paid. In 1841 a report by John Geddes revealed that at Garlaff a four-foot seam was being worked at a depth of twenty-six fathoms; it was an ' engine pit' and a tram railway had been constructed. The other workings were shallow and unimportant: the blind coal was only occasionally worked—a five-foot seam, seven fathoms deep; Coalburn employed three colliers working a two-and-a-half foot seam at eleven-and-a-half fathoms; one collier worked a 27-inch seam at seven fathoms at Craigman. Geddes considered the possibility of working blackband ironstone, and revived Taylor's idea of an ironworks: ' Either in the valley of the Nith, or near to the town of Cumnock, an Ironwork may be placed with decided advantage.' In 1843 Messrs. Whitfield and Ferguson took a lease of the coalworks of Garlaff, Knockdon, Coalburn, Craigman, Guelt, and the limeworks at Benston and Guelt. In the same year John Wilson of Coatbridge took over the Muirkirk Ironworks and the Marquess of Bute advertised for offers for the blackband ironstone on the Dumfries estate. In 1846 Wilson selected a site for another ironworks, at Lugar, and in a few years' time large-scale mining operations in Cumnock parish began.

Economic progress had to await improvements in communications. The turnpike roads of the early nineteenth century were inadequate for heavy traffic, though they were busy with the haulage of farm produce and with passenger transport. The Glasgow-Kilmarnock-Carlisle coaches passed through Cumnock, one each day in either direction. Coaches also left the town—the *Lass of Ballochmyle* and *Marquis of Bute* for Kilmarnock every other day, and the *Independent* for Ayr twice a week. Post-horses and chaises could be hired in the town. Others passed through in their private conveyances. In 1817 Sir Walter Scott, touring in the west of Scotland, spent a night in the Dumfries Arms Hotel. He wrote a rhyming epistle to the Duke of Buccleuch, whose guest he was about to become, mentioning ' Old Cumnock, where beds are as hard as a plank, sir,' probably with less regard to the truth than an attempt to find a rhyme for Sanquhar.

In 1842 there passed through Cumnock a notability of another sort, when Kirkpatrick Macmillan of Closeburn who had just invented the first bicycle rode on it into Cumnock to spend the night with a friend on his way to Glasgow. Actually Cumnock had seen a still earlier model. William Murdoch (1754-1839), the famous engineer and inventor of gas-lighting, was born at Bello Mill by Lugar. His father, John Murdoch, sometime before 1711 made a ' wooden horse on wheels, on which, by the assistance of propelling poles, he used to visit Cumnock.' Kirkpatrick Macmillan's machine superseded all previous hobby-horses. It was the first real bicycle, propelled by pedals, and was invented in 1839. He determined on a 70-mile trip to Glasgow to visit his three brothers. As he could not hope to make the trip inside one day he arranged to break his journey by staying overnight at Cumnock with John McKinnell, parish schoolmaster and student friend of one of Macmillan's brothers. At 7.25 p.m. on 6th June 1842 he set off from Courthill near Penpont. Twenty minutes after midnight James Kennedy, a Cumnock shoemaker, on his way home from courting Jean Vallance, was startled by a strange jangle and clatter—Macmillan on his 57-pound bike coming rushing down McKinlay's Brae into the Square. There he was welcomed into the old schoolhouse by an anxious McKinnell. Next morning Macmillan exhibited his invention to the wide-eyed people of Cumnock, coming down Glaisnock Street at high speed with both feet on the handle-bars. Then he set off for Glasgow, arriving in the Gorbals at 5.30 p.m., to be immediately arrested and later fined 5/- for ' obstruction of the passage.' He returned to Dumfriesshire and obscurity. Copies of his bicycle were made by George McCartney of Cumnock, Thomas McCall of Kilmarnock, and Gavin Dalzell of Lesmahagow, and the last began commercial manufacture. Only a decade after his death in 1878 aged sixty-five was Kirkpatrick Macmillan given the credit that was his due.

The greatest step forward in nineteenth century Cumnock's economic life was the coming of the railway. As far back as 1808 Scotland's first real rail track had been constructed by the Duke of Portland to convey coals by horse and truck from Kilmarnock to his new port at Troon, and on this line in 1817 a steam locomotive made by George Stephenson was tried out, not very successfully. The railway age in the west of Scotland really began in 1840 when the Glasgow, Paisley, Kilmarnock and Ayr Railway Company opened its line from Glasgow to Ayr, with a branch from Dalry to Kilmarnock. Its success was followed up by extensions, and the company (renamed the Glasgow and South Western Railway Company) set about constructing a main line to the south. Its competitor, the Caledonian Railway Company, was in process of building a line up the Clyde valley and over Beattock. The G. & S.W. planned a line from Kilmarnock through Cumnock and by the Nith valley through Dumfries. It was a mammoth undertaking and hundreds of Irish navvies were employed—innumerable cuttings had to be excavated, and a tunnel made at Mossgiel near Mauchline. Most difficult of all were the crossings of the rivers, with a great viaduct over the Irvine at Hurlford, the huge bridge over the Ayr at Ballochmyle— its 180-foot arch standing 157 feet above the river being the greatest masonry arch in the world—and the crossing of the Lugar at Cumnock by a viaduct of thirteen arches, the highest 175 feet above the river. On 9th August 1848 the line from Kilmarnock was opened as far as Auchinleck, with a branch to Lugar and Muirkirk. On 20th May 1850 the line between Auchinleck and New Cumnock through Cumnock itself was opened, linking up with the line which had been pushed up the Nith valley, and so completing a through connection. The main Glasgow-Dumfries-Carlisle line operated by the G. & S.W. Railway Company was now in operation, supplementing the Caledonian Railway Company's Beattock line which had been opened two years before. Cumnock, situated on a main line, was now in close contact with the outside world. The railway offered facilities for the convenient transport of heavy goods, and an opportunity for the rapid exploitation of the local coal resources in the second half of the nineteenth century.

SOCIAL CHANGES

The growth of population and the various economic changes in the early nineteenth century brought with them social difficulties of one kind and another. Congestion and lack of sanitation spread disease. The scourge of smallpox was declining as inoculation became accepted—though for a time there was an aversion to this. From time to time epidemics of cholera swept the country. Precautions were taken to prevent its spread by fumigating with sulphur all who entered or passed through Cumnock. Tall oblong boxes were placed at all the main entrances of the town in which visitors were placed while a mixture of sulphur and quicklime at the bottom of the boxes was set alight. A special payment was awarded by the Parochial Board to the three local doctors early in 1849 ' in recognition of their Services during the prevalence of Cholera in this parish '—Dr. Cowan receiving £4 10/-; Dr. McKinnon, £3; Dr. McGlashan, £3. Another local surgeon, Douglas Wills, died in 1849, and his tombstone records him as ' a victim to his zeal in the cause of humanity.'

To administer the public health laws, such as they were, and to cope with the growing numbers of poor people, by Act of Parliament in 1845 Parochial Boards were set up. The Parochial Board for Cumnock was typical in that it consisted of heritors, members of the kirk session, and a few elected members. It co-operated closely with the old Heritors Committee which was responsible for the church building, the graveyard, the school, and levying a poor rate to supplement the church collections. An indication of the growth of poverty is that the Heritors were obliged to expend £105 on the poor in 1837; by 1849 the corresponding figure was £532. For a time, conditions in Cumnock were so bad that nearly 20 per cent. of the parish population were in receipt of help. In 1845 the Heritors and Parochial Board appointed an Inspector of Poor—Mr. James Boyd. Besides providing for those on the poors roll, special gifts were made. For example, in 1849—' Widow Miller allowed an ear tube for her son. Widow Murdoch, Townhead, to receive chaff and straw for her bed.' There was always the difficulty of dealing with beggars. In 1851 the Inspector published handbills intimating that all persons harbouring vagrants would be prosecuted and the vagrants themselves would be arrested and imprisoned. To avoid misuse of payments, it was decided that money should not be issued, but tickets with amounts indicated, for paupers to give to lodging-house keepers, shopkeepers, etc.

To supplement the general awards, the minister and heritors had at their disposal bequests for assisting the poor—from a Miss Campbell (1860) and from Major General Campbell of Avisyard (1861); while the Marquess of Bute regularly donated gifts of meal to poor people. Rev. Ninian Bannatyne in 1837 had concluded that ' there is a sad decline of late years in the spirit of independence that used to exist.' In fact there was a good deal of self help. Three local friendly societies (Community, founded 1814; Centenary, founded in 1825; Weavers, founded 1809) had among them 273 members in 1837, making small weekly payments and awarding payments in case of illness or death. There was also a local Savings Bank founded in 1831 with over 200 depositors. And combating with some success the prevalent intemperance there was a Total Abstinence Society formed in 1838 at a time when the town had two inns and other thirteen places where spirits were sold.

All this social distress was not accepted without protest. From the later part of the eighteenth century onwards demands were being made for the reform of parliament and extension of the franchise. Until 1832 Ayrshire was represented in the House of Commons by two Members. One Member for Ayr Burghs was selected by delegates from the councils of the royal burghs of Ayr, Irvine, Rothesay, Inveraray, and Campbeltown. The county Member was chosen by freeholders whose numbers before 1832 were just over 200. In the Cumnock area, for example, the only electors were—from Mauchline: Claud Alexander of Ballochmyle, William Campbell of Netherplace, Robert Campbell of Auchmannoch, Samuel Cooper of Failford; from Sorn: Lt. Col. Matthew Stewart of Catrine, John Gray Farquhar of Gilmilnscroft; from Auchinleck: Alexander Boswell; from Cumnock: Alexander Allason of Glaisnock, and George Ranken of Whitehill who resided at Burnhead in Sorn; from New Cumnock: James Cuthbert of Dalleagles.

The new principles of liberty, equality, and fraternity were accepted by Burns and many of his friends. After the French Revolution broke out, the Society of Friends of the People was formed and delegates from Ayrshire attended conventions in Edinburgh in 1792 and 1793. The reform movement was suppressed by the government but in 1797 when schoolmasters were ordered to draw up lists of young men to be conscripted there were widespread riots, with incidents recorded at Ochiltree and New Cumnock. After the end of the wars in 1815 there was increased distress and renewed political agitation. It was reported in 1820 that Galston, Newmilns, Sorn, and Stewarton were 'seething with revolutionary madness.' After 1832 when the first Reform Act was passed more people obtained the vote, but still a minority—3,151 in Ayrshire, fifty-two of them in Cumnock parish. There was widespread disillusionment, followed by the rise of the Chartist movement with demands for universal suffrage. Dr. John Taylor of Ayr became a leading exponent of violent action and found much support in Cumnock. In 1838 a ' Dhurna Society ' was formed in Cumnock whose members pledged themselves not to purchase or use intoxicating liquors, tea, tobacco, or any other articles paying high duty to the government. In 1839, 400 from Cumnock signed the People's Charter, of whom forty declared they were ready to go to any length for universal suffrage. After 1848 the Chartist movement collapsed, but the radical spirit survived among the handloom weavers and others.

The early nineteenth century also saw continued troubles within the church. Following the death of Dr. Miller in 1819 the parish church was served by Rev. John Frazer, and after his death in an epidemic in 1829, by Rev. Ninian Bannatyne. Both were presented by the Marquess of Bute. Growing feeling within the Church of Scotland against secular control led in 1843 to the Disruption. In Cumnock the parish minister, at the call of conscience, resigned his charge and emoluments, and taking with him the entire kirk session and many of the congregation became first minister of the Free Church in Cumnock, with a place of worship erected in Ayr Road. Meanwhile a new large United Secession church with accommodation for 850 had been erected in 1831, during the ministry of Robert Brown (1823-1847). After his death he was followed by Matthew Dickie, a strong advocate of Temperance and president of the local Total Abstinence Society. Just after his ordination, the Secession and Relief kirks came together nationally, and from 1847 this church became known as United Presbyterian. The relative weakness of the established church is evidenced by the fact that the parish kirk accommodated 650; at the 1851 Census the U.P. Kirk had 600 worshippers, plus 150 at Sabbath school, while the Free Kirk had 400 plus 80.

The early nineteenth century saw these three large denominations joined in Cumnock by two new groups. In 1836 a few protestants who disliked presbyterian forms began to worship separately. In 1838 they formed themselves into a congregation meeting first in a hall belonging to the Black Bull Hotel and later forming a Congregational Church in the old parish school in the Square. In 1851 it had 120 worshipping and a Sabbath school of fifty. Then about 1840 incomers of another persuasion began to receive occasional visits from priests from Ayr and Kilmarnock. About 1850 Rev. William McCabe was appointed parish priest, using as a place of worship a hall opposite the Dumfries Arms Hotel. Under his successor, Rev. Thomas Wallace (1853-1863) the Catholics followed the Congregationalists into the Black Bull hall and then to a little chapel of their own above the priest's dwelling in the Barrhill Road. Things were difficult at first, for anti-Catholic bigotry was strong. Members of the congregation were beaten up, and on at least one occasion the celebration of Mass was interrupted. The situation was aggravated by the fact that among the congregation for a time were navvies engaged in building the railway and living in huts near the viaduct. Their rowdiness and violent differences over Irish politics did not help to endear the Catholics in general to a suspicious protestant community.

Meanwhile progress is recorded in education. A good deal of thought had gone into the new parish school erected in 1804. Originally the site was to be in the schoolmaster's garden near the foot of Barrhill; a new garden was to be bought and laid out by Dr. Miller and Mr. James Taylor; and the schoolmaster— William Simson—was to have the old schoolroom as a dwelling-house. But the proposed site was ' inconvenient for the school-master and hazardous to the Children attending School from the extreme narrowness of the public Road leading from the village to Muirkirk and immediately adjoining said Situation.' It was decided instead to sell the schoolmaster's garden and purchase an alternative site adjacent to the existing schoolhouse and dwelling-house. The project included the building of a ' new schoolroom, a Jael and Library Room, together with a Coal house, a necessary house and an Ashyard.' The work was entrusted to John Campbell, mason, and David Lees, wright, both of Mauchline. Nothing more is heard of the library room, but the jail was constructed. The schoolroom was 34 feet long, 22 feet wide and 12 feet high, and the jail at the end was 12 feet long and 22 feet wide. The old schoolmaster's dwelling was retained and repaired. The total cost was just about £350.

The new school—on the site of the present Clydesdale Bank—was under William Simson's care till his death in 1815 and thereafter James Campbell (1815-1839); John McKinnel (1839-1844), and David L. Scott (1844-1882). In 1831 there were renovations, with ' a pend to be made through the School from back to front door, flagged in the bottom.' The old desks were to be altered by taking off one side and made single so that all sitters were turned towards the master; while a bench and desk for the master were provided on a raised platform. The school about this time had about a hundred scholars. Besides the three Rs, Latin and Mathematics were also taught, while in 1845 an innovation was made with £5 spent ' to enable the schoolmaster to procure a set of chemical apparatus in order that he may introduce Agricultural Chemistry as a branch of instruction.' The fees for reading were 3/-, for writing 3/6, for arithmetic 4/-, and for Latin 6/-, all per quarter of twelve weeks. Annually the schoolmaster received about £20 in school fees, supplementing £25 from Charles Duncan's bequest for educating twelve poor children, and the maximum salary, which in 1828 had been raised to £34 4s. 4d. In addition he received minor emoluments as precentor, session clerk, clerk to the heritors, and—for a time at least—as postmaster. Then as always there were other obligations of a voluntary nature. The new Statistical Account noted that the Savings Bank ' owed its prosperity chiefly to the devoted attention of Mr. Campbell the treasurer.' Finally, once a year, on New Year's Day, the pupils in best attire brought to the schoolmaster gifts in money and kind. In response he treated them to apples, oranges, cookies and sweets—as an alternative to the drink of weak toddy sometimes offered to scholars in neighbouring parishes; and the boy and girl who had brought the most generous gifts were appointed king and queen by the master.

CUMNOCK TOWN COUNCIL and Officials, November 1966
From left : Councillor James W. McHardy; Councillor Donald MacRae; *(behind)* Mr. R. B. Lorimer, Town Chamberlain; Bailie David B. Lorimer; Ex-Provost J. K. H. McTurk; Hon. Treasurer Thomas Guthrie; Provost Thomas Finn; Mr. R. D. Hunter, Town Clerk; Ex-Provost John Edgar; *(behind)* Mr. Robert Forret, Burgh Surveyor; Ex-Provost John Weir; Bailie John King.

The Covenanter's Baptism by Sir George Harvey, P.R.S.A., 1806-1876
(Aberdeen Art Gallery)

Plan of the Colliery of Garlaff, 1780
(National Coal Board)

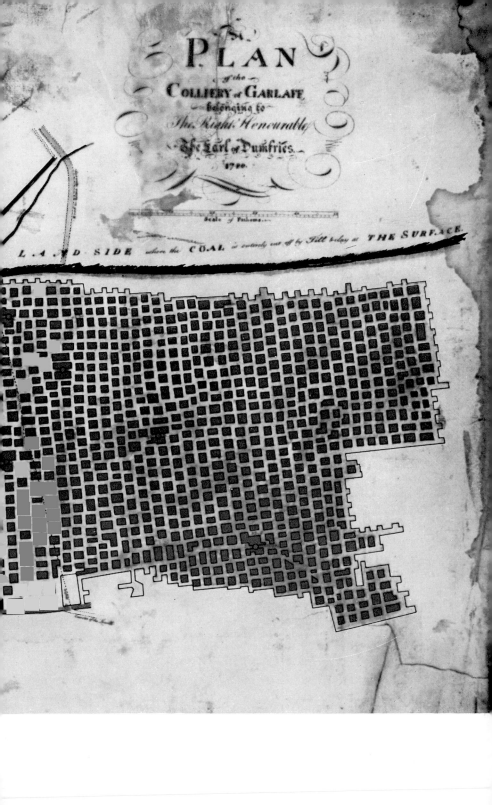

PLAN

of the

COLLIERY of GARLAFF

belonging to

The Right Honourable

The Earl of Dumfries

1780

Scale of Fathoms

L A N D SIDE where the COAL is entirely cut off by Fill below at THE SURFACE

(*Illustrations on page* 8)

Snuff boxes: (*a*) Made by Crichton, Cumnock (Lady Broun Lindsay)
             (*b*) Made by Lammie, Cumnock (N. Talbot Rice)
             (*c*) Maker unknown, (National Museum of Antiquities
                   of Scotland)
             (*d*) Made by Mirrie, Cumnock (Lord David Stuart)

Tea Caddy:
  (e) Made by Crichton,
        Cumnock
(Photographs by National Museum
of Antiquities of Scotland)

Earthenware:
  (f) From the collection in the
       Baird Institute, Cumnock
       (by courtesy of the Trustees)

(a)

(b)

(c)

(d)

(f)

Besides the parish school there were, in 1837, five private schools in the parish, and sometimes one or two additional schools during winter. These were ' adventure schools ' set up as a private venture by persons of varying qualifications. At various times such schools were run at Garlaff smithy by George Burns, in the Tanyard by Miss Mary Smith and by William McCrie, and at Baird's Place by Moses Inglis. Born in Fife in 1772, Inglis came to Cumnock in the 1820's as a clerk in the pottery, became schoolmaster at Dalleagles, then set up school in Cumnock, taking day and evening pupils till his death in 1867. There was another adventure school in the Strand, one in Tower Street taught by Miss Margaret Lammie, and Miss Susan Lamont's school in Ayr Road.

In 1843, following the Disruption in the Church, Mr. John McKinnel by joining the Free Church had to surrender the post of parish schoolmaster, giving up home and emoluments for his conscience, as did the parish minister. A year later in 1844 a Free Church School was opened beside that church, with Mr. McKinnel serving as master till 1862 when he resigned through ill health, to be succeeded in 1863 by a local man, Mr. Robert Brown. McKinnel was long afterwards remembered by a former pupil: ' He was a stern disciplinarian. In the morning we used to know by the frizzle of his hair whether we were to have a good day or a bad one with him. He had a system of spying established, the perfection of which would have put to shame the best detective agency in our larger cities. These spies were called reporters. He had a reporter for swearing, so that if you quarrelled with any of your schoolfellows there was no chance of you delivering yourself of strong language for fear of being reported. He had a reporter for striking, for tearing each other's books and clothes, for stealing, for going into George Goldie's or George McKerral's gardens, which were only separated from the playground by a small paling. He even had a reporter for kissing the lasses. After prayers every morning these reports were taken in, and all offenders had to go up to the master, and become acquainted with the red and black striped cane.' His methods of teaching were accounted effective. While there were 130 pupils in the parish school, there were (in 1853) a total of 176 in the three private schools, most of them in McKinnel's Free Church School.

In 1845, soon after the appointment of David L. Scott as parish schoolmaster, it was decided because of the dilapidated condition of the parish school and the adjoining prison to dispose of them and erect a new school and schoolmaster's house on a new site ' farther removed from the public streets.' Despite the objections of R. Campbell of Skerrington that the old school was quite adequate, it was decided to proceed with the project at a site in the park ' above the Schoolmaster's garden on the Muirkirk road ' at a cost not exceeding £450. Plans were prepared by Mr. John Baird and tenders accepted from Messrs. Campbell and Niven, Muirkirk, for mason work, and James Johnston, Auchinleck, for joiner work. In May 1847 the new school was opened, 48 feet long by 24 feet wide, with a school room and contiguous dwelling-house for the master. Thereafter three privies, a porch and coal closet were added, a well provided within the manse gate, the playground levelled, and furnishings supplied including ' three forms with backs for the younger scholars.' In 1849 the walls were roughcast, in 1852 gas was installed (at a cost of £8 13s. 1d.) and in 1854 when the Barrhill Road was widened for traffic to the railway station a six-foot-high dyke was built.

The school was open six days a week, and in 1837 the New Statistical Account had noted that ' there are very few above the age of fourteen who are not able to read and write, as parents evince a laudable anxiety to give their children the common branches of education.' There was provision for those who could not afford the fees: the Duncan Bequest paid for and provided with books twelve poor children, and the Marquess of Bute paid for twenty more. That the standard of teaching be maintained at a high level was the responsibility of the Church, and there was an annual examination of the school and its pupils by the parish minister and one or two neighbouring clergymen. The tests lasted several hours, and Bible knowledge in particular was carefully examined. It concluded with a presentation of small prizes to those scholars who had acquitted themselves particularly well.

The economic and social changes of the early nineteenth century brought changes in the way of life and manners of the people. Old habits survived. Well into the nineteenth century the townsfolk were still awakened each morning by the town drummer. As late as 1820 a few old men still kept up the fashion of a former generation. ' They wore the broad Kilmarnock bonnet, the long breasted waistcoat, the blue or brown swallow-tail coat, knee breeches, and shoes adorned with large buckles. Some, whose social position was high, dressed in pantaloons, and wore long hair, tied with ribbon.' The plaid continued in general use. A few old women continued to go to church with a mutch and a black silk hood over it. ' They carried their Bible usually wrapped in a snow-white handkerchief and holding in their hand a piece of fragrant " apple-ringie " or sweet-scented balm.' The traditional oatmeal diet was supplemented by tea, potatoes, and home-made bread. At the October fair a sheep or small bullock would be bought for winter salt meat, sometimes several households sharing this ' mart.'

Customs were in process of change, especially those relating to birth, marriage, and death. When a child was being taken to church for baptism, a gift was still offered to the first person met. At weddings, in a community where the horse was still a common feature, the custom of ' riding the broose ' was practised. The young folk attending raced on horseback from the church to the house that was to be the home of the newly-married couple. The winner received there from the mother of the bridegroom a bottle of wine or whisky, which was carried back to drink the health of the newly-weds. The last broose in Cumnock was ridden about the middle of the nineteenth century. Even after that there continued the custom of ' penny weddings ' where the expenses of a marriage supper—including the hire of a fiddler—were borne by the guests and any balance was left as a wedding gift. Another wedding custom practised in the nineteenth century—possibly a long-established one, and certainly long-surviving—is that on the eve of the wedding the companions of the bridegroom would wash his feet with soap, or even soot.

At time of bereavement, the custom of having a brief religious service at the ' coffining ' was still usual in Cumnock, but in the early nineteenth century a great change had come over the conduct of funerals. Rev. Mr. Bannatyne, writing in 1837, noted that ' it was very much the custom some time ago to give half a dozen rounds or more of spirits, wine, etc., at funerals;

but there has been a decided improvement in this respect in later years.' This change in habit was largely the result of the efforts of his predecessor, Dr. Miller, who in 1800 persuaded a group of local persons to subscribe to a ' Covenant of House-holders regarding the Method of Conducting Funerals.' Of this the most important clause read as follows:

' That none of us shall give any general or public entertainment either immediately before or after the Burial of our friends, and that, exclusive of the members of our family and those connected with the chief mourner by blood or relationship, we will not invite any number exceeding twelve to partake of the refreshment that may be provided suitable to the occasion, which we hereby agree shall not exceed three glasses of wine, or where this cannot be purchased, one glass of spirituous liquors, and bread propor-tioned; Binding and obliging ourselves to pay a penalty of Five Shillings sterling in all cases where any of us shall be found to do otherwise.'

Several years later an organisation with the curious title of ' the Whang ' was instituted. Members agreed to abstain from liquor till New Year when, after celebrating to the full, they re-pledged themselves for the next twelve-month. Another society was formed whose members abstained from all but beer and light wines—but it collapsed when some proved it feasible to be intemperate on this restricted list. Finally in 1838 at a meeting in the Pottery a Total Abstinence Society was formed and began a long and influential career. In 1851 it had 160 adult and 140 juvenile members.

One item concerning death and burial requires brief mention. In 1869 the Heritors ordered ' the small wooden house in the churchyard to be removed forthwith.' According to Warrick this was an old watch-house which was used as a shelter by those who guarded the graveyard at the time when fears of body-snatching were rife.

As ways of work changed in the early nineteenth century so did the character of leisure. In a community which was still small and had close rural connections, many of the traditional recreations continued with special opportunities for enjoyment at the kirns and fairs. But new types of leisure time activity were developing. Controversy about religion was joined by political argument. The spread of education encouraged an interest in reading and reading stimulated interest in further education. In 1837 there were two public libraries in the town. One may have been the Athenaeum, reputedly dating to 1792, though another source gives 1859 as the origin. It provided not only books on loan at moderate charges, but also lectures and concerts. The other may have been associated with the parish school. There was also a small separate library of religious books for the use of those attending the Sabbath schools, of which there were four, one in the town with 300 scholars, some of whom were probably adults. The other developing cultural activity was music. There was a strong local enthusiasm for fiddle-music from the days of John French, and this was extended. In 1841 the Heritors granted the use of the school for concerts—by the Old Instrumental Band on the evening of the May Fair, and the Senior Cumnock Band on the 31st December.

This indicates the existence at that time of two local bands. The first local brass band was instituted in the first quarter of the century, composed mainly of box-makers, but it collapsed in the late thirties. Some time later a ' New Bawn ' began, but after its formation some disgruntled members withdrew and revived the ' Auld Bawn.' Each had its adherents who followed their favourite band on practice marches round the town, and inevitably one evening both bands met head-on in the narrowest part of Glaisnock Street. An enthusiastic trombonist fortuitously struck with his instrument the ear of a passing rival, and in a moment a riot was in progress. Who won the ' Fecht of the Bawns ' is not recorded. But some years later in 1844 the ' New Bawn ' defeated the auld enemy in the band contest at an Ayr Temperance demonstration. The ' Auld Bawn ' could not overcome the humiliation and soon after broke up. The ' New Bawn ' continued alone for some years thereafter.

TOWN AND COUNTRY IN MID-CENTURY

Rev. Ninian Bannatyne in 1837 sketched the appearance of the town in words—' The town of Cumnock is snugly and finely situated in a hollow, at the confluence of the Glaisnock and

Lugar waters. The principal part of the town is a quadrangular space, called the Square, formerly the burying-ground, but now the market place, which is surrounded by houses most of them of recent erection. In the centre of the square, stands the parish church. There are besides the square, three pretty long streets, in which there are some very good houses. The rest of the town consists of very narrow lanes, irregularly built. The town in general is pretty clean and healthy. The beauty of its situation, combined with the picturesque banks of the Lugar, and the fine woodlands in the vicinity, together with the striking effect produced by some fine old trees, rearing their heads among the houses, call forth the admiration of travellers.'

The first Ordnance Survey Map of the area, surveyed in 1857, makes possible a closer inspection of the town in mid-century. The Square is clearly marked, and the irregular huddle of the old town nearby. It is possible to trace Tower Street, reached from Glaisnock Street or through Caddie's Close. From Tower Street one could go up Drummer's Brae by the Needle E'e (later the Pawn Steps) into the Square or through Bank Lane to Lugar Street; or down Elbow Lane to the Townfoot Green. Further west Tower Street met the Tanyard, with the U.P. Church and the Dubb bridge leading over the Glaisnock Water to Spout Row in Ayr Road.

The three long streets mentioned by Bannatyne were Townhead, Glaisnock Street, and Ayr Road. The first, populated by cotton handloom weavers, extended as far as Crossriggs, where the Market Cross had once stood. Off it, to the right and down by the burn stood Glaisnock Cottage beside Rakeams Green. Glaisnock Street where it bridged the burn was known as the Gorbals. Off it was the cul-de-sac called Waterside Row—or Soor-milk Row. The rising incline of Glaisnock Street was known variously as Heid Inn's Brae, or McKinlay's Brae, or Munn's Brae. Persons named Donaldson and McKinlay were proprietors of the Dumfries Arms early in the century, succeeded by Joseph McKnight, then James Murray, and Robert Munn. Glaisnock Street was built up on the west side as far as the Dumfries Arms, and on the east side behind Greenbraehead was a smithy; beyond on the main road was the Gas Works opened by a private company in 1836; and the pottery fronted by

Pottery Row. Down by the burn was the curling pond. Further out the New Cumnock Road (where the new station was later built) was known as Calstoneheads or Coldsideheads. Ayr Road, with the Free Church, was built only on that side; further down was Spout Row near Nicol's Well at the foot of Car Road.

On the north side of the town, Barrhill was still an open road. Going from the Square, on the right was French's Row, where the violinist of that name had lived. The manse stood in its own grounds, with the woollen mill to the west and the Parish School and Graveyard at Broombrae to the east. Hillside House and Broomhill had been erected. Over the Lugar by Stepends Bridge in Auchinleck parish was the land of Holmhead—popularly known as Boo't Scotland. Here several villas had been erected—Holmhead, Broomfield, and the U.P. manse, beside Woodend Farm.

In Holmhead and up Barrhill were signs of an important new development. The Stepends Coal Pit was now in operation, and up Barrhill (where Keir Hardie Hill now is) there were three pits producing coal and ironstone. Elsewhere in the parish there were coal pits at Garrallan and Garlaff, and an ironstone pit at Shankston. Miners' rows were built near Garrallan and Garlaff, and adjoining sheets of the Ordnance Survey Map show the untidy rash of pits and rows that had suddenly appeared not very far away along the Auchinleck-Muirkirk railway line by Birnieknowe, Common, and Lugar. The great age of coal and iron had begun in the Cumnock area.

The town, with about 2,600 inhabitants in 1860, was a thriving place. Rev. Ninian Bannatyne had remarked that ' from its central position in regard to the neighbouring parishes, a great deal of business is transacted in the town, much more than its size would lead a stranger to expect.' He pointed out that there were in the town ' excellent shops of all kinds.' In 1837 John McGavin had come from Sorn and set up in the Black Bull Close a bakery business long carried on by his son John, the maker of the famous Cumnock tarts. Three grocers are almost as long-established—Galbraith's founded in 1849; the firm of James Livingstone, Lugar Street, started by Mrs. Janet Livingstone in 1861; and Alex. Muir & Son, Townhead, founded in 1859. Then in 1852 Duncan Ballantine commenced business as a printer and stationer in 12 Glaisnock Street, moving in 1864 to 49 Glaisnock Street. There were in 1837 two banks in the town: a branch of the Ayrshire Banking Company, and a private agent of Hunters & Company. The Ayrshire Banking Company had bought a property on the west side of the Square in 1834, and operated a branch till 1845 when the Western Bank of Scotland took over and rebuilt the premises, which were acquired in 1857 by the Clydesdale Bank and became known as Clydesdale House. In 1838 a branch of the Bank of Scotland was opened, with its agent Matthew McKerrow, a cloth merchant, using his home as a place of business till bank premises were opened in 1870. A third bank came in 1856, with the Royal Bank renting premises till the present building in Glaisnock Street was built in 1866.

Cumnock, of course, continued as a market centre, and indeed this trade expanded in the nineteenth century. The Burgh charter of 1509 had authorised weekly markets and an annual fair on the feast day of St. Matthew, 21st September and eight days following. A charter of 1681 provided for three fairs to supplement the weekly market—the second Tuesday and Wednesday of June; the second Tuesday and Wednesday of July; and the last Tuesday and Thursday of October. By the end of the eighteenth century there were no longer regular markets, though well into the nineteenth century Thursday was still recognised as market day. The development of shops, banks, and the carrier trade made markets unnecessary for regular sales and purchases. But the nineteenth century saw an increase in the number of fairs. Three are recorded in 1813 and 1830, four a few years later, and for a time there was a fifth as well. The February Fair was a new one, on the Thursday after Old Candlemas, joined in mid-century and later superseded by the Race Fair in March, on the third Thursday after Candlemas. The May Fair was on the Wednesday after the last Tuesday of May, and so was sometimes in early June. On the Wednesday after the first Tuesday of July came the Scythe Fair. The Harvest or Hin-hairst Fair came on the Wednesday after the third Tuesday in October. Cattle were sold at all these fairs, and horses at some. They were equally important as feeing fairs, where farm workers were hired. Most of this business was transacted at the March and October fairs, though for a time the engagement of harvest workers was a principal function of the appropriately-named Scythe Fair, while at the May Fair labour was engaged for the hay. The fairs were also occasions for entertainment. ' Shows of different kinds, shooting-ranges, swings, etc., offer their attractions at these fairs to the youthful crowd, while stalls filled with sweetmeats and toys, as well as with a great variety of small articles more or less useful in their nature, tempt visitors to purchase. The sale of cloth, books, kitchen and dairy requisites, together with agricultural produce, has gradually died out.' Until the middle of the nineteenth century ' it was no uncommon thing for those who set up stalls to bring their supply of sweet-meats, nuts and toys, in little wheeled carts drawn by dogs. Two or even three dogs were sometimes yoked to one of these carts. It was a sight which evoked interest among young people, to see the dogs make a rush at the steep ascent of the old Lugar bridge and go down the other side. Frequently forty or fifty dogs were gathered together in the Square.' One special feature of the March Fair was the horse race. Formerly taking place in Ayr Road—down to Bridgend and back—it was latterly held in a field owned by Dumfries Arms Hotel, with ten to twelve entries and about £70 in prize money. In the nineteenth century the fairs were held in the Square, though with increased traffic this became awkward. By 1857 some were being held in a field up Glais-nock Street—later the site of Cumnock's second railway station.

While agrarian improvements were only beginning at the time of the first Statistical Account, forty years later in 1837 the character of agriculture had been completely changed. All farms were enclosed, with fields bounded by hedges, and areas formerly moorland were now under cultivation. Early attempts at wedge-draining with turfs had had a limited success, but now the Mar-quess of Bute had established a tile works, and supplied tiles free to his tenants, stipulating that a certain number of acres should be drained on each farm each year. Leases ran from fourteen to nineteen years, usually paid in money, though there were still some survivals where two-thirds of the rent was paid in cheese and meal. Rents varied from £4 per acre on the best lowland to 10/- for moorland pasture. Many of the farm steadings were still old, and built in an inconvenient continuous line, but new steadings were being built on the three sides of a square.

Whereas at the end of the eighteenth century the main interest had been on grazing and fattening cattle, now the parish had gone over wholeheartedly to the sale of farm produce to the folk in the growing towns, and like the rest of Ayrshire discovered with profit the merits of dairy farming. While cash crops were still being grown in considerable quantities, more land was being devoted to pasturing dairy cattle and raising fodder crops. By 1837 the cows were all of the Ayrshire breed and much care was being paid to improving the stock. There was a local Farmers' Association, patronised by the Marquess of Bute, which offered annual premiums for the best milk cows. The farmers had come to depend on the dairy chiefly for their returns, and—in days when long-distance transport was still limited—the manufacture of cheese was carried on generally. Some farmers near the town did of course sell liquid milk, or sub-let some fields and hired out cows to ' bowers ' who made a living from the sale of milk. Cumnock cheese had a good reputation, and about 11,000 stones of it were produced annually, about 1,000 milk cows producing about eleven to twelve stones each on an average. On the upland farms there were from 1,000-1,200 sheep. Though the stock population had not risen in forty years, the yield had increased manifold.

The average gross amount of raw produce in 1837 was as follows:

Oats	.	.	£10,000	Barley . . . £674
Cheese .	.	.	3,672	Bear (coarse barley) .	674
Rye-grass	.	.	1,599	Meadow hay . .	538
Potatoes	.	.	1,400	Turnips . . .	500
Peas and beans	.		900	Wheat . . .	250

The meal was ground at local mills. In 1837 there were three corn mills and one wheat mill. By 1857 the last had disappeared, but corn mills continued at Skerrington, Boreland, and Greenmill. The meal, cheese, and other produce was collected by carriers and transported mainly to Ayr. In the 1840's there were three such carriers—Alexander Findlay, John Nicol, and John Allan, plying each Tuesday and Friday. Later they were followed by the Lattas, Bryans, Vallances, and George Alexander. Robert Latta was a conspicuous figure with his dark green coat, drab breeches, rig and fur stockings, stout shoes, and tile hat. Stock was also bought and sold locally at the Cumnock fairs, though farmers were tending more and more to go to Ayr and Kilmarnock. At the Cumnock fairs, too, farm workers were hired. In 1837 the usual wages were—ploughmen from £10 to £14 a year; dairy maids from £3 to £4 a half-year; labourers from 1/6 to 1/8 a day. Most of the farm workers lived on the farms, but there was by 1857 a clachan of cottages at Roadside on the Glaisnock Road.

As well as the smithies in the town, there were others at Plantainside, Logan, Garrallan, and at Bridgend. Other country workers, besides the miners at Garlaff and Garrallan, were those labouring in the quarries—at Knockterra by Garrallan, the several whinstone quarries near Avisyard, and the quarry at Benston producing limestone from which a good quality cement was manufactured.

In the early nineteenth century the Marquess of Bute was the principal landowner, but there were other five heritors owning estates of some importance. In 1837 Glaisnock was in the hands of James Allason. His brother Alexander had purchased this estate about 1797. James Allason succeeded him in 1833 and soon after constructed the elegant new mansion house. Logan had been purchased about 1800 from Mr. Hamilton, a Glasgow merchant (who had it from the Laird of Logan) by a William Allason. After his death in 1825 it passed to his daughter, Elizabeth, who in 1834 married Captain William Cuninghame, usually known as William Allason Cuninghame. In Garrallan, an heiress had also succeeded, in 1819: Jane Douglas, who married Hamilton Boswell of Knockroon. Their son was John Douglas Boswell. The last two heritors were Robert Campbell of Skerrington, and Lt. Colonel Andrew Campbell of Avisyard, whose father, Arthur Campbell of Auchmannoch, had succeeded his uncle Dr. Andrew Mitchell in 1819. The other little estate of Boreland in 1839 passed out of the hands of the Montgomeries and was incorporated in the Dumfries estate.

Patrick, sixth Earl of Dumfries, died in 1803 in his seventy-seventh year; his wife, the Countess Margaret, had died in 1799. Of their two daughters, one died in infancy and the other lived only till the age of twenty-four. In 1792, however, while still only nineteen, Lady Elizabeth Penelope Crichton had married John, Viscount Mountstuart, heir to the Earl of Bute. Ten months later was born a boy, John, who would eventually become both Earl of Dumfries and Marquess of Bute. His father died when he was only five months old; his mother when he was four years of age. In 1803 at the age of nine he succeeded his maternal grandfather to become seventh Earl of Dumfries. Two years later, on the petition of his paternal grandfather who in 1796 had been created first Marquess of Bute, the young Earl adopted the joint surname of Crichton-Stuart, and in 1814 at the age of twenty-one succeeded as second Marquess of Bute.

Educated at Cambridge and widely travelled, the second Marquess took an active part in affairs. Politically he was a supporter of the Duke of Wellington and Sir Robert Peel. He represented the Queen as Lord High Commissioner to the General Assembly in 1842, 1843, and 1844, at the height of the Disruption troubles. He devoted much time to the improvement of his wide estates, developing particularly the lands of Cardiff which his paternal grandmother had contributed to the family fortunes. Despite his other interests, he attended to his Cumnock properties, took an active part in the work of the parish church, contributed generously to helping the poor at a time of great distress, and as a working member of the local Heritors Committee personally selected the site for the new parish school.

On his death in 1848 he was succeeded by the only child of his second marriage—John Patrick, who became third Marquess when only six months old. Educated at Harrow and Oxford, he developed a deep and abiding interest and reverence for the past. He wrote voluminously on antiquarian subjects and gave generously to the work of archaeological research and restoration. Shortly after coming of age he embraced the doctrines of the Roman Catholic Church and gave of his wealth to the building of new churches. He was equally lavish with other benefactions, both nationally and locally, until his death at Dumfries House in 1900 at the age of fifty-three.

Chapter 5

The Police Burgh, 1866-1929

The nineteenth century brought with it numerous problems arising from the increase in population and the growth of towns. Whereas in the past, in a rural community with a few and small towns, supply of water and the disposal of refuse were usually simple, by the nineteenth century with rapidly swelling numbers of people congregated together, difficulties became acute. Not only was there inconvenience, but public health became a problem, and epidemics of one kind and another swept the land. After 1832 the reformed parliament turned its immediate attention to these matters. In 1833 the old royal burghs (like Ayr and Irvine) and new parliamentary burghs (like Kilmarnock) were reformed, and householders paying over £10 a year in rent might now elect town councils to attend to such matters as watching, lighting, paving, cleansing, and water supply, and levy a local assessment to pay for them. For the smaller burghs in barony there was not the same urgency; places (like Cumnock) where the old burghal arrangements had more or less disappeared, and new towns which had grown up and had never been burghs, had to await Acts of 1850 and 1862 which permitted ' populous places ' to adopt the ' police system ' and become new burghs. In Ayrshire this was in fact done in Maybole (1857) and Galston (1862); in Cumnock (1866); followed by Stewarton (1868), Newmilns (1872), Darvel (1873), Largs (1876), Ardrossan (1877), Saltcoats (1885), Girvan (1889), Kilwinning (1889), Troon (1896); in the twentieth century, Prestwick (1903) and most recently Stevenston (1952).

THE FORMATION OF THE BURGH

Early in 1866 a petition was presented to the Sheriff of Ayr to have Cumnock declared a populous place in terms of the General

Police and Improvement (Scotland) Act, 1862. It was signed by nine local gentlemen—David Crichton, grain merchant; William Dalgliesh, manufacturer; Daniel King, manufacturer; William Ettershank, banker; David Lawson Scott, schoolmaster; Duncan Ballantine, bookseller; John McCowan, innkeeper; Anthony McClymont, solicitor; and Alexander Muir, grocer, residing in Holmhead in Auchinleck parish. The boundaries were defined by a line running from near the railway station south towards the New Cumnock Road, north-west to Bridgend on the Ayr Road, over the Lugar Water to include the Holmhead area, and up the Lugar thereafter to the railway station.

After various legal formalities, the Sheriff decided that this was a populous place as defined in the Act and called a meeting of £10 householders ' at Cumnock within the Hall in or near Glaisnock Street in the yard of the Dumfries Arms Inn there ' at 11 a.m. on 2nd November 1866. At that meeting it was proposed by Messrs. McClymont and Scott, two of the petitioners, that Cumnock be made a burgh.

There was opposition, however, and an amendment that the Act be not adopted, moved by William Johnstone and seconded by George Macarvail, was carried. But the petitioners were able to demand a poll and this was arranged to be held in the same place three days later, 5th November, between 9 a.m. and 4 p.m.

Meantime feelings were running high, and though few people had the right to vote, the town was sharply divided on the issue. The local Chartists, whom one would suppose to have favoured the scheme, were violently antagonistic, for the reform of parliament and universal suffrage was for them the first and only prerequisite. They held meetings in the Square denouncing ' the idiocy of municipality.' Rev. William Hutton, the U.P. minister, was a powerful advocate for the Burgh and as a result many of his congregation left his church. Challenged by an opponent, he was defended by a supporter and after the ensuing fight the minister's friend was taken to Ayr and fined for assault—the fine being paid by the supporters of the movement.

The result of the poll was declared on 6th November at 11 a.m., when by thirty-five votes to thirty-two, the Act was adopted and Cumnock became a police burgh. The majority was small but, says Warrick, ' it was sufficient.' It was thereafter decided that the burgh should be known as the Burgh of Cumnock and Holmhead, that the council should comprise nine commissioners, and that it should not be divided into wards. Just over a month later, at 11 a.m. on 7th December 1866 at a meeting of householders as before, the following Commissioners were elected by public poll, to form the first Council:

William Dalgliesh, draper	20 votes
David Lawson Scott, teacher	20 votes
William McLetchie, wright	20 votes
Thomas Barrowman, contractor	20 votes
Daniel King, wool manufacturer	20 votes
William McGavin, miller	18 votes
John Drummond, engineer	18 votes
John McCowan, inn keeper	18 votes
Duncan Ballantine, bookseller	16 votes

The first meeting of the Council was held in the Parish School at noon on 10th December, and at an adjourned meeting at the more convenient hour of 8 p.m. on 13th December when all could be present, William Dalgliesh was appointed Senior Police Magistrate and Messrs. King and McGavin after a vote were elected junior police magistrates. Thereafter the Commissioners settled down to make plans for the appointment of the officials who would be required to assist them in the execution of their duties. By Act of Parliament there were certain mandatory duties (things that must be done) and others which were permissive (things that might be done if so minded). It should be mentioned that though this was designated a police burgh, such a burgh was not responsible for police, since county police forces had in fact been set up in 1858.

On 24th December 1866 a start was made by appointing as Clerk and Collector Andrew White, agent of the Royal Bank, at a salary of £15 per annum; and as Inspector of Nuisances at the modest sum of £4 per annum, David Smith who already was the Inspector of Poor for the local Parochial Board. In the New Year it was decided that meetings thereafter should be held in the Clerk's Office at the bank in Glaisnock Street, and to get down to business the Council formed committees—a Sanitary committee (January), a Water committee (February), and a Finance committee (June). The enthusiasm with which the council proceeded can be gauged from the work accomplished in the first year of office, before the December 1867 elections. The Sanitary committee made plans for collecting street sweepings and rubbish, provided six street dust receptacles, and arranged to purchase a large two-wheeled dust barrow. It selected sites for privies in Rakeams Green and Townfoot Green. It investigated nuisances in Townhead Street, and consulted the County Road Trustees regarding the repair of that street. It conferred with a committee of townsfolk who had a scheme for street lighting, took over their funds, obtained lamps, put them on posts, and made arrangements with the Gas Company. It appointed a scavenger and lamplighter at 16/- a week. The Water committee was no less energetic. Obviously the provision of a water supply was one of the prime intentions of the new council. What made the matter particularly urgent was that the spouts were drying up as pits were sunk. In February they considered analysing water from various sources—which next month was reported by Professor Penny of the Andersonian University, Glasgow, as 'suitable in every respect for dietetic purposes.' They engaged Mr. Blackwood, Civil Engineer, Kilmarnock, to draw up a plan. He selected the stream near Boreland farm as the best place for a reservoir. By August an approach was made to the Curators of the Marquess of Bute regarding land for reservoir, filters, and water courses. The Finance Committee in turn investigated the possibilities of a loan, and in October to prepare for future commitments appointed Thomas Shields as the Burgh Treasurer at an annual salary of £3 10/-.

Apparently satisfied with their first Council, on Saturday, 7th December 1867, only nine persons turned up at the householders' meeting in the Court House and by a show of hands re-elected the three retiring commissioners—Messrs. Drummond, McCowan, and Ballantine. The Council thereafter reconstituted its three committees, created another for the formulation of byelaws, reappointed its officials, and continued with its work. By March 1868 the lands and premises in the burgh had been valued at £4,280. The Council's proposed expenditure had been estimated at between £130 and £140. The first year's assessment for 15th May 1867 to 15th May 1868 was thereupon levied on all occupiers at 8d. in the £. The organisation of burgh affairs was completed some time later in October 1869 when a Burgh Court was set up to deal with offences against the byelaws which had been prepared. Andrew White, the Town Clerk, was to be Clerk to the Court at an additional salary of £5 5/-, and Archibald Brakenridge, solicitor, became Burgh Prosecutor at from £7 to £10 per annum. The County Police Committee authorised the local policemen to enforce the byelaws, and cases were to be heard in the existing Court House.

PROGRESS IN PUBLIC SERVICES

As time passed, while the Council extended its range of activities, throughout its history one of the most important duties has been the humble, uninteresting, but essential one of keeping the town clean, healthy, tidy, and safe—the work mainly of the Sanitary committee. It was decided in May 1868 that David Richmond, the scavenger, should go round daily with the dust barrow, at 8 a.m. in summer, and 9 a.m. in winter. Offers were taken for the street sweepings, and for many years after 1868 they were disposed of, at 2/2 per cart, to John Stevenson, Garrallan. The primitive state of affairs existing is indicated by the first of the Burgh's byelaws, as revealing for what it permits as for what it forbids:

' it shall not be lawful to empty privies, or to place, or allow to remain, for the purpose of removal, on any street, lane, close, etc. within the Burgh any dung, manure, or other offensive matter at a later hour than nine a.m. from April 1st to October 1st and eleven a.m. during the rest of the year.'

For thirty-two years David Richmond was Burgh Officer and scavenger till he retired in 1899 due to ill health. By that time he had an assistant to help cope with the work, and a man, horse, and cart were also hired as required. In 1903 the Council decided to purchase its own horse and cart.

The actual negotiations for acquiring a horse were protracted, and stimulated Alexander Barrowman, the journalist, to one of his best efforts:

A TALE OF A ONE-HORSE TOWN

A Provost and a Bailie,
Both men of high resource,
Did undertake, quite gaily,
To buy a burgh horse.

They knew the thing they wanted
Had a body somewhat round,
Four legs, for they had counted,
Just length to reach the ground.

A head upon its shoulders,
Projecting well in front,
And, to draw those whinstone boulders,
A big stern, broad and blunt.

A neck, too, quite elastic,
To bend about, or rise,
And a tail that could be drastic
With the buzzing summer flies.

Their horse should have no vices—
Not any trace of guilt,
And though they paid two prices,
They'd have one pure Clyde-built.

But here the tale gets comic,
For, alive to what they did,
Their colleagues, economic,
Set a limit—fifty quid.

Then the two, both much insulted,
Said that wouldn't get a cob.
And the meddling all resulted
In them chucking up the job.

A draper and a grocer
Then stepped into the breach,
For each of them did know, sir,
All the horsey art can teach.

They visited the Crosslar,
And out for miles around;
They talked with groom and ostler,
But no horse could be found.

At length these men, so zealous,
Tramp, tramping here and there,
A postcard wrote to Wallace,
Who sent them on a mare.

She's said to be a beauty,
Quiet, active, young, and fresh,
And bunks at no one duty
That's fitting to horseflesh.

And thus we see in Ayrshire,
From this lesson ta'en from life,
Good horses are getting scarcer,
Though donkeys may be rife.

The Clydesdale mare actually cost £55, more than was originally stipulated. A dust cart and box cart were also purchased.
And Robert Grant was engaged as the burgh's first carter. To
a later Council the system was thought unsatisfactory, and in
1911 the horse, carts, harness, and stock were disposed of, the
stable in Barrhill let, and for the next twenty-three years con-
tractors were hired to undertake the burgh cleansing and other
cartage.

Though a scheme for burgh drainage was suggested as early
as 1870, in fact many years were to pass before an adequate
system of sewage disposal was possible. All that the Council could
do for long enough was to deal with public nuisances, insist that
proper cesspools should be provided, and latterly arrange for
effluent to be carried by sewer pipes down to the Glaisnock
Water. So long as there was a good flow of water in this stream
all was more or less well, but in dry summers the situation was
both unpleasant and unhealthy. In 1886 therefore the Council
was pleased to agree to a suggestion of the Cumnock Curling
Club that their pond should be repaired and enlarged to provide
a reservoir from which the Glaisnock could be flushed in the
summer. After negotiations with McCartney & Co., who required

a constant supply of water for power and whose interests had to be safeguarded, the flushing scheme was introduced in 1887. Difficulties increased in the twentieth century when waterclosets became more common—120 were installed in the years just before 1911. But in 1902 the Council had considered there was no necessity for a drainage system. It was not until 1920 that the Council decided on a comprehensive linking up of drains and sewers, with an eye towards a scheme of sewage disposal, which was initiated in 1929.

The Council had certain special responsibilities for public health and when epidemics threatened they had to take precautions—the dangers of outbreaks of cholera were noted in 1883, 1885, 1892 and 1893, and of smallpox in 1872, 1874 and 1901, while in the influenza epidemic of 1918 twenty-three died in the burgh. To control possible sources of infection, the Inspector of Nuisances, David Smith, was appointed also Inspector of Cattlesheds in 1868 at £1 per year extra and the following year a burgh slaughterhouse was erected at ' the north west corner of the field at Barrhill in which the Eglinton Iron Coy's Ironstone Pit is situated.' A Slaughterhouse committee was thereafter constituted, letting the slaughterhouse annually, and prohibiting killings elsewhere in the burgh. Another possible source of infection was from the coming and going of beggars and casual labourers, especially from Ireland. At the 1871 Census it was noted that of Cumnock and Holmhead's population of 2,903, 190 were Irish-born, 48 English, and 10 foreigners— and some of these incomers must have been migratory workers. The inspection of lodging houses was one of the Burgh's duties; in 1893 there were eighty-seven licensed beds in local lodging houses, and it was estimated that through the year there was an average of fifty persons per night using them. A Model Lodging House was suggested and in fact one was built under private auspices in 1902 in Elbow Lane. In 1910 besides the Model, there were other eight lodging houses: Carter's, Bryan's, Digby's, Whitten's, Lorimer's, Moorhead's, Phillips', and Hamilton's. Finally, to report on the state of public health it was agreed in 1893 to have a Burgh Medical Officer of Health at £10 per annum, and Drs. Lawrence and Kerr were appointed jointly. The former died in 1895, the latter resigned in 1899, and thereafter the County M.O.H. performed the work at £15 per annum.

Though the maintenance of the streets was not the responsibility of the burgh till 1892, the Council was always concerned with the convenience of the public. Shopkeepers were periodically reproved for leaving boxes and rubbish in the public thoroughfare, and the Square was a particular concern. This was the site for markets and fairs and by the old charter of 1509 the Marquess of Bute had certain traditional rights. In 1869 the Council applied to him for authority to uplift the ' customs of the town ' and apply the proceeds to their own purposes. The factor to the Marquess believed that the late Mr. A. McCowan had been the last person authorised to collect the customs and the Council was given this privilege, which had apparently fallen into neglect. Thereafter they drew up a scale of charges for those wishing to use the Square. Congestion was already a problem, but the Square was let regularly for shows in March and September to the occasional annoyance of shopkeepers, passers-by, and the kirk session.

The lighting of the streets the Council made its responsibility from the beginning, taking a supply of gas from the private local Gas Company. Until 1876 David Richmond, the scavenger, was lamplighter, and as the number of lamps was extended he was granted appropriate recompense, eventually obtaining 22/- per week for his main duties and £5 per year specially for lamp-lighting. For a time thereafter the care of the lamps was contracted out. In 1881 John Sime, plumber, agreed ' to execute the lighting and repairing of your lamps for one year of seven moons for Fifteen pounds, or for eight moons Fifteen pounds ten shillings.' When the burgh staff was increased they took over lamplighting duties again, but later still it was once more contracted out each winter. In 1920, for example, James Little, gas fitter, was given the job at 25/- per week. In 1898 an advance was made when the new Diamond Jubilee Fountain in the Square was illuminated by an incandescent gas lamp. After 1905 incandescent lamps were extended throughout the town. In an excess of enthusiasm even the Market Cross had been crowned with a gas lamp in the 1880's, but this was removed in 1911. In 1899 a forward-looking Council talked of ' fitting up apparatus for engendering Electricity for the purpose of lighting the Public Streets and to supply all private parties who wish,' and in 1906 this was again considered. In 1921 Kilmarnock Corporation sought powers to initiate an electricity supply undertaking to serve a wide area throughout the county. By 1925 this Ayrshire Electricity Board was extending lines towards Cumnock, but there were delays and it was only in 1928 that Cumnock was in fact reached. It was decided that the main streets should be lit by electric power, and a beginning was made with five lamps at the Square—two of 300 watts, two of 200 watts, and one of 60 watts.

As early as 1870 the Water committee was instructed to place fire plugs throughout the town and provide a hose, and a fire brigade of sorts must thereafter have been formed. In 1876 a house was erected in Waterside Place to hold the barrow and hose. In 1879 the brigade was reorganised, when 29 persons volunteered and were formed into four teams under J. Sime, H. Morrison, David White, and Andrew Murdoch, who were elected captains. The four captains were to arrange for practices and to have sole charge at any fires, ' the first on the scene to have the preference in command.' By 1896 a smaller (though presumably more efficient) brigade was under the sole charge of Hugh Morrison as captain. There were six assistants, with four practices a year, paid 10/- each per annum, with a fee at fires of 3/- for the first hour and 1/- per hour thereafter. They were to be insured for £250 each. In 1913 these scales were increased, and new equipment was purchased, including an old barrow obtained from Kilmarnock Fire Brigade at £4 4/-. The Burgh Surveyor, Thomas Small, was in charge, as superintendent, and his brigade consisted of A. Harvey (captain), A. McLellan, J. Merry, H. Merry, William Arthur, and James Morrison. In 1915 proposals for a new shed for the fire engine had to be deferred, and it was arranged that the fire equipment should be stored in the Craighead Inn.

The provision of a water supply engaged the earnest attention of the first Council in 1867. From the very beginning there were difficulties. Their first ambitious plans had to be modified for reasons of cost, and as a compromise it was decided that the reservoir to be established at Boreland should contain six weeks' supply only, but with the possibility of later enlargement. A cash credit of £2,000 was obtained from the Clydesdale Bank and throughout the latter part of 1868 the work was put in hand. By January 1869 fifteen street wells had been erected, the first dozen better-off householders had applied for a private supply, an offer had been accepted from Mr. David Johnston of Kame, Lochwinnoch, to erect a ' fountain and jet d'eau ' in the Square, and arrangements made for the opening of the water-works. The total cost had risen to £2,400, and a further loan had to be obtained. At the second annual assessment, though the rate for general purposes was reduced, a new water rate of 6d. pushed the total rate up from 8d. to 11d. in the £, and the following year it went up to 1/2 in the £. Nor was it possible to make any reduction till 1877.

Gravitation water was preferable to water from the river or spouts like Nicol's Well (Ayr Road) and Robin's Well (Barrhill). But inadequacies in the new supply soon made themselves felt. In 1872 the Water committee sought to extend the catchment area. In 1873 the water main was extended up Barrhill and in 1880 to the miners' row at Glengyron, and at these higher levels the pressure was often inadequate. In 1880 and 1885 the Auchinleck Parochial Board applied for an extension of the water main to Auchinleck, but these requests had to be turned down. In 1885 plans were made to clean out and heighten the reservoir, and in 1889 to install new filters and relay the pipes, but the supply to Barrhill was only temporarily augmented. As general consumption of water increased and reserves went down, there just was not enough of a head for the people at the top of Barrhill. In 1895 and later summers when there was a drought it became necessary indeed to shut off the entire burgh supply for some hours daily. In 1896 angry Barrhill residents unsuccessfully petitioned for relief of rates because of the chronic water shortage. Borings were made in search of more water in 1896 and 1897, but though some improvements were made, by 1902 the Barrhill water supply was again under consideration. In 1903 additional work was done, but complaints continued in 1904, 1906, and in 1908. In 1912 the *Cumnock Chronicle* described the burgh water supply as ' the Banquo's ghost of the Town Council table.' There were many jokes about efforts to scour the pipes with a contrivance nicknamed ' the monkey.' Major improvements were proposed in 1908 but not accomplished till 1913. Even so, by 1917 shortage of water was again a problem and in 1919 thoughts turned to a completely new water scheme up Glenmuir, possibly in association with the County Council. This ambitious proposal fell through, and a search for alternative additional sources of supply proved unsuccessful. But in 1922 work was initiated on a large-scale extension of the reservoir at Boreland, with new filters, at a cost not far short of £10,000, and after its completion in 1924 the situation was eased, for a time.

The public services so far detailed were the concern of the Council since its inception in 1866. New duties, however, were added. In 1885 a Town Hall was erected and taken over. In 1892 the Council acquired responsibility for road maintenance. In 1903 the Council, always concerned with the approval of new buildings, formally constituted itself as a Dean of Guild Court. In 1912 it moved into the new field of council house building. In 1928, under Council auspices, a Municipal Bank was instituted.

The want of a public hall had long been felt. The only available accommodation for meetings, concerts, and elections was—apart from the school and the U.P. Church—in halls connected with the Black Bull and Dumfries Arms hotels. A proposal to consider the erection of a town hall was first mooted in Council in 1880, and because they had no authority to borrow for this purpose it was decided to make an approach to the Marquess of Bute. This was done late the following year, with the welcome response that the Marquess would offer a site free of charge and a monetary contribution of £500. Three sites were considered—in Ayr Road; on the Jail Park in Barrhill Road opposite the graveyard; and a field in Glaisnock Street opposite the Gas Works, which was selected. A subscription list was opened, a committee formed with representatives of the Council and subscribers to select a suitable design, and the foundation stone was laid in October 1883. By the beginning of 1885 subscriptions had passed £2,000 and the Hall was in fact opened on the evening of 7th January 1885, followed by an amateur concert and ball which raised £70, leaving a deficit which was cleared by a bazaar in 1896. Public generosity built the Hall and helped to equip it, from John Baird's special subscription ' for ceiling ornament of Large Hall, £5,' to a Union Jack presented by Captain Campbell of Glaisnock on

the occasion of the Queen's Jubilee. The Council became responsible for its maintenance. Furnishings were purchased, including
Dr. Lawrence's piano at £35. A Hall committee was appointed,
and arrangements made for a hallkeeper. Conveniently, David
Richmond the scavenger, who had also been holding the post of
Inspector of Nuisances since 1874, decided to resign the latter
post in 1884, and applications were invited for ' a man of good
character honest and obliging, cleanly and tidy with himself
and his work,' who would combine the posts of Inspector of
Nuisances and Hallkeeper. John McCallum, mason, was appointed at £30 per annum, plus free house, coal, and gas.

The Town Hall proved its immediate value and was in constant
demand for social, religious, and political functions, and the
Council was always generous in reducing or rebating charges for
worthy charitable purposes. The facilities of the Town Hall
were also utilised by the Council for its own purposes. A Council
room was furnished for meetings, the Inspector had an office, and
the annual elections could be held here. Other bodies found the
Hall equally useful. The Athenaeum moved from the old Court
House and took a room for its Library. The County Council
hired the Lesser Hall for the J.P. Court in 1893 and until a new
Court House was built in 1895.

The Parish Council obtained the use of the Town Council
Room until a fearful row broke out in 1898. The Parish Council
had had a group photograph of themselves taken and had hung
it up without the permission of the Town Council. This was in
January. After much correspondence, in March the Parish
Council were ordered out. In August they surrendered, took
down the photograph, and the Council Room was re-let to them
the following January on new terms. The Town Council recom-
pensed the Parish Council who had shared in purchasing the
furniture—' paying them one half of the furniture and to obtain
a Receipt therefor.'

Normally the Town Hall committee's work dealt with more
humdrum items—purchasing a lightning conductor (1893), new
seats (1896), a new flag (1902), a new piano (1908), and a clock
(1909); dealing with dry rot (1891, 1911); relaying the floor
(1905); improving the heating (1911); providing two new
bedrooms for the hallkeeper (1899); and making periodic

renovations (1912). Occasionally matters of principle involved the whole Council. In 1891 following a petition from the Peden Thorn Lodge of Good Templars it was decided that no intoxicating liquors might be served at any function in the Town Hall. This was in June. In December the decision was rescinded. Similarly, in 1908 an application to hold a Christian Socialist meeting in the Hall on a Sunday was turned down. Later—but this time after ten years—in 1918, Cumnock Independent Labour Party was granted the Hall for a Sunday meeting. Innovations always caused discussion. In 1913 the Town Hall was let for cinematograph entertainments (on nights not otherwise engaged). Elaborate precautions had to be taken—the screen had to be dismantled and re-erected to the Council's satisfaction, care had to be taken with the four-ton portable engine and dynamo, no smoking was to be permitted during the shows—and the hallkeeper asked for an increase in salary. After 1918 work continued, to keep the Hall in good order and adequate for local needs. To raise funds for extensive renovations (1919, 1922) two fancy dress balls were held, a whist drive and dance, and a musical and dramatic recital. Then the heating was improved (1925); electric lighting was installed (1928); and the post of hallkeeper became a separate job (1923). It was decided (1921) that at dances only ' plain-soled shoes or slippers ' might be worn, and later (1923) there were purchased ' Smoking Strictly Prohibited ' notices. In 1925 a new piano was gifted by Mrs. Kerr on behalf of the Gray family.

In 1892 the Council became responsible for the maintenance of highways. Before that it dealt with various public nuisances in the streets; in 1876 it named them and numbered the houses; and when necessary it made representations to the County Road Trustees about the conditions of the roads themselves. In 1875 when the Trustees proposed establishing an additional toll bar on Barrhill the Council objected, because of the number of existing toll bars and the unsatisfactory condition of the roads in general. Growing traffic made changes in administration necessary. Tolls were abolished and replaced by a road assessment in 1878, the new County Council took over from the Road Trustees in 1889, and by the Police Burghs (Scotland) Act of 1891 the local roads and streets became the responsibility of the Town Council.

The surfacing of the streets imposed extra expense and work and worry. In 1895 the local merchants successfully petitioned for the streets to be watered in summer. In 1898 when the old wooden bridge over the Glaisnock near McCartney's works was carried away in the big flood, a replacement was necessary and an iron bridge built. This became known as Betty's Brig, after Betty Howatson or Goudie of the nearby Candlehouse who was rescued from the flood by James Davidson. Joe's Brig was named after Joe Hunter ('Pottery Joe') who for many years entertained the Hecklers' meetings with his wit, campaigning for a bridge to replace the stepping stones at the Greenholm. In 1900 the council removed the iron tram rails on Barrhill Road—this action was contested in court by J. Keir Hardie and others. From 1902 the council decided to take over and maintain footpaths. The same J. Keir Hardie in 1903 asked for a footpath outside his house in Holmhead, and obtained it on payment of the usual contribution by the householder. Nine years later he complained of the state of the footpaths in Auchinleck Road and became involved in a dispute with the council over responsibility. The maintenance of footpaths in fact became a burning election issue and the council had to fight several court actions. To improve the roads, in 1903 it was decided to macadamise the Townhead; in 1909 the council purchased a tar boiler, and in 1912 a tar spray; in 1913 it was decided to acquire a horse-drawn sweeping machine and a snow plough.

These miscellaneous items concerning the maintenance of the highways were accompanied by other difficulties relating to the traffic on these highways. In 1895 Bostock and Wombwell's Menagerie was charged 5/- for damage their vans did to a lamp in the Square on their way through the town. Wombwell is said to have described the Glaisnock Street corner in Cumnock as the worst between Hell and New York. In 1893 complaints had been made to the Council about 'the high rate of speed at which Bicycles were ridden through the Burgh' and a byelaw was proposed three years later to restrict the speed of bicycles to six miles per hour. Eventually it was stipulated in 1898, with the authority of the Secretary of State, that the speed limit should be eight m.p.h., and that all vehicles should carry lamps at night. New developments in road traffic brought a further problem and in 1903 the speed of motor vehicles in the burgh was restricted to ten m.p.h., and in 1907 for the convenience of through traffic the Scottish Automobile Club agreed to erect direction posts. In 1901 a novel speed trap was successfully operated. As a car passed through Cumnock the police telegraphed Sanquhar. When the car ultimately arrived there, it was halted by the local police, a calculation made, and the driver charged with exceeding the stipulated general speed limit of 12 miles per hour, by 22½ minutes. In 1908 there were complaints against boys playing marbles and football in the streets—a long-established practice, but a new danger because speeding by cars and bicycles continued, noted for example in 1913, and in 1916 when motor hirers in the town were approached regarding their ' high and dangerous rate of speed.' Motor traffic increased rapidly after the first World War. By 1924 the Council discussed with other local authorities the need for byelaws relating to the new passenger road services. There were numerous complaints about the high speed of buses, about the noise and smell, damage was being done to kerbs, and a lamp was knocked down in Auchinleck Road. They brought increased expenses in road maintenance.

In 1926 the Council allocated £2,400 for the repair of Class I and Class II roads within the burgh. Work was undertaken in widening the foot of Barrhill Road in 1925, and in the following year the Commercial Bank corner in Glaisnock Street was improved, to cope with the new flow of traffic. In 1927 additional work was done at the Barrhill, Lugar Street was widened at the Clydesdale Bank, and in 1928 Munn's Brae in Glaisnock Street was improved. In the same year asphalt was used for the first time and all the main thoroughfares had been improved and resurfaced by 1930 when the County Council took them over. Congestion was also relieved when in 1928 the fountain was removed from the Square to the Oval facing Gray Street, though James Neil's proposal (in 1925) also to remove the Old Market Cross had to be dropped after a public outcry. The greatest advance was made when it was finally decided that it was quite impossible to continue having the shows in the Square. Bostock and Wombwell were allowed to have their menagerie on 4th August 1927, and in 1928 Lawrence was given his last let for shows at the March Fair.

As a result of the passing by Parliament in the early years of the twentieth century of various Acts for the housing of the working classes it became possible for the first time for councils to contemplate, if they so desired, the construction of houses for letting. In Cumnock the opportunity was seized at once, for here in the early years of the century the housing position was becoming acute. In the early days of the burgh, Cumnock was not as badly off as many places. At the Census of 1871, figures of numbers of persons per room showed that Cumnock with 1.86 was better than the burghs of Kilmarnock (2.11), Galston (2.62), Newmilns (2.60), Stewarton (1.99), and Kilwinning (2.03) and many parts of the landward area (the county average was 1.90). In the following decades Cumnock's figures improved to 1.74 (1881), 1.53 (1891), and 1.48 (1901). But while local overcrowding was being relieved it was not by further building. In fact, it was because people were leaving the town. Numbers had risen steadily from about 800 in 1800 to 2,903 in 1871 and 3,345 in 1881, but thereafter declined to 3,104 in 1891 and 3,088 in 1901. The number of houses in the burgh, 425 in 1871, had risen to 500 in 1881 and 642 in 1891. But in the next ten years less than thirty were added and the number was only 670 in 1901. The trouble was the difficulty in obtaining leases on favourable terms. In the 1880's the thatched house of Peggy Baird in Lugar Street and several other old properties, having run their ninety-nine year lease, were taken possession of by the Marquess of Bute. This action caused consternation among other owners. Public meetings were held and the Marquess was interviewed by Provost McLetchie and a deputation from the Council. Sandy Barrowman summed up the feeling against the feudal superior and the settlement:

> *Oh it's when was a Stuart e'er cautious?*
> *Or free frae that mean selfish greed?*
> *They should aye be reminded, when fashous,*
> *O' yin o' them losin' his head.*

> *The upshot o' a' oor endeavour,*
> *Is noo pretty publicly kent:*
> *We're tae get oor ain house, as a favour,*
> *By paying his Lordship's rack rent.*

As a result of all this, private house-building seemed a chancy business. In 1893 the Council petitioned Parliament regarding building land. In 1903 they again approached the Marquess of Bute regarding the difficulties of getting ground to lease from him. Warrick in 1899 noted this difficulty of obtaining sites on favourable terms from the feudal superior, to whom practically the whole of the land on which the town was built belonged. He pointed out the large amount of building twenty-five years previously whereas since then the building of new houses had practically ceased. Though the position was eased with getting leases in Holmhead from Auchinleck estate, and feus in the glebe after 1898, difficulties persisted. After 1901 the burgh population started growing again, from 3,088 to 3,407 in 1911, continuing to 3,541 (1921) and 3,653 (1931). Overcrowding became worse— 1.48 persons per room in 1901, 1.49 in 1911, 1.50 in 1921. An acute shortage was felt, and at a time when the houses in the town, built most of them just about a century before, were proving increasingly inadequate. In 1911, of the burgh's 752 houses, 135 (18 per cent.) were single-ends, and another 305 (40 per cent.) were two-room dwellings.

The Council therefore, on 10th June 1912, accepted the motion of Councillor James Neil: ' Being fully aware of the deficient state of many dwellings, and the serious inadequacy of housing accommodation within the Burgh, it is hereby proposed that the Council should consider the advisability of erecting a number of suitable houses to meet the needs of the community in this department.' A Housing committee was appointed under the convenership of Provost Richmond, and the Council proceeded cautiously on this novel venture. It was decided to erect twelve houses on land belonging to the Baird Trustees on the new thoroughfare laid out in 1908 and known as John Baird Street. The total costs would be £2,658 8s. 8d. and it was resolved to borrow £2,700 from the Public Works Loan Commissioners, repayable over a period of sixty years. According to the Housing of the Working Classes Act, 1913, preference had to be given to ' respectable working class people.' The rents were fixed at £13 5/- per annum for a ground floor dwelling and £13 for an upper floor. These, Cumnock's first council houses, were ready and occupied in March 1915, and the following year it was decided they should be named Urbana Terrace. Some time passed before this first scheme was joined by others. Wartime economy measures were in force. In any case there had been some difficulties with the builders of the first houses over defective workmanship. And they were proving expensive. A housing assessment had to be added to the rates from 1918 onwards. Thus while the Council in the autumn of 1918 began considering possible sites for new housing schemes, the following year they were recommended by the Cumnock branch of the Miner's Union not to build any more till the government would offer housing loans free of interest.

Plans for a second council housing scheme were passed in 1920. These 36 houses, in Cairn Road, Car Road, and Shankston Crescent, were ready for occupancy in October 1921. The rents were fixed at £22, £27, and £31 per year for three, four, and five apartment houses respectively. In 1922 additional houses in Glaisnock Street were planned, and sixteen such houses were ready by 1924. Another scheme was approved thereafter and thirty-two bungalow-type houses erected on the site of the old Racecourse in 1925, forming the four new streets named Hall Terrace, Latta Crescent, Gemmell Avenue, and Gray Street. The first took its name from the adjacent Town Hall, the others from local benefactors—Sir John Latta, Bart., the late Alexander Gemmell, and the late James Gray.

A further eighteen houses were added to this scheme in 1926 and plans made to erect another fifty-two, and three more were added in 1927. In 1929 twenty more were built in Urbana Terrace, thus providing the burgh by that date with a total of 189 council houses. At the same time efforts were being made to bring up old properties to reasonable standards, by insisting that owners should install water closets and other facilities, and from 1928 Closing Orders were made on old houses which required to be condemned and demolished. The number of houses in the burgh increased from 752 (1911) to 767 (1921) and 887 (1931). The ratio of number of persons per room improved from 1.50 (1921) to 1.34 (1931). But there was still plenty of scope for further improvement. There were in 1931 still 125 single-ends. And though some of the 340 two-apartment dwellings were new council houses it was an unsatisfactory position when more than half of the people were still living in one and two roomed houses. Overcrowding, it is true, was worse in Kilmarnock (1.52), Galston (1.72), Newmilns (1.38), Darvel (1.37), Kilwinning (1.53), Irvine (1.55) and in the landward area of Ayrshire (1.39). But advances were being made everywhere—in 1926, for example, the County Council built twenty-eight houses at Skerrington Mill. In 1931 the county average for number of persons per room (1.33) was now rather better than Cumnock (1.34).

The provision of all these various local services involved an annual reckoning of costs. Large capital outlays were spread over many years by loans, and latterly increased grants from government sources for more expensive projects became available, but even so day-to-day expenditure and the repayment of loans involved increases in the annual assessment of rates. The first levy of householders in 1868 of 8d. in the £ was followed by a rise in the next two years to 11d., then 1/2. Thereafter there was no change in the next six years and an actual drop over a period—1/1 in 1877, 11d. from 1878-1883, 10d. from 1884-1885, and 9d. from 1886-1889. But the twentieth century saw a new upward trend. This was due to the extension of the various public services, at a time when prices and costs were rising. The local rates were also inflated when in 1892 the burgh took over from the county responsibility for road maintenance.

In 1893 a new system of levying rates was introduced, which continued in operation till 1947. For roads, and after 1900 for sewage, water supply, and public health as well, owners and occupiers shared the costs while an additional general assessment was levied on occupiers only. In 1893 owners paid 2¼d. in the £, occupiers paid 1/2¼ (and owner-occupiers paid a total of 1/4½ in the £). Rates rose slowly though erratically over the next two decades. In 1914 owners were paying 1/- and occupiers 1/8½ in the £. After 1918 there were sudden and dramatic increases, reaching a peak in 1923 (2/6 owners, 3/11 occupiers) with a drop thereafter. A tidying-up step was accomplished by the Valuation Act of 1926. In succeeding years the Town Council was made responsible for collecting in the burgh also the rates previously separately levied by the Parish Council and the County Council. In 1929 Cumnock Town Council collected a consolidated rate of 4/7 in the £ from owners, 5/7 from occupiers, of which 1/3½ and 2/3½ respectively was the burgh assessment.

During the period of the police burgh, from 1867 till 1929, other public local authorities were in operation. There was a Parochial Board (1845-1895) superseded by a Parish Council (1895-1930), responsible for poor relief throughout the parish and for certain minor duties in the landward area. It co-operated from time to time with the burgh council on matters of common interest, from concern over unemployment to the arrangement of coronation celebrations, and members and officials of the one council often also served the other. Its meeting place and office were for a time in the Cumnock Town Hall, which was the occasion for the spirited ' photograph ' dispute in 1898. Friction was more frequent with the County Road Trustees and with the County Council who were responsible for roads before 1892. The County Council had been formed in 1889, taking over from the old Commissioners of Supply the levying of a county rate, and becoming responsible for police, roads, and a widening field of public health functions. The proposals of the County Council in 1893 to erect a hospital in Cumnock resulted in dissension over the most suitable site. The town council objected to the choice of Barrhill Road.

Sandy Barrowman complained:

> *What's this the County Council want?*
> *What gumption they disclose, man!*
> *A fever hospital they'll plant,*
> *Aneath our very nose, man!*
>
> *They'll put it where the Slauchter-house*
> *Emits its pleasin' odour!*
> *Objection's no' the slightest use—*
> *We're prejudiced; they're broader!*
>
> *Though Cumnock may hae choice sites*
> *On sunny braes a' roon, man,*
> *That's naething to sic knowin' wights;*
> *They'll plant it in the toon, man!*
>
> *Nae fear o' them, they've got the brains:*
> *They'll no' mak' ony blunder!*
> *But place it where the railway trains*
> *Gae rushin' by like thunder!*

> *What's that ye speer? Can they rely*
> *On sure supply o' water!*
> *Just note their ready, smart reply,*
> *' That, really, does not matter!'*
>
> *What though a' roon' the country-side,*
> *We gather in infection,*
> *There's cause, at least for civic pride—*
> *'Twill be a grand erection.*

Eventually in 1898, with the approval of the Marquess of Bute, they were able to persuade the County Council to place the hospital outwith the town, at Holmhead.

Friendly co-operation however was the general rule. No complaint ever had to be offered over the efficiency of the local police provision. J.P. Courts met in the old parish school in the Square (with jail attached) till 1839 and thereafter in a Court House built in the Townhead. This became also the police station after the creation of a County Constabulary in 1858. A new Court House was built behind it in 1895.

As time went on the town council was called upon to appoint representatives to numerous bodies constituted on a county basis. In 1907 the county and the various burghs collaborated in the establishment of Glenafton Sanatorium for pulmonary cases and continued to do so till the County Council took it over entirely in 1915. In 1903 the town council agreed to participate in forming an area Juvenile Delinquency committee, and representatives were annually appointed to a variety of committees dealing with social welfare, child welfare, and old age pensions.

One special public service with which the town council was never directly concerned was education. This had been the concern of the local parish Heritors Committee, which lost its supervision of poor relief in 1845 and (though it survived till 1931) surrendered in 1872 its other main function of providing education. In 1873 the Old Cumnock Parish School Board was formed, with elected members, and through the Parish Council levying a school board rate to maintain the local schools. In 1919 an elected County Education Authority replaced it and continued till 1929, with a subordinate Cumnock Area School Management Committee to which Cumnock Town Council sent one of its members as a representative. In 1929, with the passing of the Local Government (Scotland) Act, the whole system of local government authorities was reorganised.

THE COUNCIL AT WORK

When the police burgh was instituted in 1867 its nine elected members were designated police commissioners, and from among that number they selected a senior police magistrate and two junior police magistrates. It was not till after the Burgh Police Act of 1892 that the titles of provost and bailies were introduced; and by the Town Council Act of 1900 the police commissioners became councillors. In December 1893 the council chose as its common seal a device ' shewing the Old Cross in the Square, with a Weaver's Shuttle on the one side and a sheaf of corn on the other.' In August 1916, to commemorate the 50th anniversary of the burgh, a Provost's Chain was presented by Alexander Gemmell, a native of the town who had gone from the local branch of the Royal Bank eventually to become an important representative of Barclay's Bank in the Bradford area.

Originally the annual elections were conducted by the Sheriff of Ayr, until in 1869 the council obtained the right to supervise its own elections. Before 1872 these elections were carried out at a meeting of the £10 householders by a show of hands, but by Act of Parliament the secret ballot was then introduced and this stimulated participation. The numbers of persons proposed did not exceed the number of vacancies till 1871 when a choice of three had to be made from among four contestants. A year later (under the secret ballot) there were five candidates and thereafter a contest became usual each November. Over the next thirty years, a poll had to be held on twenty-one occasions. The numbers taking part in the elections were increased when the franchise was extended to all ratepayers, and interest was augmented by the keen party rivalries between Conservative and Liberal, the intervention of fierce issues like temperance, and the rise of the Labour Party. In 1872, 290 votes were cast among five candidates; in 1896 in similar circumstances there were 1,049 votes, cast by 425 electors.

The nine members of the original council set a good record for service to the community. McGavin served only two years, Drummond seven years, and King served nine. Ballantine's was cut short by death after eleven years. Dalgliesh was in the chair for his entire period of twelve years and was succeeded in that office by McCowan, who was fifteen years a councillor. Scott and Barrowman had respectively twelve and thirteen years' interrupted service. The last was McLetchie, narrowly defeated after eleven years on the council, but returning two years later to begin another eleven years and become the burgh's fourth provost. Only four later councillors could surpass that record. Long service was almost always rewarded by eventual appointment as provost, though William Kay was twenty years on the council without achieving that honour. On the other hand, seldom did anyone hold the provostship for more than one term of three years in the period of the police burgh. The first served four terms; Samson served two. The only other was James Richmond, who in the hurly-burly of party politics was a councillor from 1885-1901 and 1905-1917, was provost once, then again at a later date, and after another interval served for a third and fourth term, dying while still in office—a total of twenty-eight years' service to the burgh.

Each council, after the November elections, made when necessary the appointments of provost and senior and junior bailies, and occasionally appointed former magistrates to be police judges. At the same meetings appointments were made to the various committees through which the work of the council was expedited. In 1867 finance, water, and sanitary committees were constituted, and in 1868 a Slaughterhouse committee added. The widening scope of public service required additions and re-organisations from time to time. The Sanitary committee became a Sanitary and Streets committee in 1871. In 1893 a separate Streets and Lighting committee was formed—with an additional Footpaths committee between 1911 and 1919. The Sanitary committee became in 1905 the Sanitary and Public Health committee and thereafter was known as the Public Health committee. In 1910 the Slaughterhouse committee was superseded by a Cleansing committee, responsible for Cleansing and Property after 1913. In addition there had been added a Town

Hall committee in 1884, a Dean of Guild Court in 1903, and a Housing committee in 1912. By the 1920's therefore the council's committees had increased to eight—finance, water, public health, cleansing and property, streets and lighting, town hall, housing and Dean of Guild Court.

Each committee met under the chairmanship of a convener selected by the council. As one would expect, newly-appointed councillors were rarely given such appointments, or only a relatively unimportant convenership. The very important finance committee was for its first ten years continuously under the convenership of Duncan Ballantine, who though ' brusque in his manner ' was recognised as ' a man of mind, energy, and good business habits, with a peculiar aptitude for statistics.' After his early death aged 49 it was taken over by Bailie Samson, who retained this convenership when promoted to provost and from 1893 till 1947 the provost was always finance convener. When the dean of guild court and the housing committee were instituted, the convenership of these was also always given to the provost. There was less continuity with the other committees. Until the late 1880's it was quite common for the same convenership to be held by one councillor for a number of years, but thereafter the annual allocation seems to have become quite irregular apart from the war years when there were no elections and reappointment of committees was the rule. After the war, constant change became the rule. To cite one instance: in the years from 1919 to 1924 one councillor served in turn as convener of each of the five committees available—the other three being reserved for the provost.

From its inception the burgh was required to appoint certain paid officials—a clerk, a treasurer, and another whose duties extended from being an inspector of nuisances to become eventually the superintendent of the burgh's various public works.

Andrew White, agent of the Royal Bank, was appointed Clerk and Collector in 1866 and held these part-time posts for twelve years, his remuneration being increased in 1875 to £25 per annum, plus a supplement for his work at elections, £5 if there was a poll £2 if not. He was also Clerk to the Burgh Court, which usually earned him five guineas a year. He died in 1878 and the council mourned the passing of this man of ' stainless character and sterling integrity.' Archibald Brakenridge, who had been the

Burgh's Procurator Fiscal and also burgh treasurer, succeeded him as clerk and collector (and also as agent of the Royal Bank). Twenty-two years later in 1900 he acquired the assistance of John Hume, solicitor, as depute town clerk, who in 1903 took over as Clerk, with Brakenridge retiring to become depute. Hume was joint agent of the Royal Bank from 1916 till his death in 1923. Brakenridge continued as bank agent till his own death in 1933, but his 54 years of service as a burgh official had ended after Hume's death in 1923. In that year R. D. Hunter succeeded as town clerk, at an annual salary of £100. He was a local solicitor, agent of the new Commercial Bank in Cumnock, and he continued to serve bank and town till he died in 1941. He was assisted by a depute town clerk, from 1925, in which year the council took the novel step of appointing to that post Miss B. S. Meikle, its first lady official.

The post of burgh treasurer was in the days of the police burgh less responsible than it later became, being then concerned mainly with keeping the burgh accounts, the town clerk and collector taking charge of the rates. It was less remunerative, and two holders of the post used it as a stepping-stone to becoming town clerk. The first treasurer, Thomas Shields resigned in 1873, succeeded by Archibald Brakenridge, who became town clerk in 1879. His successor was David Smith. He was a son of James Smith, shoemaker, and at an early age was appointed Inspector of Poor by the Parochial Board. David Smith was a prominent local figure, Preses of the U.P. Kirk, Superintendent of its Sunday School, and active in the cause of Temperance. Besides being Inspector of Poor he was the burgh's first Inspector of Nuisances (1866-1873) and later Treasurer for a longer period (1879-1901). After Smith's resignation came George Begg; following his sudden death in 1908 the post was taken by John Henderson, bank accountant. Henderson resigned in 1922, and was followed by R. D. Hunter, who became town clerk a year later. Thereafter there was a redivision of duties and John Allan, the Cumnock Inspector of Poor, became also both treasurer and collector, at a salary of £90 per annum, from which he had to provide his own office accommodation.

When David Smith, Inspector of Poor, took over the additional post of the burgh's Inspector of Nuisances in 1866 it was worth

only £4 per annum, and even adding the duties of Inspector of
Cattle Sheds in 1868 brought only £1 extra, so that he resigned
in 1873, to be succeeded by William Thomson, and a year later
by David Richmond who did the job between 1874 and 1884
in addition to his work as town scavenger.   John McCallum
followed in 1884, combining the job of Sanitary Inspector with
that of keeper of the new Town Hall till 1897, and thereafter as
Inspector only, till his death in 1906.   In 1897 it had been resolved
to create an additional post of Burgh Surveyor and Inspector
of Cleansing, and Thomas Goldie was given also the duties of
hallkeeper, at a combined annual salary of £65 plus free house,
coal, and gas.   He resigned in 1907 and it was decided to combine
his duties with those of the vacant Sanitary Inspectorship.   The
responsibilities of the council were now so considerable that it
was decided to advertise nationally for a man of experience,
and twenty young married men who might be expected to settle
down in Cumnock were considered.   Thomas Small from South
Queensferry was selected to be the Burgh Surveyor, Master of
Works, Sanitary Inspector, and Hallkeeper at £85 per annum
with the usual extras.   But a year later he gave up his hallkeeping
duties and in 1914 went off to a better job in Dunbar.   Thereupon
for his successor was chosen a fully-qualified man with a certificate
in Sanitary Science, Robert Forbes from Buckie.   He got rid
of the vexatious duties of Town Hall keeper in 1923, which thereafter became a separate post.   His responsibilities were vastly
increased with the extension of council house building.   His
initial salary of £100 had risen to £300 by 1925, and he continued
to serve the council till 1956.

The council was also served well by its employees in a lesser
capacity.   David Richmond, appointed scavenger and lamplighter
soon after the burgh's inception, served for thirty-two years,
helping out as sanitary inspector for ten of them.   One of his assistants, Andrew ('Bammey') Harvey, was employed before 1889
(when his salary was increased by 1/- to 20/- a week), went on
to assist with the fire brigade, and during the first World War
took over the duties of Burgh Surveyor and Sanitary Inspector
while Forbes was away in the Army.   In 1917, when he celebrated
his golden wedding, the Provost and some friends presented
him with a gold watch.   In 1922 he was kept on as an odd-job

man; he could retain his house rent-free and his old age pension was made up to £2 a week. He died soon after, having served the burgh for over thirty years.

The Minute Books of the Council reveal from time to time glimpses of events, great and small, as they affected Cumnock. In the early years the shadow of the feudal superior still fell over the burgh, and the council never omitted to pay its respects. In 1868 it offered its congratulations to the Marquess who had just attained his majority. In 1876 and 1883 it congratulated him on the birth of children. In 1900 it offered condolences on his death. In 1901 it expressed its pleasure at the twentieth birthday of the new Marquess and the following year on his twenty-first birthday invited him to a luncheon and presented him with an address. In 1907 it congratulated him on the birth of an heir. But thereafter the personal link was less close. In 1928 messages were sent when Lady Jean Crichton Stuart was married, and when the Earl of Dumfries came of age, but in each case some Labour councillors dissociated themselves.

National events found a local echo. In 1898 a fountain was erected in the Square to celebrate the Queen's Jubilee. A jubilee bonfire set Shankston bing on fire, and had to be extinguished by Andrew Harvey's fire brigade. Queen Victoria's death was noted in 1901; in 1901 and again in 1911 arrangements were made in association with the Parish Council and the School Board to celebrate the coronation of Edward VII and George V respectively. There was rejoicing in 1900 at the relief of Mafeking, and the following year the smallpox epidemic in Glasgow meant that no shows could be held in the Square. Local events were noted. Floods are mentioned in 1869, 1898, and 1901, and recurred in 1916, 1923, and 1927. Current high wages in 1875 are remarked upon—' which here as elsewhere had an unfortunate effect in increasing the number of Police Cases.' The problem of unemployment was giving concern in 1893. New ideas were in the air. While in 1897 the council declared by four votes to three against supporting women's suffrage, it agreed to support this in 1910, and in 1914 even sent delegates to a Glasgow conference on the matter. In 1914 it refused to subscribe to the Bannockburn anniversary; but in the 1920's it paid annual subscriptions to the Scottish Home Rule Association. In 1920

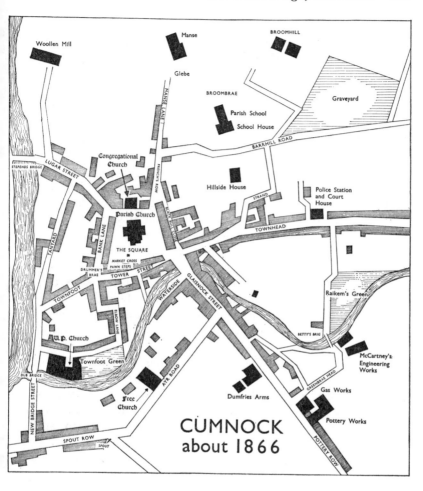

Woollen Mill

Manse

BROOMHILL

Glebe

BROOMBRAE

Parish School

School House

Graveyard

BARRHILL ROAD

STEPENDS BRIDGE

LUGAR STREET

Congregational Church

MANSE LANE

FRENCH'S ROW

Hillside House

STRAND

Police Station and Court House

Parish Church

BACK STREET

TOWNHEAD

TANYARD

BANK LANE

THE SQUARE

MARKET CROSS

PAWN STEPS

DRUMMER'S BRAE

TOWER   STREET

Townfoot

ELBOW LANE

WATERSIDE

GLAISNOCK STREET

Raikem's Green

BETTY'S BRIG

U. P. Church

Townfoot Green

AYR ROAD

McCartney's Engineering Works

DUB BRIDGE

Free Church

Dumfries Arms

GREENBRAE HEAD

Gas Works

NEW BRIDGE STREET

SPOUT ROW

SPOUT

Pottery Works

POTTERY ROW

CUMNOCK
about 1866

it sent petitions to the Prime Minister and to the President of the U.S.A. in favour of introducing the metric system; and in 1928 (by the provost's casting vote) declared its opposition to capital punishment.

The shadows of the first World War first darken the pages of the Minute Books in 1911 when it is noted that manoeuvres were to be held in the area. At the meeting of the council on 11th August 1914, just after the outbreak, war makes its immediate impact. The Town Hall has been requisitioned for the Ayrshire Yeomanry, a public meeting is called to help form a local company of volunteers, and support is given to a national fund for the relief of war distress. In succeeding meetings they consider special constables to guard the reservoir; they note that Joseph Handley, a burgh workman, has enlisted, and agree to pay his wife 10/- a week during his absence; they grant the first of many requests for a free let of the Town Hall for a whist drive to raise funds for comforts for soldiers. In 1915 they gravely note the first local casualty—the death of Pte. Thomas Gilchrist of the 1st R.S.F.; they hear that a new county battalion is to be raised; and news arrives of the Cumnock Company of the 5th R.S.F. in action in the Dardanelles; they form a local Tribunal for appeals under Lord Derby's recruiting scheme. Municipal elections are to be postponed for the duration; and burgh workmen need higher wages because of increased war prices. At the beginning of 1916 it is recorded that the burgh has lost twenty-four dead, and four missing; later in the year the death of Lord Kitchener is mourned. A War Savings Committee is formed, allotments laid out, and the gas supply is to be cut off in the event of an air raid. The fiftieth anniversary of the burgh's formation is celebrated by a brief historical statement read by Provost Richmond.

Tension eases in 1918. The end of the war passes unmentioned. The new Council refuse the offer of a damaged machine gun from the War Office. In 1921 they attend the opening of the War Memorial in the new cemetery; and in 1922 agree to support the formation of a local branch of the British Legion. But already they are immersed not only in the problems of post-war reconstruction, but in the new post-war difficulties. In 1921 they give the Town Hall free to the Miners' Union for a concert in aid of the Communal Kitchen Fund, and after the coal strike is over they ask the miners to cover in the open casts in the Bank where they had been working coal for their own use. The following year the council are faced with a strike immediately concerning themselves. The workers engaged on the new reservoir down tools when the government orders a reduction in the wages of publicly-employed workmen. In 1926 the council expresses its concern at the General Strike, and co-operates with the Sheriff in enrolling special constables.

Meanwhile the composition and the outlook of the council reflect the rise of Labour influence. In 1916 immediately after Keir Hardie's death a proposal in council for a statue in his memory had been turned down. In 1919 the matter was considered again, and a committee formed, but the establishment of a suitable memorial took a long time. The spread of Keir Hardie's socialist ideas are clearly seen in 1920. In that year it was proposed to purchase High Auchengibbert farm ' to cultivate for the benefit of the burgh ' and a similar plan for a wide extension of municipal ownership came with a suggestion that the Gas Works, the Model Lodging House, and the Picture House should each be taken over and run for the benefit of the ratepayers. In fact enthusiasm was focused on building of a series of council house schemes. And in 1928 Cumnock Municipal Bank was formed. Its first shareholders were seven members of the town council, and its first chairman was the man whose idea it was. He was Emrys Hughes, who in 1927 was elected to the town council at his second attempt, and served on it for twenty years till after his election as M.P. for South Ayrshire in 1946.

In 1929, with the passing of the Local Government (Scotland) Act, a chapter in the burgh's history came to an end. Negotiations were set afoot for the transfer of certain duties to the County Council, and the title of ' police burgh ' was abandoned in favour of that of ' small burgh.' By coincidence, an interesting ceremony took place in Cumnock that year which afforded an opportunity to assess the sixty-three years of the police burgh's work. James Richmond, a native of Cumnock and son of the old scavenger, who had become an engineer in Australia, sent a donation to supply the provost with a gown, hat, and chair. On 12th August, in the presence of the council and several excouncillors, Provost Neil was formally robed. The presentation was made by Ex-Provost Thomas Hunter, who had served from 1878-1896, and who reminded his audience of the tremendous changes that had taken place in the police burgh's history. Sixty-seven persons had voted on the issue of establishing the burgh in 1866; now there were 1,903 electors. The valuation of the burgh had increased from £4,280 to £20,299. The first assessment of 8d. in the £ raised £142. In 1929 the burgh rate of 4/7 raised £4,630, and the total consolidated rates collected by the Burgh Treasurer amounted to £10,290.

Chapter 6

Keir Hardie's Cumnock

No one born in Cumnock has achieved great fame. But for over thirty years there lived in the burgh a man—James Keir Hardie—who was to play a decisive role in the political history of Britain. As the founder of the Labour Party, a well-known parliamentarian, and an outstanding figure in the international socialist movement, he earned for himself a place in history. When he came to make his home in Cumnock in 1880, a young man of twenty-four, no one could have suspected what his future held. As time went on, his vigorous work and his powerful personality made their influence felt. From one point of view the impact he made on local affairs was slight compared with that of some of his contemporaries. Yet in retrospect we cannot but place him in the centre of the picture when reviewing life in Cumnock in the late nineteenth and early twentieth centuries. It was in Cumnock that he worked out his political philosophy, and the kind of Cumnock he knew determined its character. When he went on to become a national figure, he kept his roots in Cumnock, and here was his home for the rest of his life. After his death in 1915, his influence continued. The character of modern Cumnock has been shaped by people who followed in his footsteps; and indeed for Britain as a whole many of his dreams have been realised in the better way of life we have come to enjoy.

James Keir Hardie was born on 15th August 1856 at Legbrannock near Holytown in Lanarkshire. He began work at the age of eight in Glasgow, where the family had moved. Returning to Lanarkshire, at the age of ten he became a trapper in the pits, in which he worked for the next twelve years. He studied at night school. He joined the temperance movement. Brought up as an atheist, he was converted to Christianity in 1878 and joined the Evangelical Union church. The poverty and distress he and his workmates knew turned him to agitate for better conditions. For this, and trying to help form a trade union, he was sacked and refused work in Lanarkshire pits. At this dark moment, aged twenty-three, he married Lily Wilson and set up house in a single-end in Hamilton, his only income the little sum the miners could pay him to be their agent.

In 1879 he received an invitation to become secretary of the Ayrshire Miners' Association, and he came to live in Cumnock. Setting up house in a single-end in Waterside Place, he later moved to a two-room-and-kitchen dwelling in the Barrhill Road. He travelled around Ayrshire trying to organise the miners and led them in the big strike of 1881. But after an ordeal of ten weeks the men had to return to work, and the Miners' Association could hardly support a secretary. Fortunately for Hardie, in 1882 he was offered a job reporting for the *Cumnock News*. Writing news items, poems, and his own column, he earned £1 a week, and he lived as a journalist for the next four years. Meantime he had thrown himself into local activities. He founded a Good Templars Lodge and played an active part in the local temperance movement. He organised a Cumnock Shorthand Writers' Association and taught them (without fee) each Wednesday evening in the old parish school. He was secretary of the Cumnock Flute Band. In 1882 he joined Cumnock Congregational Church and two years later in association with the pastor led a secession to form a separate E.U. church. From 1885 till 1887 he was an elected member of Auchinleck School Board. He was at this time also a member of the local Liberal Association. In 1886 he was an unsuccessful candidate for Cumnock Town Council. In 1889 he stood for the new county council against R. B. Angus, manager of William Baird's.

In 1886 a new chapter in Hardie's life began, with the formation of the Ayrshire Miners' Union. Ever since the 1881 strike, efforts had been made to set up a more effective trade union organisation, and the new union came into being after a meeting in Mauchline at which there were present James Neil (later provost of Cumnock), Andrew Fisher of Crosshouse (later Prime Minister of Australia) and Keir Hardie. Hardie was appointed organising secretary at a salary of £75 a year, and gave up his job with the *Cumnock News* to devote himself wholetime to union work. His political views had now developed towards the aim of an inde-

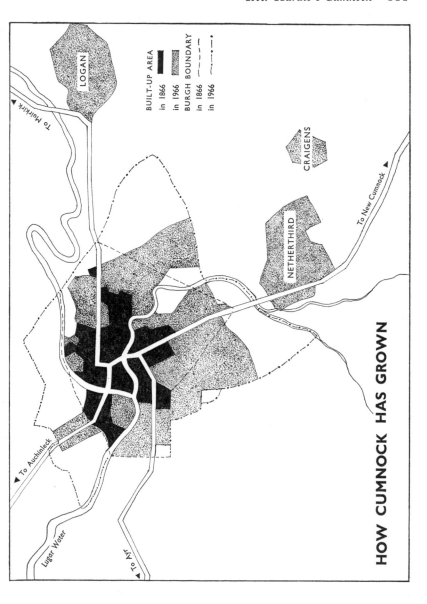

LOGAN

To Muirkirk

BUILT-UP AREA
in 1866
in 1966
BURGH BOUNDARY
in 1866
in 1966

CRAIGENS

NETHERTHIRD

To New Cumnock

To Auchinleck

Lugar Water

To Ayr

HOW CUMNOCK HAS GROWN

pendent working-class political organisation, and the following May at demonstrations on Irvine Moor and at Craigie Hill the Ayrshire miners adopted the following resolution: 'That in the opinion of this meeting, the time has come for the formation of a Labour Party in the House of Commons, and we hereby agree to assist in returning one or more members to represent the miners of Scotland at the first available opportunity.' Hardie had in January 1887 begun publishing *The Miner*. Though it was discontinued after two years, by the autumn of 1887 he had succeeded in having established the Scottish Miners' Federation, with himself as secretary (at £5 per annum); and on 26th August 1888 the Scottish Labour Party was formed.

Keir Hardie had early in 1888 stood as an Independent Labour candidate against both Tory and Liberal in the Mid-Lanark parliamentary by-election, and though he gained only 617 votes, the campaign there marked the beginning of his national political career. Four years later in 1892 he was elected M.P. for West Ham, and in January 1893 at Bradford the Independent Labour Party was formed with Hardie as its national chairman. When he made his first appearance at Westminster he was conveyed in a horse-drawn wagonette and accompanied by a mass of enthusiastic supporters. The Members of the House of Commons, dressed traditionally in silk hats and morning suits, were scandalised when Hardie appeared wearing a tweed cap and a brown homespun suit (made by Hugh Lorimer, the Cumnock tailor). They were even more scandalised when in the Commons he began an uncompromising campaign to bring to public notice the distress of the unemployed and to demand social justice for the common people. He lost his seat at West Ham in 1895 but he continued as the recognised leader of the new independent labour movement. From 1894 he edited and published the weekly *Labour Leader*. He opposed the war against the Boers in South Africa, and attended international socialist conferences which sought to organise international working-class action against the coming world war. In 1900 he took a leading part in associating the I.L.P. with the T.U.C. and the Fabian Society to form the Labour Representation Committee, which six years later became the Labour Party. In 1900 Hardie was re-elected to Parliament as Member for Merthyr, and held this seat for the remainder of his life. He had the satisfaction of seeing the Parliamentary Labour Party, of which he was elected chairman, grow in numbers from two in 1900 to twenty-nine in 1906 and forty in 1910. From time to time he visited the Continent; in 1907 he set off on a world tour, visiting Canada, India, Ceylon, Australia, New Zealand, and South Africa. Through all his travels he kept his watch at ' Cumnock time,' for it was to Cumnock he always returned, from the conferences, and meetings, and demonstrations that filled his life. Here in Cumnock he had built for himself in 1891 a new house in Auchinleck Road called ' Lochnorris '—with the help of a £600 interest-free loan from a wellwisher. Here his family grew up. James, the eldest, had been born in 1881. Sarah, a second child, died at the age of two. Agnes was born in 1885 and Duncan in 1887. To his home in Cumnock he returned for the last time in the summer of 1915, aged 59, a sick man, and troubled by the horrors of the war he had fought against. On 26th September in a Glasgow nursing home he passed peacefully away. Three days later at Maryhill were cremated the remains of this great man. The *Cumnock Chronicle* in its obituary notice appropriately declared: ' No single man has had greater influence in forming the opinion . . . of the age in which we live.'

THE AGE OF COAL

Cumnock's Age of Mining began when John Wilson, the Coatbridge ironmaster, moved into the area. In 1843 this firm took over the old Muirkirk ironworks which had been established in 1787. In 1846 they set up another ironworks at Lugar in Auchinleck parish not very far from Cumnock. This provided an immediate demand for the accessible coal and blackband ironstone which lay below Cumnock. In 1850 the completion of the Kilmarnock-Dumfries railway line provided facilities for the transportation of these heavy raw materials to Lugar and the despatch of the iron goods manufactured there.

In the Old Statistical Account (1793) and the New Statistical Account (1837) it had been noted how rich the local mineral resources were, but because demand was as yet limited, mining occupied an insignificant part in the local economy. In 1837 the only coal workings were small-scale undertakings ' on the high lands towards the south-west side of the parish.' By the time of the Ordnance Gazetteer (1886) coal mining is noted as Cumnock's staple industry.

The first area to be intensively exploited was around the town and near the railway line. Here outcrops beside the Lugar water had been worked from the beginning of the eighteenth century if not before. The first sinking to be made was at Stepends in Auchinleck parish about 1848. By 1853 the Stepends pit was working minerals under the glebe on the Cumnock side of the Lugar. About this time also sinkings at the top of the Barrhill were made by Messrs. Lancaster and Cookney. The first edition of the Ordnance Survey Map (1857) shows Stepends pit and three coal and ironstone pits on Barrhill. Just south of the town at Shankston also, ironstone was being wrought from about 1850. The O.S. Map shows two pits at Shankston (one abandoned). There were also the remote small coal pits at Garrallan (one abandoned, one operating) and at Garlaff.

In the 1860's the pits around the town were further developed. In 1856 the Eglinton Iron Company—the Ayrshire subsidiary of William Baird—bought out John Wilson and took over Muirkirk and Lugar Ironworks. Ten years later their new Lugar Works were opened and production vastly expanded. Baird's took over from the Portland Iron Company the Barrhill pits and also the Stepends pit. About 1860 the Townhead pit was sunk and ironstone carried up the steep ' Bogey Incline ' to the railway station. New sinkings were also made at Stepends and Shankston, and a beginning made at Glengyron. The minerals in the town area were intensively exploited, and as the seams became exhausted the pits closed down. The Barrhill pits were abandoned before 1875; the Townhead pit followed in 1884. Of the Shankston pits the first was closed in 1875 and the second before 1884. The Stepends pit continued to work the seams under the centre of Cumnock. In 1873 the minerals under the glebe were acquired for £1,000; in 1875 the Eglinton Iron Company also purchased the minerals under the old churchyard for £246, and under the old school for £103. Finally in 1892 the Stepends pit was closed.

Meanwhile the field in the south-west of the parish was being developed, a process which was rapidly accelerated with the opening in 1872 of the Ayr-Cronberry railway line and the laying of mineral branch tracks in this part of the parish. Glengyron pit was sunk in 1865 and thereafter developed, and a miners' row built beside the railway. At Garrallan new pits were opened after 1875—there were in all eight sinkings in this area—and another miners' row was established. Nearby, Knockterra pit was opened about 1880. Further away at Dykes a pit was operating from about 1865 till 1894. Around 1870 at Skares a mining village was established by Baird's to house miners at Dykes, at Hindsward (opened c. 1880) and Whitehill (1897).

At the end of the century there were five pits working in the parish. All those near the town were now closed. Glengyron, Garrallan, Knockterra, Hindsward and Whitehill were together producing 141,000 tons of coal a year. Ironstone was no longer worked. Barrhill, Townhead, Shankston and Stepends which had supplied it were closed, and Glengyron produced coal exclusively after 1878. There were in the parish just over 400 miners—350 working underground, 60 above. Only a few lived in the burgh itself—some of them travelling to Auchinleck pits. Most lived in the mining rows at Skares and Garrallan.

The early decades of the twentieth century saw the slow but steady decline of the local coal industry—symptomatic of the general decay of Scottish heavy industry. In the second half of the nineteenth century the landward part of Cumnock parish had grown steadily in population, with miners coming from other parts of Scotland and abroad to find work in the new pits. Numbers increased rapidly from 1,138 (1871) to 1,515 (1881), 1,608 (1891) and a dramatic rise to 2,056 (1901). But thereafter numbers declined to 2,048 (1911) and 1,950 (1921), as pits were closed and miners left the district. Baird's gave up working Glengyron (1905), Knockterra (1914) and Hindsward No. 1 (1925). At Garrallan the Carriden Coal Company abandoned successive workings in 1909, 1916, 1927 and 1931. Closure of the ironworks at Muirkirk (1923) and Lugar (1928) was part of the general contraction of Scottish heavy industry and the declining demand for coal.

When Keir Hardie came to Cumnock in 1880 to organise the Ayrshire miners the working and living conditions of those in the coal industry can only be described as shocking. Until the Act abolishing serfdom in the mines in 1799 Scottish colliers had virtually been slaves of their masters. It has often been said that memories of this old state of affairs long affected the status of the miner. Certainly conditions were bad throughout the nineteenth century and even after. In the 1830's local miners were being paid from 3/- to 4/- a day. Women and children were still employed underground till the 1842 Mines Act. Little obvious progress was made as the century advanced. By the 1840's wages had gone down to 2/- a day, and the first Ayrshire coal strike, in 1842, failed to effect any improvement. Later strikes led to eviction of strikers from tied houses, and again and again blackleg labour was brought in from other parts of the country or even from abroad. In 1857 the miners were petitioning for an eight-hour day, an enquiry into ventilation and a just system of weighing coals at the pit-head. One of the great troubles was violent fluctuation in wages. In the 1860's wages were rising and in 1872 reached a peak of 10/- a day. But in three years' time they had dropped sharply to 4/- a day, and with miners working on one day's notice they could never be assured of a full week's work. After the 1871 Trade Unions Act, however, workers could organise themselves more effectively and in the 1880's throughout Britain new unions of unskilled workers became established. In each instance determination had to battle against difficulties and success did not always come at once. In 1880 the Ayrshire miners under Keir Hardie's leadership went on strike for a 10 per cent. increase in their 4/- a day wage and the occasion was described many years later:

' On Monday, long before dawn, there was stir on the Ayrshire roads. At two in the morning the Annbank brass band came playing through Trabboch village and every miner, young and old, jumped out of bed and fell in behind. Away up towards Auchinleck they went marching, their numbers increasing with every mile of the road. On through Darnconner and Cronberry and Lugar and Muirkirk, right on to Glenbuck by Aird's Moss where the Covenanting Martyrs sleep, then down into Cumnock, at least five thousand strong. Never did magic muster such an army of the morning. It was as though the fairies had come down amongst men to summon them to a tryst. Over in the Kilmarnock district similar scenes were being enacted. The bands went marching from colliery to colliery and

> *the rising sun ower Galston Muir*
> *Wi' glorious light was glintin'*

upon processions of colliers on all the roads round about Galston village and Hurlford and Crookedholm and Riccarton, making as by one common impulse, towards Craigie Hill which had not witnessed such a mustering of determined men since the days of William Wallace. Ere nightfall a miracle had been accomplished. For the first time in its history there was a stoppage nearly complete in the Ayrshire mining industry. At last the Ayrshire miners were united and, win or lose, they would stand or fall together. The fields were ripening to harvest when the men ' lifted their graith.' Ere they went back to work the Cumnock hills were white with snow and by that time Keir Hardie was at once the most hated and the best respected man in Ayrshire. It was the Lanarkshire experience over again—an experience of sacrifice and endurance. The Bands went out collecting money. The women folk and the children went ' tattie howkin' ' and harvesting. Thrifty miners' families who had saved a little during the prosperous years of the early seventies, threw their all into the common stock. The farmers, many of them, gave meal and potatoes to keep the children from starving. Here and there was an occasional break away, and the pickets were out, and the police and the military and there were skirmishes and arrests and imprisonments. Hardie toiled night and day directing the relief committees, restraining the wild spirits from violence, advocating the men's claims temperately and persuasively in the local press, addressing mass meetings all over the county and keeping the men in good heart. " God's on our side, men," he declared. " Look at the weather He's giein' us!" And it seemed true. It was the finest fall of the year in Ayrshire within the memory of man, and, but for the pinch of hunger, was like a glimpse of Heaven to men accustomed to sweat ten hours a day in underground darkness.'

After ten weeks the men went back without having been granted their increase. But within a month, with improving trade, wages were advanced. In 1886 a more effective Ayrshire Miners' Union was born out of the experience of the Big Strike. In three months Keir Hardie enrolled two thousand members. A year later the Scottish Miners' Federation was formed. Even so, this was but the beginning of the long campaign for better conditions.

In 1887 miners were being paid only from 2/6 to 4/- a day, and with unsteady work, the average weekly pay was only about 12/- a week. In that year Parliament took a step towards improving conditions by prohibiting the employment underground of boys under the age of 12. For many families, however, this praiseworthy advance meant only a drop in the total family income and more difficulties. In 1899 the School Board, noting the irregular attendance at Garrallan school, asked Wm. Baird & Co. to discontinue employing children during school hours. Apart from the difficulties and dangers of their work, for those who lived in the miners' rows there were many inconveniences. The houses belonged to the local coal companies, and loss of job meant also eviction. The condition of the houses was perhaps little worse than many of those in the town—cramped accommodation, outside water supply, dry closets, lack of properly paved footpaths—but the miners' rows were isolated, almost segregated communities. Although various Truck Acts had forbidden payment in kind or by token, in fact the shops the companies operated held a virtual monopoly of trade and profited accordingly. But—to look at the brighter side—Wm. Baird & Co. did provide a reading room and hall at Skares, a Mission hall was erected in 1911, and the school rooms there and at Garrallan also provided places for social gatherings. The School Board minutes provide glimpses of such activities. At Garrallan there were evening music classes (1876), a quadrille band (1884), a magic lantern entertainment (1886), a branch of the Lugar Temperance Society (1897), the Ancient Free Gardeners (1900) and dancing classes (1915). At Skares there were the Free Gardeners (1904), the Rechabites (1904), the Skares Juvenile Football Club (1907), Skares Brass Band (1907), a dramatic club (1908), a quoiting club (1908), a phonetic class (1911), Good Templars (1912) and an ambulance corps (1912). In 1922 a Skares War Memorial Hall was built to commemorate the fourteen Skares men who had been killed. For a number of years thereafter annual Skares reunions were held. Nevertheless the general isolation was unsatisfactory. The miners who lived in the town had a better time of it, even though wages and conditions of work were slow in improving.

In the 1840's Cumnock's principal trades had been the manufacture of textiles and snuffboxes. By the 1880's coal mining had become the staple industry. The older crafts suffered not only a relative but an absolute decline. The making of snuffboxes and similar wooden articles was given up. The handloom weaving of cotton goods slumped in the sixties and never revived. The factory manufacture of woollens survived for a time. Spinning, weaving, and dyeing continued at the long-established Lugar Mills; weaving was also carried on at the Greenholm factory after 1870; and for a time there was a small woollen mill at the top of the Barrhill. But these had all closed down by the early years of the twentieth century. A similar fate overtook the pottery works, which ceased manufacture in 1907, though the firm continued a retail business for some years thereafter. As against this, there were some new developments. McCartney's engineering works continued to make threshing mills. In 1858 James Drummond left McCartney's and set up his own works, first in Ayr Road, latterly up the Barrhill, producing various types of agricultural implements. In 1901 Charles and Andrew Taylor took over McCartney's and a few years later extended their interests by beginning the manufacture of electrical switchgear for use in factories, shipyards and mines. Various other developments in this period included the extension of the gasworks in 1898 and the establishment in the succeeding decades of a series of new small miscellaneous undertakings—a jam factory, two manufactories of aerated waters, a bicycle maker, a steam laundry, and a creamery company. Some of these small businesses absorbed part of the available supply of female labour, but—as in most mining communities—there was a shortage of jobs for women and for others unfit for pitwork. Thus while the expansion of the coal industry brought immigration to swell the population, the incomers were predominantly male; and there was a corresponding exodus of girls and of families who could not find work for their daughters. So the local population became somewhat unbalanced, with a predominance of males in the community.

In the late nineteenth century it was obvious that Cumnock was too dependent on the single trade of coalmining. Some first faltering steps were taken to try to bring alternative trade to the town, by publicising Cumnock's attractions as a holiday resort. It was easily accessible by passenger railway services from the north (Glasgow and Kilmarnock); the south (Dumfries); and after the opening of the Ayr-Edinburgh line in 1874, from Lanarkshire and the east as well. The mining industry had failed to despoil the town or its immediate environs. Warrick in 1899 pointed to the plentiful supply of ' facilities for healthy recreation ' and advocated several improvements in these amenities. Even before this, in 1896 the town council sought to entice holidaymakers by advertising houses to let in the town during the summer months. In the first decade of the twentieth century both the *Cumnock Chronicle* and the Merchants' Association made efforts to attract visitors. Later, various publishers felt it worthwhile to sponsor Guides to Cumnock, in 1915, 1920, 1923, 1925 and 1927. The first, locally-produced by James P. Ballantine, listed the attractions of the town and district, described a series of walks and cycle runs, advertised a bus tour to Ochiltree and other facilities for holidaymakers. As an inland resort Cumnock did in fact attract some visitors, but the appeal remained limited.

In the country part of the parish the nineteenth century saw continued progress in agriculture. The profits of commercial farming had in the early part of the century encouraged the improvement of existing arable land by draining and other methods, and the bringing under cultivation of land previously fit only for rough pasture. This process continued to the end of the century. By 1907 a maximum of 9,562 acres in Cumnock parish was under crops and grass, while the area of moorland had been reduced to 1,049 acres, just about half of what it had been two generations before. During this period, too, the parish had followed the general pattern for Ayrshire of developing a specialised intensive dairy farming. The farms of the parish, which had at the beginning of the century maintained about 1,000 cattle, by mid-century had doubled their stock, and before 1900 had passed the 3,000 mark. And while at the beginning of the century many of the cattle had been raised for beef, dairy cattle of the Ayrshire breed had become almost universal. To feed the augmented stock, the area of land under improved grass and meadow had been increased to over 8,000 acres by 1907, almost ninety per cent. of the farmland. Of the remaining fraction devoted to crops, almost all was for growing fodder, principally hay and oats with lesser amounts of turnips, potatoes, and some green crops. The beginning of large-scale importation of cheap foreign agricultural products in the late nineteenth century, which ruined the fortunes of arable farmers in other areas, was turned to advantage by the dairy farmers. Increasing proportions of fodder could be purchased, more land devoted to pasture, and the acreage of crops grown in Cumnock parish declined from 1,598 acres in 1867 to 1,365 acres in 1907. By that time only one corn mill was still operating in the parish, at Boreland. The attractions of dairy farming meant not only the ousting of beef cattle, but of some other types of livestock. The sheep flocks of the parish had grown from some 2,000 to 6,000 in the first half of the nineteenth century, but thereafter numbers declined towards their former level. The pig population, however, remained fairly constant, as farmers found them a useful sideline to fatten with the whey by-product of the cheesemaking. The manufacture of cheese on the farm was the basis of nineteenth century Ayrshire dairy farming, though there was always a certain sale of liquid milk to the people of the towns, a market which extended as population continued to grow. A good deal of the milk consumed in the town was purchased from cowfeeders who lived in the town and grazed their few cattle in convenient small holdings. The first farmer to sell milk in the town was William Anderson, Burnside, followed by his son Charles and by Gib Murray of Skerrington. Well into the twentieth century a feature of a morning street scene was the local farmer with his horse and cart, and housewives buying jugs of milk and perhaps butter and eggs as well. Regular supplies were also being sent out of the area—in 1907 the railway company dispatched over 5,000 cans of milk from Cumnock.

The twentieth century saw changes in the pattern of farming. Certain processes continued. With increasing dependence on purchased fodder, the amount of cropping continued to decline— except in wartime when, with imports restricted, government direction compelled more land to be brought under the plough.

Farmers increased the size of their herds of dairy cattle. But there were signs of difficulty. Some land formerly under cultivation was allowed to revert to rough pasture and given over to sheep, whose numbers began to grow again. Demand for cheese became less certain, and more and more farmers gave up production—and also gave up keeping pigs. And while improved transport facilities made it now possible to distribute liquid milk over wider areas, marketing was difficult and the dairy farmers suffered. In 1916 local farmers formed a Cumnock and District Dairy Association and planned to establish a co-operative creamery. Things did not improve till the establishment of the Scottish Milk Marketing Board in 1932. Some farmers, however, were profiting from sales of pedigree Ayrshire stock. In 1920 Jacob S. Murray, Dalgig, sold his champion ' Carston Bridesmaid ' to an American purchaser for the record price of £1,000.

The nineteenth century countryside was still dominated economically and socially by the great landowners. The Dumfries estate covered the greater part of Old Cumnock and adjoining parishes, amounting in all in 1872 to 43,734 acres—exceeded in Ayrshire only by the 76,000 acre properties of the Marquess of Ailsa. The Marquess of Bute as the principal landowner retained tremendous local influence. His Ayrshire estates alone had a gross annual value of £22,756, plus £2,506 minerals value. He owned most of the land of the parish and was superior of many of the town properties as well. But with the extension of the franchise and in particular the introduction of the secret ballot in 1872 the end was approaching of the dominating political control of the great landowners.

The end of patronage in the church after 1874, coupled with the adhesion of the third Marquess to the Roman faith, plus the fact that he was only occasionally resident at Dumfries House, meant a diminution of the social influence of the Bute family over the parish. Glaisnock estate in mid-century passed from the Allasons into the hands of Captain Robert Campbell of Auchmannoch in the parish of Sorn, whose combined properties in 1872 extended to 3,928 acres with a gross annual value of £2,156. He resided at Glaisnock and interested himself in parish affairs. The Logan estate was entirely in Old Cumnock parish, comprising 3,783 acres of £1,976 annual value plus

£860 for minerals. From Elizabeth Allason, who inherited it from her father in 1825, it passed after her death in 1851 to her husband, William Allason Cuninghame, who held it till his death in 1885. The third of the smaller local estates—Garrallan—was only 594 acres in extent, and an enclave in the Dumfries property, but it was rich in coal resources, whose annual value of £1,015 was in fact greater than the estate's gross annual value of £723. Acquired through marriage by a cadet branch of the Boswells of Auchinleck, Garrallan was from 1863 till 1892 owned by a prominent figure in the local scene—Patrick Charles Douglas Boswell.

In 1887, the four landowners among them owned eighty-three out of eighty-six farms in the parish, while only three farmers had farms of their own. The situation did not materially change till after the first World War when a great revolution in land-ownership took place. Here as elsewhere fiscal impositions undermined the position of the great landowners and resulted in the breakup of many of the great estates. In 1919 and 1920 the Marquess of Bute sold twenty-two farms in Old Cumnock and forty-one in adjoining parishes, on favourable terms to the sitting tenants usually. At the beginning of the century Glaisnock and later Logan and Garrallan were sold off, the estates broken up, and the mansion houses were occupied by successive owners. By 1927 only forty-seven of the eighty-three farms in Old Cumnock parish were still rented, and with the process of selling-off continuing, soon after that most local farms had passed into the ownership of the farmers themselves.

In 1927, of these eighty-three farms thirty-six were between 100 and 300 acres, mostly around the 200 acre average. There were only four local farms with more than 300 acres; but there were forty-three smaller holdings of one kind or another with less than 100 acres. The farms were worked by the farmers and their families, with the further assistance of 170 employees—two or three on most farms. Most of these were full-time men, ninety-five in all, including forty lads under 21; fifty-six women; and a score of casual workers. The total number engaged in farming was probably not very different from a century before, but the productivity of the land had increased manifold. The place of farming in parochial life had also been transformed. Farmers were looking beyond the parish both for sales and for labour and supplies. In the early years of the twentieth century, Cumnock Auction Market was still running fortnightly sales, and there was an Annual Show and Sale—in November 1901 involving 239 cattle and 87 sheep. But after the first World War these local markets were heading for extinction. At the same time the numbers finding a livelihood in other pursuits had grown to such an extent that the farmfolk had become a small and separate minority in a community of burgh and mining villages.

'THE GOOD OLD DAYS'

The second half of the nineteenth century saw the continued growth of the population. Numbers in the parish as a whole grew from 2,834 (1841) to 3,777 (1851), pausing at 3,721 (1861) but showing further increases to 4,041 (1871), 4,861 (1881), and after another check to 4,721 (1891), continuing to 5,144 (1901), 5,465 (1911), 5,491 (1912) and 5,637 (1931). The erratic character of this growth can best be explained by considering burgh and country separately. During the first three decades of the burgh's existence conditions were extremely unsettled. The collapse of cotton handloom weaving in the 1860's brought distress to many townsfolk and some emigration, only partially compensated by the opening up of the pits around the town; and when these closed down, at a time when the housing situation in the burgh was particularly awkward, in the 1880's some people again had to move out. But from 1900 onwards, despite various economic problems, the burgh community became more settled and there was a fairly steady growth of population thereafter. As compared with the town, the landward area shows a different pattern of population growth. There was, if anything, a decline in the numbers of people engaged in farm work, but with the opening up of mines in various parts of the parish in the second half of the nineteenth century the landward area shows a steady and dramatic increase in population. Miners' rows had been set up at Glengyron and Garrallan before 1855. The mining village of Skares was established about 1870. The total numbers in the landward area increased from 1,138 (1871) to 1,516 (1881), 1,608 (1891), and 2,056 (1901). But thereafter the closure of pits brought decline. Landward numbers decreased from 2,048 (1911) to 1,950 (1921).

The fluctuation in trade in the coal mining and other industries in the nineteenth and early twentieth centuries gave everyday life a frightening insecurity. The incidence of poverty and distress had become so acute in the 1840's that Parliament was forced to make public provision for poor relief. The Parochial Board (1845-1895) comprised heritors and representatives of the kirk session and ratepayers. At its half-yearly meetings (in the parish school till 1885 and thereafter in the Town Hall) the board appointed committees to draw up the roll of paupers and consult with the Inspector of Poor—James Boyd (1845-1849), Archibald McCowan (1849-1866), David Smith (1866-1905). The board had its own little poorhouse (till 1886). It sent some cases to the Ayr Poorhouse or to asylums. It settled with other Parochial Boards the maintenance of paupers who had moved from one area to another. While its main function was poor relief, as time went on other duties were added. Local doctors were retained to help care for the sick poor; latterly they were appointed as medical officers to report on sanitary conditions in the landward part of the parish. They were Dr. Stewart (1847), Drs. Robertson and McGlashan (1850), Drs. McKinnon and McGlashan (1851), Dr. Lawrence (1877-1895) and Dr. Kerr (1895-1907). In 1854 the board was made responsible for the now compulsory registration of births, marriages, and deaths and appointed registrars— D. L. Scott (1854-1887), Adam Urquhart (1887-1907). In 1873 the board (in association with the old Heritors committee) proposed a new cemetery and when it was opened in 1877 the Parochial Board became responsible for its maintenance. Several town councillors served from time to time on the old Parochial Board, but the leading figure was P. C. D. Boswell of Garrallan, chairman for quarter of a century till ill health forced him to resign in 1891.

The Parish Council which replaced the board in 1895 and took over all its functions was entirely elected by ratepayers. It had originally eleven members. Four were from the landward area; seven were from the burgh—including Holmhead, which was thus detached from Auchinleck parish in 1895. The first chairman of the Parish Council was James Gray, who served till his death in 1904. It was he who in 1897 presented the council with a group photograph which caused the famous dispute with the town council. And in 1898 he took the members of the board on an excursion round Arran—and they held an official meeting in Ardrossan. He was succeeded as chairman by David Reid (1904-1910), Robert Livingstone (1910-1919), George McTurk (1919-1920), George Bridges (1920-1925), John Craig (1925-1928), and George McTurk again in the last year of the Parish Council's existence. In 1906 on the death of David Smith, John Allan from Renfrew had been appointed Inspector of Poor, Clerk to the Council, Collector of Rates, Clerk to the Cemetery Committee, and a year later Parish Registrar. In 1916 the Parish Council gave up its parish office and meeting place in the Town Hall and acquired its own premises at 40 Ayr Road.

The main function of the Parish Council was the provision of a bare minimum relief to the destitute, so that the phrase ' on the pairish ' became synonymous with the direst of poverty. Such figures as the minutes of the board and the Parish Council afford give some indication of the extent and variations in poverty. In the 1850's conditions were bad. The numbers of persons in receipt of poor relief were eighty-four (1857), seventy-seven (1858), and seventy-four (1859). In the 1870's there was an improvement. Numbers were less at a time when population was growing, dropping from eighty-three (1872) to just under fifty (1877, 1879, 1880). In the 1880's when the parish population was becoming less, with bad trade and emigration, numbers remained in the fifties, but in the last decade of the century there was a slight improvement. In the early twentieth century numbers increased and around 1910 times were bad, but the proportion of paupers in the population thereafter declined.

The introduction of old age pensions in 1908 and National Insurance in 1911 mark the beginning of a new view of social welfare. Nevertheless, the amount expended on individual persons by the Parish Council was small indeed. Until the end of the nineteenth century it amounted to a few shillings a week— an average of less than £14 per year per person. Increases in the early twentieth century hardly kept pace with rising prices and even after the first World War less than £1 a week was usual.

Parish Councils had a reputation for meanness and all but the most needy were reluctant to beg for help from a council of local people. Even so, the total commitments of the Parish Council were considerable. In the late nineteenth century, in most years between £600 and £700 had to be raised by poor rates. In the early years of the twentieth century the annual assessment was uniformly higher, often over £1,000 and after the first World War the Parish Council was spending over £2,000 a year on poor relief. The council found it impossible to ignore the periodic and widespread distress occasioned by mass unemployment and industrial disputes—and the Labour members on the council sought to extend the assistance of the Parish Council in these cases whenever they could. In 1922, for example, the numbers on the poors roll increased by twenty to sixty-five and with eighty-six dependants made a total of 151 people supported, and there was no decline in following years. In 1926 with the General Strike and the miners' strike connected with it, nearly 250 families sought assistance, and over £2,000 was paid out in emergency relief, bringing the annual poor rate assessment to over £4,000 for one year. In 1929 with still sixty-one on the poors roll and ninety-six dependants, and £2,619 to be levied, the burden was becoming too great for a parish authority. On 15th May 1930 the old Cumnock Parish Council met for the last time. Parish councils had been abolished by the Local Government (Scotland) Act of 1929, and thereafter the county council took over responsibility for poor relief.

Despite the spectre of poverty which haunted life in the nineteenth and early twentieth century, the picture was not uniformly drab. Old people later recalled these times and with sincerity regarded them as the ' good old days.' One notable feature of social life was the widening range of recreational opportunities. True, working hours were long and spare cash was limited. But with more people about and most of them congregated in a growing town, there was scope for new kinds of leisure activity, many sponsored by voluntary organisations formed for that specific purpose.

The fairs had previously been the only occasions for organised entertainment. They still retained their popularity, but were now supplemented by a series of other functions so that a whole

programme of recreational activities was available throughout
the year. From the middle of the nineteenth century circuses and
menageries started visiting Cumnock regularly. In 1902 Lord
George Sangers recalled the first visit of his circus to Cumnock
fifty-one years before. Once the Town Hall was opened in 1885
touring companies came to offer drama, music, and even (in
1905) grand opera. For several years after 1895 indeed, a portable
wooden theatre was set up for a season of three or four months
in Munn's field off Glaisnock Street. As novelty passed, dis-
crimination followed. In 1902 the *Cumnock Chronicle* criticised
' travelling incompetents who arrogated to themselves the title
of professional.' As well as commercial entertainment, Cumnock
people could now sample, on winter evenings, concerts and shows
presented by local amateur groups, or participate in soirees,
balls, and (after 1918) whist drives organised for pleasure, profit
or charity by cultural, sporting, or political organisations in the
town. From 1913 onwards regular entertainment of a new kind
was available. For a number of years cinematograph shows had
been offered at the fairs in the Square. Mr. Green, who sponsored these now began regular shows in the Town Hall. These
were superseded when a picture house was built and opened on
31st March 1913. The first show was the film *Monte Cristo*.
There were twice nightly performances and a children's matinee
on Saturdays. Prices of admission were 6d., 4d., and 2d.

Sport became organised in the later nineteenth century.
Before that handball had been played against the wall of the
old parish kirk, there was some curling in the old pond by the
Glaisnock, and cricket was played with the permission of the
Marquess of Bute in his park at Townhead. Curling continued,
and a club was formed with a pond at Woodhead, given up in
1905 for a more convenient site off Ayr Road. Cricket was still
being played in New Station Park in the last decade of the
century. But new sports succeeded. In 1868 a bowling club
was formed, laying out a second green in 1882 and flourishing
thereafter. In 1888 a tennis club was also set up. Golf was
played in various fields—first to the north of the town, then
successively near Ayr Road, Cairn Road, and the Coachworks.
Around 1900 a nine-hole course was opened at Netherthird,
moving in 1922 to Drumbrochan. These sports of course catered

Keir Hardie, at home in 'Lochnorris'
(*Cumnock Chronicle*)

Market Cross,
about 1900

Glaisnock Street, about 1850
(*Cumnock Chronicle*)

Weather Cock from
Old Parish Church
(Baird Institute)

Employees of Geo. McCartney & Co., Engineers, Cumnock
between 1890-1895 (Alex. Parker)

The " good old days " in the " raws "
    (*a*) Glengyron Row, about 1916 (Mrs. Scott, 4 Gemmell Avenue)
    (*b*) Skares Row, about 1920 (D. Smith, 13 Ayr Road)
    (*c*) Sunday in Skares, about 1920 (D. Smith)

The men who won the coal
    (*d*) Burnock Hill Pit, 1924 (Mrs. Scott)
    (*e*) Hindsward Pit, about 1920 (D. Smith)
    (*f*) Whitehill Pit, about 1918 (D. Smith)

Killoch Colliery, near Cumnock (National Coal Board)

Compressed air hoist for loading/unloading heavy equipment,
in this instance self-advancing roof supports (National Coal Board)

Harvest time in the Cumnock area

Milk distribution from Changue Farm, (McCallum, Ayr)

Swimming Pool,
1958
(*Cumnock Chronicle*)

The Night of the Flood, Ayr Road, 1 a.m., 14th August 1966
(Scotsman Publications Ltd., Edinburgh)

Visit of H.M. Queen Elizabeth and H.R.H. Prince Philip,
Woodroad Park, 3rd July 1956

The Crowning of the Carnival Queen, 1962
(*Cumnock Chronicle*)

for fairly small numbers. A cheaper sport was quoits, played at Townhead in mid-century, later on several pitches attached to public houses, and by the first decade of the twentieth century there were local and district competitions. General interest in athletics was fostered by annual sports which were run for several years, and in 1905 a wrestling exhibition in the Town Hall provided the first such display in Cumnock.

The most popular of the new sports was football, which swept into widespread and general favour in the seventies. In May 1877 an Ayrshire Football Association was formed, with its first secretary, John Wallace, who had a business in Cumnock before going off to Kilmarnock and later Australia. Every mining village formed teams and by the early twentieth century the district had a formidable array of junior and juvenile clubs. These included, at various times, Cronberry Eglinton, Common Thistle, Darnconner Britannia, Auchinleck Rangers, Auchinleck Talbot, Lugar Boswell, Muirkirk Athletic, Glenbuck Cherry-pickers, Glenbuck Thistle, Skares Victoria, Skares Athletic, Skares United, Skares Brunton Lads, Afton Thistle, Afton Lads, Lanemark. One of these teams, Lugar Boswell, which had been formed in 1876, in a match against Mauchline in 1879 abandoned the traditional line-up of six forwards and two half-backs in favour of a new formation of five forwards, and Lugar's idea was eventually universally adopted. In Cumnock itself there were originally two teams—nicknamed the Roughs and the Swells. Later came such teams as Cumnock Thistle, Cumnock Celtic, Cumnock Craigbank, Springbank, Glaisnock Lads, Townhead Thistle and—since 1913—Cumnock Juniors. In 1904, to raise funds for the proposed Glenafton Sanatorium, a Cumnock Select challenged Glasgow Rangers, who came and won by 4-1 at Station Park. For enthusiasts of other sports, there were local horse races at the March fair each year till 1909, and the September meeting at Ayr has since 1900 always been a local holiday in Cumnock. An alternative interest was supplied in 1908 when a whippets handicap was organised in a field behind the Stepends bing.

Miscellaneous sports and hobbies were catered for by a variety of local organisations. The Cumnock Horticultural Society held its first exhibition in 1880 and regular annual shows were held

thereafter, with additional shows for sweet peas, rose, and carna-
tion enthusiasts after 1928. In 1899 the first poultry and pigeon
show was held, and after a relapse the society was reformed
in 1927. In 1909 a Cumnock and District Canary and Cage Bird
Society was formed and held shows for a number of years. In
1927 a Canine Club was set up to organise shows. In 1919 a
Cumnock and District Angling Association came into existence.

Cultural interests in Cumnock were catered for by a number
of societies. The long-established Athenaeum Library was
reconstituted in 1880, in 1885 moved from the old Court House
to a room in the Town Hall, and also sponsored lectures and
penny readings. By 1901 its reading membership had dwindled
to seventy-two, but in 1923 it was reorganised and saw a new
lease of life. Cumnock also had in the late nineteenth century a
lively Literary and Debating Society, resuscitated in 1909 and
revived after the war as a Literary Guild. Then there were
several Burns Clubs. The Winsome Willie Club was formed in
1856 and met in the Craighead Inn and later in the Hotel Royal.
The Cumnock Burns Club was instituted in 1887 and held its
annual celebrations in the Dumfries Arms. There were also
for a time the Cronies Club meeting in the Burns Inn, the Tam
Samson Club in Buck's Head Inn, and the Jolly Beggars Club
in the Craighead Inn. For a number of years the Total Abstinence
Society held a teetotal Burns Supper in the Town Hall each
January. Another cultural development was a growing enthusiasm
for drama, and by 1901 there were three local groups producing
plays.

Cumnock had also a well-established musical tradition. The
Musical Association with an amateur orchestra was formed in
1877 and though it lapsed it was revived for a time after 1917.
In 1879 and for some years after there was a Choral Union and
in the last decade of the nineteenth century the various congregations all formed church choirs. But as the *Chronicle* complained
in 1902, ' Cumnock, we venture to think, is musical, but it is
more critically musical than it is practically musical.' Musical
societies tended to have a limited life. Public interest was fitful.
A promenade concert presented in Cumnock Town Hall in
1903 by the Muirkirk Orchestral Society got little support.
While early in the nineteenth century the town had for a time

two brass bands, efforts in 1904 and 1912 to form a new brass band came to nothing. Local enthusiasts had to content themselves with listening to visiting bands from Lugar, Auchinleck Birnieknowe and New Cumnock. Particularly embarrassing must have been the fact that in 1907 Skares was able to form its own band, while Cumnock couldn't. More successful were the various flute bands associated with the friendly societies. But general appeal was reserved for popular music purveyed by such groups as the amateur local Christy Minstrel troupe— the Cumnock Coons, formed in 1907.

The cultural and recreational facilities of Cumnock were augmented in 1891 with the opening of the Baird Institute, with its reading room, small museum, and facilities for various indoor games. John Baird was a local draper with interests in literature, art and photography. When he died unmarried in 1888 at the age of 76 he bequeathed money for this worthy local purpose. In Baird's time and after there was in Cumnock a small coterie of people actively interested in a wide variety of cultural pursuits. Among the earliest was Thomas Barrowman who came from Lanarkshire in 1859 to manage the Barrhill pits, played a leading part in burgh affairs, and whose interest ranged from horticulture and poultry-keeping to pioneering penny readings. A prominent figure in the musical life of the town was Dr. James Lawrence who set up practice in Cumnock in 1851. There was D. L. Scott, interested in mathematics, astronomy and music. Mary Maxwell Campbell (1818-1886) who wrote *The March of the Cameron Men* was a daughter of Dugald John Campbell of Skerrington. John Crawford (1829-1887) and Hugh C. Wilson (born 1845) were minor Cumnock poets. Versification was also practised by Alexander Barrowman, one of Thomas Barrowman's eight sons, an engineer turned journalist, who wrote for the *Cumnock News*. James Neil was both flautist and versifier, and even J. K. Hardie tried his hand at poetry. John Walters Crawford, founder of the *Cumnock Chronicle*, was interested in literature and was an accomplished violinist. His wife, Helen J. Steven, wrote histories of Cumnock and several other Ayrshire parishes. Rev. John Warrick wrote his local history and other works. Another who grew up in Cumnock was John Smith, geologist and author of *Prehistoric Man in Ayrshire*. The most outstanding local literary figure was Adam Brown Todd. Born near Mauchline in 1822 and brought up to the tile-making trade, in 1863 he moved into Cumnock to become the local editor of the *Cumnock Express*. In 1846 A. B. Todd published a volume of poems, followed by others in 1876 and 1880. In 1888 these were joined by two volumes on *Homes, Haunts, and Battlefields of the Covenanters*. In 1892 he had the satisfaction of seeing the Peden Monument in the old kirkyard inaugurated by Professor J. S. Blackie in the presence of an audience of three or four thousand. He was a noted Burns orator who often presided at the Cumnock Club, for instance at the celebrations of the centenary of the poet's birth (1859), the centenary of the death (1896) and the 150th anniversary (1909). He was a staunch conservative, who squabbled furiously with Keir Hardie. Altogether he was a colourful figure in the life of the town, and in 1903 he was entertained in the Dumfries Arms to a public luncheon in his honour. In 1906 he published his *Poetical Works*, with an autobiography. In 1911 came his last book—*Covenanting Pilgrimages and Studies*. He died in 1915 aged 93. Cumnock seventy years ago was obviously a lively place, with all sorts of communal ventures, successful and unsuccessful, great and small. Club-making became a popular pastime. There were, for example, the September Club after 1876 when David Smith and some friends went off for outings on Ayr Race holidays; the Bute June Club formed in 1906 which celebrated for a few years the Marquess's birthday; James McKechnie's ' Kechie Club ' and later Sandy Barrowman's Dynamite Club, for political and philosophical discussion. One curious body was the Cumnock Tart Club, comprising a dozen master tradesmen and shopowners who celebrated one another's birthdays by treating fellow-members to one of McGavin's tuppenny Cumnock tarts. In 1901 a Glasgow Cumnock Association was formed, with February reunions in the city for several years; and in 1907 Cumnockians in Edinburgh tried to follow suit.

Meanwhile the various friendly societies of the early nineteenth century were superseded by branches of national organisations— the Good Templars, Shepherds, Free Gardeners, Rechabites, Foresters, Oddfellows, the Ancient Order of Hibernians, and the Bute Jewel Friendly Society. The local Total Abstinence Society lost its place with the rise of the Templars, but survived under the presidency of David Smith, recovered in the 1890's, and celebrated its seventy-fifth anniversary in 1913. A No-Licence Association was formed in 1920 and a branch of the British Women's Temperance Association a year later. But in a local poll taken in December 1920, while 434 voted for a dry Cumnock, 785 preferred ' no change.'

Among long-established local organisations was the Freemasons Lodge St. Barnabas No. 230. Founded in 1809, the lodge was constituted a Royal Arch Chapter in 1909 and acquired its own premises in 1912 with the opening of a Masonic Temple in Ayr Road. In 1913 there was instituted for local women a lodge of the Order of the Eastern Star.

From time to time new bodies were set up in support of a variety of worthy causes. In 1907 the *Cumnock Chronicle* sponsored a Bare Feet Fund to aid necessitous children. In the same year a District Nursing Association was formed, followed a year later by a Cumnock Ambulance Corps. Various organisations ranging from the Literary and Debating Club to the St. Vincent de Paul Society ran regular charity concerts. In 1926 Ayr students began a Charities Day and collected in Cumnock for hospitals. In 1927 an annual Old Folks' Party was instituted, organised by the Order of the Eastern Star.

Another activity that for long attracted strong local participation was the Volunteer movement. The Ayrshire Yeomanry Cavalry formed in 1798 set up a Cumnock troop in 1803 and found a ready supply of recruits from farmers and farmers' sons. From 1860 those with military inclinations had also the opportunity of enrolling for infantry training. After a meeting in the school in that year a local company was set up, the 12th Ayrshire Rifle Volunteer Corps. William Ettershank was appointed captain and Andrew White lieutenant. The corps met for training sometime in the Dumfries Arms Hall, sometimes in the school, till a Drill Hall was built and opened in September 1914. In 1902 the Volunteers had a muster of 114. In 1908 with the formation of the Territorial Army the Volunteer Corps was superseded by E. Coy. of the 2nd Volunteer Battalion Royal Scots Fusiliers. The Yeomanry and Volunteers were keen shots. There was a rifle range at Burnside and later at Muirside. Several local men indeed were members of Ayrshire Yeomanry teams which in the last decades of the nineteenth century had a national reputation. An outstanding local Yeoman was Will McLanachan of Boreland farm, winner of local and national shooting, riding, and sporting events. In 1899 he and other seventeen local men saw active service in South Africa. Later in 1914 the Yeomanry and Volunteers were mobilised and many local men served in these regiments during the war. Altogether in the first World War 662 men from Old Cumnock parish enlisted; sixteen were decorated; 117 were among the fallen.

Politics was another lively local interest. With the extension of the franchise and the growth of national parties, political controversy became a feature of Cumnock life, with crowded meetings and acute controversy at parliamentary and municipal elections. Before the introduction of the secret ballot in 1872 elections were sometimes even occasions for violence. A. B. Todd wrote: 'The conduct of the rowdies was generally bad everywhere, and in no place was it worse, or perhaps so utterly bad as in the town of Old Cumnock and it was like going through a campaign in an enemy's country for a Conservative to go to the poll and record his vote. On one occasion, in addition to the local police and special constables, thirty picked police constables were brought from Glasgow.' Later elections were more orderly, but controversy among the parties remained keen. Among the local Conservative and Unionist stalwarts were men like Provost Andrew, D. L. Smith, G. B. Cree, D. Baird, A. B. Todd, Provost William Hill and David Reid of Milzeoch. The Liberals numbered among their supporters Provosts Hunter and Richmond, James Merry, James Dunsmor, William McGeachin, William Baird. From the local Liberal Association in 1886 broke away working-class supporters led by James Neil and James Keir Hardie, and to this secession the modern Labour Party owes its genesis. Hardie had brought Henry George to Cumnock to lecture in 1884; the next year James Patrick, who had joined the Social Democratic Federation, returned to the town and converted James Neil to Socialism; the opposition of the Liberal Party in Parliament to an eight-hour day for miners brought matters to a head; and following a debate in the Dynamite Club Hardie decided to leave the Liberals. Thereafter he played his leading part in organising nationally an independent labour party; locally various Labour groups were formed—I.L.P., Fabian Society, Christian Socialists. From the beginning of the twentieth century the Labour Party began to make an effective impact locally. In the post-war years it held frequent public meetings, annual Keir Hardie Memorial demonstrations, and in 1924 opened I.L.P. rooms in McGavin's Close. In the early years of the century another political movement for a time demanded attention, when the cry of ' Votes for Women ' was heard, and in 1907 Mrs. Pankhurst addressed a meeting in the Town Hall under the auspices of the I.L.P.

Other societies for advancing mutual interests were being formed. There was a Cumnock and District Farmers' Association before 1899 holding annual cattle shows; and a Cumnock and District Ploughing Society ran competitions for a time. In 1916 the farmers also established a local Dairy Association. In 1902 a Cumnock Merchants' Association was formed to look after shopkeepers' interests. In July 1890 a Cumnock Co-operative Society had been instituted. The first Co-operative store was sited on the south side of the Square. After some difficult years more elaborate premises were built in 1913 in Hamilton Place at the foot of the Barrhill. Finally in 1927 the Cumnock Society was incorporated in the Auchinleck Co-operative Society. Throughout the nineteenth century various short-lived trade unions had been attempted; the formation of the Ayrshire Miners' Union in 1886 by Keir Hardie may be taken as marking the beginning of the modern trade union movement locally.

In Cumnock, as elsewhere, one type of organisation had to await the twentieth century for full development—those catering specially for young people. There were, of course, Sunday schools. The temperance societies always took special interest in young people. Gala days with children's sports were arranged each summer after the schools closed, and on special occasions treats were provided by the Marquess of Bute and others. But apart from that, children were left very much to themselves, raking the countryside, playing football in the streets, getting up to mischief, and conducting the intermittent war between the ' Cumnock Covies ' and the ' Affleck Cubs.'

The establishment of youth organisations with regular recreational activities began in Cumnock in 1895 when the parish church started a Boys' Brigade company. A decade later this was followed by the Boy Scouts. In 1908 two troops were formed in Cumnock; they had a short career but a new and more successful troop was formed in 1921. For girls, a company of Girl Guides was set up in 1924. The inter-war period also saw the beginnings of inter-schools football, the expansion of school sports, and with the formation of the West Church Young People's Association in 1923 a new development in church work among young people.

Cumnock had for many years the benefit of two weekly newspapers—the *Cumnock Express* beginning in 1866 and the *Cumnock News* from 1880. These were not locally produced. The first was simply a local edition of the Conservative *Ayr Observer*, and the latter of Arthur Guthrie's *Ardrossan and Saltcoats Herald* advocating the Liberal cause. They were joined and eventually ousted by the *Cumnock Chronicle*, founded by John Walters Crawford. The son of a local tailor, he went into journalism, followed Keir Hardie in the *Cumnock News* and decided to set up for himself. The first issue of the new paper, printed and published locally in Ayr Road, came out on 8th November 1901. It proclaimed itself as a non-partisan paper, devoted entirely to town and district news and opinion, and that policy it has always maintained. The *Chronicle* soon established itself. At the end of its first year it was selling 2,160 copies. In 1914 a linotype type-setting machine was installed. By 1916, after fifteen years, circulation had risen beyond 4,000. By the time the *Chronicle* passed its thousandth issue in 1921 it had ousted its two rivals and was thereafter the sole local paper. J. W. Crawford had died suddenly in 1916, but the *Chronicle* was fortunate in its new owners continuing its policy and standards; it was taken over by James Ballantine and Charles Gibb, who ran the long-established local printing business; and after 1929 it was under the sole control of James P. Ballantine.

The community by the twentieth century was coming into closer contact with the outside world. There had been, of course, railway services since 1850, extended with the opening of a second station on the new line in 1872. There was still also a limited amount of road traffic—Andrew Carnegie twice stayed overnight in the town. But day jaunts to Ayr, Kilmarnock and Glasgow and holiday excursions further afield were not enjoyed by many till the twentieth century. In 1902 the town council took a trip to Leadhills. Travelling has become more common for pleasure and with increasing frequency to work. In 1907 the two local railway stations booked over 100,000 passengers. The new century brought new forms of transport. In July 1911 Cumnock had its first view of flying when two monoplanes passed over. Of more immediate importance was the beginning of motor traffic. Andrew Reive and James Parker in 1902 built for themselves what was Cumnock's first motor car. William Hunter, brother of the provost, was an ironmonger keenly interested in all new developments. He had begun cycle-making in 1902 and opened a 'gramophone saloon' in 1912. In 1914 he opened a motor garage, offering open and closed cars for hire and provided a twenty-four-seater motor charabanc. About the same time Guthrie Bros. operated a service between Cumnock and Skares. After the war more regular bus services were begun. In 1923 the Ayr and District Motor Services began to operate. They took over Munn's hayshed as a garage. A year later in 1924 they built a new garage in Pottery Row. In 1923 a Cumnock and District Motor Cycling Club was formed.

Improved transport also made national newspapers more easily available, and from 1922 the BBC began radio programmes. The following year the town council decided to allow a tenant to erect an aerial on a council house. The development of communications can also be instanced in the expansion of the postal services. The first local post office had been run by Archibald Slimman in Lugar Street. Later offices occupied successive shops around the Square. In 1880 George Stoddart became postmaster, with premises in Ayr Road. Thirty-one years later in 1911 a new G.P.O. was opened in Lugar Street, where George Stoddart continued till he retired and died in 1917 after thirty-six years' service. During this period the amount of business transacted had grown many times. The staff increased from five to eighteen. In the new G.P.O. a telephone exchange was installed in 1912, when the Post Office took over the telephone service. The National Telephone Company had extended lines to Cumnock in 1902, with exchanges, first in Glaisnock Street, then above Boreland's shop in Ayr Road, and with Miss Baird (later Mrs. Hyslop) as operator.

By the twentieth century Cumnock was being equipped with a wider range of new social facilities. The shopping centre was extending up Glaisnock Street, and in 1904 a row of new shops in Ayr Road was built by Crichton of Hillside.

Though the community was becoming more settled, it still had a quota of unruly members. Immigrants to the coal mines usually contained a rowdy element—especially the Irish and the Poles. At a J.P. court in 1907 it was remarked that ' rarely a month passes but one or more Poles figure as the accused.' There was a floating population resident in the Model and the other lodging houses who too often made themselves a nuisance. The town was also pestered by vagrants, as it had been for a long time. In 1903 a tramp census of the parish was made and eighty-eight counted. One day in 1907 a hundred ' tinklers ' were counted in Townhead park where they had made an encampment. But apart from the usual misdemeanours, the burgh's history is remarkably free from instances of serious crime and indeed the public records suggest on the positive side a high standard of honesty.

EDUCATION, 1872-1929

By the Education (Scotland) Act, 1872, School Boards were set up in every parish to be responsible for providing and supervising public schooling. When the Old Cumnock Parish School Board was instituted in April 1873 it found a situation that was far from satisfactory. With population increase and growing demand for education, facilities had become increasingly insufficient. The Parish school, erected at Broombrae by the Heritors Committee in 1847, was in good condition but accommodation was quite inadequate. Only seven years after the opening, it was already inadequate by 1854 and had been overcrowded for nearly twenty years since. In 1873 it had a roll of 189, though 144 was as many as existing standards deemed it could contain. David L. Scott had been parish schoolmaster since 1844 and offered not only the elementary subjects of reading, writing, and arithmetic but also Higher English (including History, Geography and Composition) and Latin as well. Pressure on the Parish school was somewhat relieved by the Free Church school where Robert Brown and a female assistant coped with 220 pupils. Overcrowding here was actually worse—ninety-seven and fifty-one were the estimated capacity of the two classrooms behind the Free Church in Ayr Road. In fact many parents with no Free Church connection sent their children. The fees were cheaper— an average of 3½d. a week compared with 4½d. at the Parish school; Mr. Brown was a properly qualified teacher whereas Mr. Scott had not yet taken a certificate; and the Free Church school offered all the subjects available at the Parish school, plus mathematics as a higher subject for those who wished it. A few other parents paid 4d. a week and sent their daughters (twenty-seven of them) to be taught the three Rs with some music at a private adventure school in Ayr Road. This was run by Miss Susan Lamont who came to Cumnock in 1852, was the first pianoforte teacher in the district, later played the harmonium in the parish church, and died in 1914 aged 78.

In the country two small schools offered the three Rs at 3d. a week. At Garrallan was a tiny school maintained by private subscription, able to accommodate twenty-eight pupils, but with forty-eight squeezed in and many more collier children unprovided for. At Benston the Marquess of Bute had set up a little school, where John Johnston, a veteran of Trafalgar, had taught till he retired in 1871 at the age of 90, dying in 1880 aged 99. He was followed by a sixteen-year-old local lad, John Thomson, who went off in a few years to university. His successor, a Mr. Crerar, was a qualified teacher. But there was little demand among the farm folk for schooling. Even taking fifteen pupils from New Cumnock parish, there was room for the forty-seven on the Benston school roll and usually only a couple of dozen children attended. The fact that this was a denominational school may have scared some parents. Altogether in 1873 there were in the parish 845 children between the ages of five and thirteen. Five hundred and thirty-five were on the schools' rolls; 453 attending; and adequate accommodation for only 403.

The new School Board took over the Parish school from the Heritors Committee, while the Free Church school and the two country schools were also handed over to the board. Scott and Brown were retained at a salary of £150 in their respective schools, renamed Cumnock Public School and Ayr Road Public School. A qualified assistant for Brown and several pupil teachers were engaged and part-time sewing and music teachers appointed. To relieve overcrowding, a room was hired from the U.P. Church for an infants' class and Miss Annie Clarke appointed to take charge. Meantime preparations were made for a rebuilding scheme and Messrs. Ingram, architects, Kilmarnock, were engaged to design two large new schools, in the town and at Garrallan.

For the first, three sites were considered, Greenmill Holm, Car Road, and beside the old school in Barrhill. The last was preferred, and on 19th August 1875 the foundation stone was laid with masonic honours. At a cost of £2,700 the new building was erected on a commanding site. In its belfry the old parish church bell was installed (by William McCartney & Co. at a charge of £8) and Mr. Black, the jeweller, presented a clock. Just over a year later it was almost complete—' a very elegant and commodious edifice, among the finest in the South of Scotland.' At the beginning of the new session the building was ready, but furniture was slow in arriving. On 6th October 1876 Mr. Scott and his pupils moved in from the old Parish school. The following May, Mr. Brown's pupils and Miss Clarke's infants joined them. One important point had to be settled—who was to be in charge? The School Board ' felt great difficulty and resolved to send a Memorial to the Scottish Education Department.' A novel compromise was decided upon. Scott and Brown became joint headmasters. The former (with three pupil teachers) was responsible for Standards I, V, and VI; the latter (with an assistant and four pupil teachers) for Standards II, III, and IV; while the new Infants' Mistress, Margaret Ann McCulloch, with one pupil teacher, looked after her own children. This arrangement continued for five years till Scott retired in 1882; Brown continued as headmaster till 1899. One other interesting arrangement was made. Matthew Smith, shoemaker and parish church precentor, who had been appointed part-time music teacher in 1873, was in 1876 given another £1 a week to become janitor of the new school and also ' Compulsory Officer' (i.e., Attendance

Officer) for the parish. In 1892 he was relieved of his musical duties and became a full-time janitor, but after he retired in 1899 his successor, Andrew Dunlop from Paisley, combined janitation and truancy work with giving instruction in drill.

The board's plans for Garrallan came to fruition in 1876 when the new school, to accommodate 130 pupils, was opened, with Mr. J. B. Wilson from Kilmarnock as the new headmaster, who would serve here till he retired in 1914. With two fine new schools for the parish, the School Board could congratulate itself. Little more seemed necessary. The little Benston school on the New Cumnock border was discontinued in 1878 and was used thereafter only for Sunday school and social functions. Some children in outlying parts could go to Ochiltree school, others to the Glenmuir school which the Auchinleck board maintained till its closure in 1916.

In fact, the School Board was soon faced with new demands. The first was in 1886 when they were called upon to assist with books and equipment for a denominational school newly set up by the Roman Catholic Church. There is note of an earlier R.C. school in Cumnock parish in 1867—this was almost certainly the little school at Benston which the Marquess of Bute had set up and which was described in the 1873 report as a ' denominational school.' R.C. children in Cumnock went to the public school, being excused Bible lessons. In 1886, however, St. John's School was set up—a wood and iron building in Bank Avenue off Barrhill—replaced by a more substantial building in 1907. It was another of the Marquess of Bute's many benevolences. Its first teachers, Miss Kate McCarrick and Kate Malloy, had 66 pupils. In a few years' time, in 1890, the Sisters Servants of the Sacred Heart took over the teaching duties and the Diocesan Inspectors reported in 1896 on ' its high state of efficiency.' By 1899 there were 99 pupils, growing to 109 by 1903. Though this school was outwith the control of the School Board, it was entitled to, and received financial aid.

Another demand arose with the opening of new mines and the building of other miners' rows. The capacity of the new school at Garrallan was soon overtaxed. Additions were made in 1886, but even so by 1900 it had 228 pupils. A new brick school was built at Skares, capable of holding 200 pupils. This relieved the pressure, and by 1903 the two schools held between them 149 (Garrallan) and 129 (Skares).

When the new Cumnock Public School was being built, there were in the town many and loud complaints, from A. B. Todd and others, that it was too expensive and far beyond what would be required. In fact, it was soon too small. Indeed, it was as well that Mr. Scott continued to occupy the schoolhouse in the old parish building and that there were no thoughts of demolishing the old parish schoolroom attached to it. After only three years, in 1880, the old parish building was brought into regular use again, for the 140 infants. Even so, the new building was over-crowded, with well over 400 pupils taught in three large rooms. Cumnock with 611 pupils in 1881 was now the second biggest school in Ayrshire—only Maybole (with a roll of 628) was larger. In 1883 the raising of the school leaving age from 13 to 14 raised new difficulties. Following suggestions by Her Majesty's Inspectors, glass partitions were installed in 1882 to provide a larger number of smaller rooms, and an extra classroom was added in 1886. Fortunately there was no significant increase in the school roll in the last two decades of the nineteenth century. But the situation remained unsatisfactory. When John Dick came as the new headmaster in 1899 he found a staff including the Infants' Mistress (Agnes Dalziel), four assistants and nine pupil teachers, working in congested conditions; and in the early years of the new century the school population once more began to increase. Plans were therefore made for a new infants' building to be erected behind the main school, but before this was ready in 1905, the 195 infants had in 1904 overflowed from the old parish schoolroom into temporary additional accommodation in the Church Mission Hall nearby.

Until 1889 fees had to be paid. These were due in advance for each four weeks—Infants 10d.; Standards I and II, 1/-; Standard III, 1/2; Standards IV, V and VI, 1/4; extra subjects, 1/8. Until 1881 (when heating by hot water pipes was installed) pupils might also be called upon to pay in winter a levy of 2d. a month to pay for coals. Fees were abolished in 1889, but in 1909 the board turned down Hugh Lorimer's proposal that books should also be free. The board, however, was not particularly ungenerous. It was responsible for building and maintaining schools, and providing improvements—like a play-shed (1885), new lavatories (1906), cloakrooms and a corridor (1914) at the Public school. It appointed extra teachers as required, gave individual teachers salary increases when their requests seemed to justify it and in 1914 agreed to a definite scale of salaries. They even paid travelling expenses by railway for teachers going to Garrallan. The Board was generous enough in supplying equipment and furniture. There were miscellaneous expenses to be met, as when the piano at Skares school was gnawed by rats (1904); in 1909 and 1913 because of new traffic dangers it purchased ' Caution ' signs from the Scottish Automobile Club; in 1915 to meet black-out requirements, dark blinds had to be provided for evening classes. In 1879 it instituted prizes for attendance, in 1900 introduced merit prizes and in 1915 medals for the best in each class with a dux medal for each school. In the 1912 miners' strike it organised school meals for necessitous children, in a soup kitchen in the Mission Hall, and repeated this for a short time after the outbreak of war in 1914.

The School Board was responsible not only for the schools but for the schooling therein. One of its first decisions in 1873 was to stipulate that the Bible and Shorter Catechism be taught for half-an-hour each morning and for five minutes each afternoon before dismissal. The general work of the school was also supervised. Applicants for posts were interviewed and often heard teaching a class. Each session on the closing day members of the Board visited the schools and examined the classes; and the reports by Her Majesty's Inspectors following their annual visits were studied. In 1882 the Board considered that corporal punishment should no longer be administered by pupil teachers. In 1894 they felt that more time should be devoted to drill and in 1902 even thought of acquiring a playing-field. In 1895 they arranged for the teachers to instruct pupil teachers between 8.30 and 9.15 each morning. In 1899 the teaching of drawing was begun with all classes. In 1900 they introduced Band of Hope lectures on temperance to school pupils and in 1908 lectures on the evils of smoking.

The School Board was also responsible for arranging holidays. The summer vacation usually lasted for five weeks or so. There was also a spring holiday of about a week and a New Year holiday of the same length. Only occasionally was Christmas

Day a holiday. In 1881, however, Captain Campbell of Glaisnock provided for the pupils a party, with a Christmas tree, and in 1913 Lady Bute arranged a similar entertainment. There were single day holidays for the March Races, the May Fair, the Hin Hairst Fair in October, and latterly the September Ayr Races. The school was also closed twice yearly on the Friday Fast Day before Communion Sunday in the Parish Church, and (until 1877) for the special church services on the Monday following. It was also customary to grant a holiday after the annual Inspectors' visit, in 1899 for the Queen's birthday and in 1902 when the Marquess of Bute visited Cumnock. From time to time there was a day off for ' recreation on the ice '; in 1880 a half-holiday was declared ' on account of the town being visited by a circus '; in 1896 the school was closed in the afternoons one Thursday and Friday because of the Town Hall bazaar, and there were similar closures in 1899 and 1904. Sometimes the schools were shut because of epidemics of measles, mumps ('the branks'), scarlet fever, or typhoid—and for a fortnight in 1918 because of influenza. Quite often in winter there was an early closing because of the weather conditions. In March 1881 the headmaster recorded in his log book that roads and railways were blocked with snow, the heaviest fall since he came to Ayrshire thirty-seven years since. On 2nd December 1898 the school could not meet. The Glaisnock in flood had swamped Waterside Place and it was impossible that morning to get from one side of the town to the other. There were also holidays when the school was required for parliamentary elections and for the triennial elections to School Board, County Council, and Parish Council. There was in 1887 a special Jubilee holiday when all school children in the parish, led by New Cumnock Brass Band, marched off to Glengyron farm for sports, buns and milk; and similar festivities were organised for the Coronations in 1901 and 1911. In 1900 three special half-holidays were granted to celebrate the relief of Ladysmith, the relief of Mafeking, and the capture of Pretoria; a year later the end of the Boer War gave a whole day's holiday. In the first World War, when local schools savings passed £1,000 in 1918 the pupils were rewarded with a holiday and on Monday 11th November, at the Armistice, the school bell was rung, the flag hoisted and the pupils dismissed.

Even with all these holidays pupils tended to take days off when their parents (or they themselves) felt inclined. In 1874, for example, two congregations arranged Sabbath School outings on a school day. In 1881 there was poor attendance because the town was on holiday on the occasion of the Volunteer Review in Edinburgh. Smith (the musical janitor) was away as quarter-master-sergeant, with other 138 men of the local volunteer company. The school log-book adds that the day was 'very wet'—this was the famous 'Wet Review.' In 1900 low attendance one day was blamed on 'the Glasgow holiday, the New Cumnock races, flitting and the Glaisnock roup.' And each year at harvest time, many pupils were kept off to help. Despite parents being summoned before the Board and occasionally fined at the J.P. Court, attendance in general was poor. School was apparently a less attractive place in the good old days.

The annual reports of Her Majesty's Inspectors indicate that, to begin with, Cumnock Public School's standards were not very high—very unsatisfactory work and poor discipline were noted. In the 1880's there was a pronounced improvement in the work of the school. By 1891 it had acquired a 'reputation for thorough and successful work' and the infants' department under Miss Dalziel was year after year singled out for special praise. As early as 1879 the Board had considered the possibilities of developing 'higher class education' at this school and certain 'specific subjects' were taught, but nothing very much was done till 1894. In that year the new County Committee for Secondary Education made its first grants, including £50 to Cumnock Public School. A curriculum of secondary studies was drawn up, it was decided that some teachers should specialise in certain subjects, and pupils from Muirkirk and other parishes were enrolled in the new senior classes. English, Latin, French, Mathematics, and Physiology were among the subjects. But accommodation was limited and teachers had commitments to their large elementary classes. It was impossible to provide a complete secondary course; from 1898 older pupils were given the chance of competing for places at Ayr and Kilmarnock, and from the Duncan Bequest bursaries were provided.

With increased staff, better work was possible. By 1902, Mr. Dick had on his staff the Infants' Mistress (Elizabeth Orr), eight assistant teachers (two of them graduates) as well as seven pupil teachers and H. B. McCulley—the Parish Church organist who had been teaching music part-time in the local schools since 1892 and who continued till 1930. The H.M.I. report of 1903 noted that ' the Advanced Department is fast growing to be one of the very best in the district.' The Board decided that better accommodation was needed. The new Infants' building which was being contemplated should, they decided, include laboratories for the teaching of science. But the Scottish Education Department laid down the law that no grants would be available for this. The new building was modified and only a cookery and laundry room provided in addition to the infants' rooms. But when the infants in 1905 evacuated the old parish schoolroom, the Board was able to convert it for the teaching of science and art. On 1st July 1905 the school was recognised as Cumnock Higher Grade Public School. Two years later the timetable was reorganised better to accommodate the 1½-hour periods in the higher grade department. The school now met from 9 to 12.15 in the mornings and 1.15 to 4 in the afternoons. A year later the morning opening time was advanced to 8.30 for the convenience of pupils arriving by train from Muirkirk and New Cumnock.

The school roll now began to rise rapidly, reaching 796 in 1913 and 901 in 1916. In 1909 an unexpected opportunity arose of obtaining additional (though somewhat unconventional) premises. Just opposite the school was Hillside House, which came on the market at a price of £1,500. This was an impressive large villa, with a beautiful garden ' kept in the most exquisite order and its flower-beds, with ribbon-style of gardening, are bright with all the colours of the rainbow.' There was a conservatory and vinery and greenhouse ' in which every kind of fruit and flower in their season may be found.' The grounds were enclosed with shrubs and trees.

Hillside House had since its erection in 1846 been in the possession of the Crichton family. The first had been factor to the Marquess of Bute. His son, Hew Crichton (1795-1891), became head of the Edinburgh firm of Tait and Crichton, Writers to the Signet. The third generation was James Arthur Crichton (1825-1891), an advocate who became Sheriff of the Lothians and Peebles. Hillside House was tenanted by his brother Hew Hamilton

Crichton, who died in 1906, and an unmarried sister who died two years later.

The School Board borrowed from the Public Works Loans Board the total of £3,500 for purchase and conversion and in 1911 the 143 Higher Grade pupils moved across the Barrhill into the new premises. The highest class met in the parlour and the old kitchen became a staff room. Visiting specialists came to teach Art and Physical Training. Gardening was successfully taught in the grounds (until staff shortage during the war). It was even possible now to offer cookery and woodwork classes in the H.G. School for pupils from St. John's R.C. School. But the old parish schoolroom had still to be kept in use.

The School Board provided not only elementary and higher grade schooling but as early as 1874 considered arranging evening classes. Though nothing was done till 1889, they regularly granted the use of school premises for evening meetings of various kinds, some of which would now be regarded as further education. In 1876 Matthew Smith started an evening music class at Garrallan, and from time to time choral, orchestral and band practices were held in the Cumnock school. The Athenaeum arranged courses of lectures and in 1881 there were penny readings at Garrallan. On 19th October 1882 J. K. Hardie was granted the use of the old parish schoolroom for one hour each Wednesday evening for meetings of his Cumnock Shorthand Writers' Association (and he gave instruction without fee). In 1893 painting classes on Saturdays were tried and in 1896 Monsieur Navarné from Gilmilnscroft began evening classes in French and German. In 1889 the Board instituted its own evening classes in science and in later years courses in mining and shorthand were added. For these a fee of 2/- was charged, refunded for satisfactory attendance. In the early years of the new century, in co-operation with the County Secondary Committee, a scheme of courses was offered. Classes in elementary subjects were provided for pupils who were thereby allowed to leave school at an earlier age. Other classes were offered in commercial arithmetic, book-keeping, shorthand, art, mathematics, physiography, machine construction, needlework, cookery, French, German, mining, engineering and horticulture. Demand, however, was limited—156 enrolled in 1902, but in the winter of 1907-8 none at all were held. But vocational classes became well-established after war-time difficulties were over.

The Parish School Board which (under the supervision of the Scottish Education Department) was entirely responsible for educational provision was a committee of seven men, elected triennially and with Archibald Brakenridge as their Clerk and Treasurer for the forty-six years of the Board's existence. The first Board consisted of Messrs. Barrowman, Baird, Samson, and Mackervail—two of whom were at that time also town councillors; Rev. James Murray; from the country Charles George Shaw (factor to the Marquess of Bute) and Patrick Charles Douglas Boswell of Garrallan who was elected chairman for the first twelve years. This pattern of membership continued; most members served several terms. The one who served longest, from 1876 till 1911, was David Reid, farmer, Milzeoch. The outstanding figure of the Board's history was ex-Provost Hunter, who was elected to the School Board in 1885 and was its chairman from 1897 till its dissolution in 1919. It was he who inspired many of the progressive developments and pioneered the development of secondary education in Cumnock, including the acquisition of Hillside House.

The schools and properties maintained by the Old Cumnock Parish School Board were in 1919 handed over to the new county authority. Under Ayrshire Education Authority from 1919 to 1929 the schools were organised on standard lines and lost a good deal of their individual character. This was so even with local persons elected to the Authority and with a subordinate local School Management Committee to deal with minor items of administration. School holidays, for example, were determined at eight weeks in summer and about a week at Easter and New Year. Christmas Day was a separate day's holiday, becoming attached in due course to the New Year break. The fortnight's September holiday (1921) became contracted to a long week-end in autumn. A few odd days were left over for special holidays, including the local factory holidays which the town council since 1900 had always made the Ayr Cattle Show in April and Ayr Races in September.

Despite differences in details of administration, one general problem recurred, to provide staff and accommodation for a widening curriculum in a growing community. By 1919 Cumnock H.G. School was again overcrowded. The old parish schoolroom was still occupied; another class was being held in the central hall of the Infants' building; and the Mission Hall was once more called into use. Army huts were erected in the grounds of Hillside House in 1920 and preparations made for additional building. At this moment of renewed crisis the laboratories in the old parish building were threatened when the old two-storey schoolhouse, which was attached to it, was burned down in February 1925.

On Tuesday, 31st October 1926, a new secondary building in the grounds of Hillside House was opened by ex-Provost Thomas Hunter. It was, the H.M.I. report remarked, ' a handsome building . . . splendidly equipped in every respect for the purposes of a secondary school.' It contained a dozen classrooms, two staffrooms, laboratories, and a gymnasium with a small swimming pool. Music, art, and technical subjects were provided in the old Hillside House, to which the new building was connected by a covered-way. A full five-year secondary course had been instituted the previous session, with departments of English, Latin and Greek, French, Mathematics, Science, Art, Educational Handwork, Music, Needlework, and Physical Training. In December 1927 the new designation of Cumnock Academy was granted to the school. It now had a roll of over 900 pupils. When John Dick, headmaster and first rector, resigned in 1929 the next H.M.I. report noted his waygoing—' He had served the community faithfully and well for the long period of thirty years and had seen his efforts rewarded by the gradual growth of educational facilities till now the school has attained to a full secondary curriculum.'

Over the period from 1873 till 1930 a steadily-increasing annual expenditure on education was required and this was included in the rates assessed and levied by the Parochial Board and the Parish Council which succeeded it. In its first year the School Board spent £250, which amount grew to £700 five years later and by 1901 had passed £1,000. By 1918 over £2,000 a year was required and there were protests when the new Education Authority needed £4,500 in 1920. But it continued at over £4,000. Indeed it passed £5,000 in 1925, and continued to grow thereafter.

THE CHURCHES, 1843-1929

The Disruption of 1843 left the pews of the Established Church in the Square almost empty. The minister, Rev. Ninian Bannatyne, had given up his living, so had the parish schoolmaster John McKinnell, and many parishioners followed them to help form the new Free Church. Indeed the entire Kirk Session left, and in ' the peculiar circumstances of the Parish, as being destitute of a kirk-session ' the Presbytery of Ayr had to appoint a special committee of three neighbouring ministers till a new session could be appointed. To fill the vacancy of parish minister the Marquess of Bute presented Rev. James Murray, a young man of literary tastes—author of *Songs of the Covenanting Times* (1861). Though he was not the man to revitalise a depleted congregation, yet during his long ministry of thirty-one years the foundations were laid for later revival. In 1846 the Marquess was presented with a petition by the remaining 207 parishioners and heads of families regarding the ' damp, dilapidated and otherwise unwholesome state of their present church.' The old church, built in 1754, had been renovated in 1822 when outside stairs had been added. Further repairs were made in 1846, and again in 1854, but it was not till 1863 that a decision was reached that rebuilding was needed. Proposals were made for a grand new church, which would possibly cost £3,500, even without the spire and tower originally contemplated. Early in 1864 the demolition of the old church was begun. From the old church the weather-cock was rescued and put up on top of Munn's stables in Glaisnock Street and rested there till 1965. The old church bell was similarly saved. It was hung on what came to be known as the Bell Tree at the foot of the Strand, and continued to be rung daily at 5.30 a.m. and 8 p.m. by Hugh McLelland, the bellman and gravedigger. In time this plane tree became unsafe, and the town council had to cut it down in 1872. The Heritors Committee kept the bell till 1875 when they offered it to the School Board for erection in the belfry of the new school. There it was installed, with 80-year-old Hugh McLelland climbing up to satisfy himself that his bell was properly housed. The bell, cast by Quirinus de Visscher of Rotterdam in 1697, is 20⅜ inches in diameter, an excellent casting with a good tone, and ornately decorated with geometric designs and a hunting scene round its border.

On 22nd March 1864 the foundation stone of the new parish church was laid with masonic honours. The congregation was meantime granted the use of the U.P. Church for Sunday services at 2 p.m. Throughout 1865 the new building grew, and with it the cost. Finally on 15th November 1866 it was opened. Including heating and furnishing it had cost a total of £6,227 14s. 8d. It was an imposing church, set right in the heart of the police burgh that had been formed just ten days before the church was opened. Built of white freestone in Gothic style, the parish church provided 1,100 sittings as well as a gallery for the Marquess of Bute as patron of the parish. It was enhanced by stained-glass windows presented by him, and a town's clock gifted in 1872 by Captain William Allason Cunninghame of Logan and Afton at a cost of 100 guineas.

When Rev. James Murray died at Mentone in the south of France in 1875 at the age of sixty-four following a period of ill health, a new chapter in the life of the Established Church began with the ordination of Rev. John Spence Robertson. He came as a young man of 25, called by the congregation (for patronage had been abolished in 1874). He served with enthusiasm and effect and after more than fifty years in this his only charge, died in 1934. In the early years of his ministry church services were revitalised. In 1875 the traditional sitting during praise and standing at prayer was abandoned and it was decided ' that the congregation stand while singing and kneel during prayer ' but with a new tolerant spirit ' allowing each individual member to act in the manner as he may think right or expedient.' In 1880 an organ was installed, replacing a harmonium that had been in use for some five years. By 1879 the number of members had risen to 555 and efforts were being made to extend the work of evangelism. Students were engaged to act as missionaries in the town and the miners' rows, and regular services were instituted at Garrallan and Skares, where a new Mission Hall was built in 1911. By 1888 the church had a choir and a Sabbath School well enough established for each to have a summer excursion. In 1895 a Boys' Brigade Company was formed in connection with the church. The fabric of the church was modernised—a new heating system installed in 1886 and a general renovation made in 1894. In 1900 a Mission Hall was erected on the glebe, providing scope for the extending range of congregational activities in the twentieth century. In 1924, for example, the session agreed to allow badminton in the hall, provided there was no smoking or dancing. During all this time Rev. J. S. Robertson made his effective presence felt, both in the congregation and in the community as a whole.

While the Established Church was recovering from the Disruption, those who had left in 1843 were firmly establishing their own congregational life. A Free Church was built in Ayr Road, and with earnest enthusiasm they committed themselves also to the creation of a Free Church School, providing all that the parish school could offer and more, and eventually handing over to the new School Board in 1873 the town's leading educational establishment. For the first three decades of its life the Free Church was served by Rev. Ninian Bannatyne. He retired in 1873 and died a year later at the age of 72. After the short ministry of Alexander Adamson (1873-1882) there followed Rev. John Warrick who served from 1883 till his death in 1931 at the age of 76. Two great monuments of his ministry were the new church erected in 1896 and his own history of Cumnock published in 1899. The latter bears witness to his keen interest in the community which he made his own, and his energy and skill in compilation. The former, the new church, was made possible by the generosity of Miss Crichton of Hillside, as a memorial to her father Hew Crichton and her brother Sheriff Crichton, both of whom died in 1892 within two days of each other. The Crichton Memorial Free Church, with 500 sittings, is built of red sandstone in ornamented English Gothic style and has a spire 140 feet high which has made it an outstanding local building.

Meanwhile the third presbyterian congregation continued through the nineteenth century. In 1831 a large new church of the United Secession was erected, a sign of the congregation's vitality, and in 1847 as a result of national advance it became the United Presbyterian Church. Locally the ministries of Matthew Dickie (1848-1857) and William Hutton (1857-1867) were short. But they made a forceful impact on the community, the former by his temperance work, the latter by his contribution to the

establishment of Cumnock as a police burgh. Each went off
to bigger charges. Their successor, Alexander Macdonald,
continued their good work between 1871 and 1913. During his
ministry an organ was installed in the church; and in 1904 a
hall, vestry and session house added. He sponsored evangelistic
work at Glengyron, Garrallan and Skares. From 1897 till 1913
he took an active part in the work of the School Board. When he
died in 1913 the Town Council recorded in its minutes that he
had ' endeared himself not only to his own congregation but to
the whole community.' He was succeeded by two ministers,
each of whom stayed only briefly—Stewart Richard Scott (1913-
1922) and Hugh McKniven Agnew (1923-1929). The latter
wrote a history of the church to celebrate its 150th anniversary
in 1923.

While the three presbyterian congregations had followed their
own separate paths, the early decades of the twentieth century
brought formal ending to such differences as remained. 1900
saw the coming together nationally of the Free and U.P. churches
to form the United Free Church of Scotland. Thereafter with
two U.F. congregations in the town—the Crichton Memorial
U.F. in Ayr Road and the West U.F. in the Tanyard—the
established church had become a minority. In 1929, however,
came the great national reunion and thereafter all three congregations were together within the Church of Scotland.

Throughout the nineteenth century the Congregationalists
showed a marked advance. Beginning in 1838 with twelve
members meeting in the Black Bull Hall, by 1847 they were
able to purchase and adapt the old parish school in the Square
as a chapel at a cost of £700, and twenty years later a manse at
£500. There were difficulties in a small congregation getting
and keeping ministers. In the first half-century there were seven—
Mr. Sime (1840-1842), P. W. Grant (1844-1853), John McAuslan
(1854-1865), Thomas Brisbane (1866-1872), John Murray (1873-
1876), Francis Lamb (1877-1881), A. N. Scott (1882-1884).
Nevertheless membership was rising—eighty-eight in 1881 and
115 three years later. Some were incomers into the town, like
Keir Hardie. In the Minutes for 9th July 1882, it is reported:
' This day, at a meeting after communion, Mr. and Mrs. James
Hardie were admitted on certificate from E.U. Church, Hamilton.'

He came at a time when the congregation had undertaken an ambitious programme. The old church was sold off to the Clydesdale Bank, the old manse disposed of to G. T. Samson, and a fine new church with manse adjoining built at Stepends on the other side of the Lugar at a combined cost of £2,100. The church, with seating for 350, was opened on 18th February 1883. A year later, however, came an internal dispute over the disciplining of members and the opinions of the pastor. At a meeting of 28th March 1884, following an ' inflammatory speech of Mr. Hardie,' he and other thirty-seven members resigned and with the pastor set up a separate congregation attached to the Evangelical Union. Though this E.U. congregation failed to become established and most of the seceders found their way back into the Congregational Church, by 1890 membership was still only ninety and did not reach one hundred till 1902. Under the long ministry of William Mathieson (1884-1913) definite advances were however made. From 1891 till 1897 under the auspices of this congregation a Band of Hope was formed to conduct temperance meetings, reaching a peak with 494 adherents in 1894. In 1892 a bazaar liquidated the debt on the manse and the surplus helped to provide an organ costing £225 in 1894. Mission service services were conducted by the pastor at Auchinleck, Lugar, and in Glaisnock chapel. When William Mathieson died in 1913 after thirty years in the charge he was followed by Mark N. Robson, who ministered for over twenty years to this small but vital congregation. Despite small numbers its influence in the community was marked—three of its members having been provosts of the burgh.

The influx into town and parish in the second half of the nineteenth century of many pitworkers brought members of other religious denominations. Assemblies of Christian Brethren were formed in Ayrshire from the 1860's onwards, preaching the doctrines first promulgated at Plymouth. After the Moody-Sankey revival, enthusiasts from various protestant groups combined to form the Ayrshire Christian Union in 1878 and Keir Hardie took an active part in its work in Cumnock. When the Salvation Army invaded Ayrshire in 1882 it found in Cumnock not only a small detachment of ready recruits but many enthusiastic camp-followers.

Then in 1875 two Baptists from Kilmarnock came to work at Gaswater and helped found a congregation of their church in Cumnock. In 1876 they welcomed Rev. J. Houston as their first minister. After occupying various temporary premises—including the parish school from 1879 till 1881—they erected in 1887 their own church in Barrhill, with accommodation for 200. Three years later New Cumnock adherents hived off to form their own congregation, and the congregation suffered from short ministries—ten in the congregation's first half-century. Membership remained small, numbering only fifty-three in 1926. But there was compensation in the enthusiasm and faith of the select few—like the Senior Deacon A. White and Mrs. White who contributed much to the work of the church in the early years of the century.

During the nineteenth century the Roman Catholics enjoyed a growing strength. From 1850 onwards Rev. William McCabe (1850-1853) and Rev. Thomas Wallace (1853-1855) had held office as parish priests, conducting local services. Under Rev. John O'Dwyer, however, when it was decided to build a chapel, the site chosen was at Birnieknowe in Auchinleck parish, and there Cumnock Catholics had to go for a number of years after 1867. After Father O'Dwyer's death in 1873, to Birnieknowe came Rev. John McGinnis, in 1874 Rev. Patrick A. Wright, and in 1882 Rev. John O'Neill. With increased numbers, in 1882 Cumnock became a separate charge, under Rev. Daniel Collins. Thanks to the third Marquess of Bute, who followed the Roman faith, in that year St. John's Church was erected at the head of Glaisnock Street. A beautifully-furnished place of worship, it has served the congregation ever since. In 1885 it became the first ecclesiastical building in the country to be lit by electricity. Until the congregation became self-supporting, the Marquess defrayed the entire costs of maintaining the incumbent and the church. Also in 1882 Lady Bute erected a Cottage Hospital in Barrhill Road, staffed with trained nurses from the Sisters of the Sacred Heart. With ten beds and three children's cots, it was equipped for dealing with surgical cases from the pits and the surrounding area—and it offered its services to persons of all creeds. In 1886 Lord and Lady Bute extended their generosity by building the new St. John's School in Bank Avenue beside the Cottage Hospital.

After Father Collins left in 1885 he was succeeded by Rev. John Hourigan (1885-1889), Rev. Henry Stuart Laverty (1889-1890), and the Rev. Charles J. A. O'Malley. The congregation had now become well-established with—in 1895—687 members of all ages. Of these 314 lived in Cumnock, twenty-two in Glengyron, eleven in Skares and five at Garrallan. The other half came from further afield—from Lugar (102), Auchinleck (61), the New Cumnock area (93), Kirkconnel and Sanquhar (17), Ochiltree and other places (62). Over 300 performed Easter Duties annually. Under Father O'Malley's charge congregational life flourished. Annual congregational reunions and summer excursions were organised, a Sunday school and youth groups formed, various societies set up—including the St. Vincent de Paul Society, 1894—a lending library opened and a parish magazine attempted. O'Malley's successors, Daniel Keogh and Henry J. Langley, stayed only briefly, but Martin Meagher served his parish from 1906 till 1936. The congregation was in good heart, now an accepted minority within a predominantly protestant community. Progress was signified by such things as the erection of a new school (1907), the transfer of the fabric of the old school to be used as a congregational hall, and the building of a new presbytery (1914).

The passions of sectarian controversy had not entirely died out by the end of the nineteenth century. Anti-Catholic feeling was long in waning. On 25th July 1900, for example, a Protestant conventicle was held in the Square by Jacob Primmer, and the presence of Ulstermen among the immigrant Irish resulted in the formation of a lodge of Loyal Orangemen. There was a continuing tendency to ostracise those of the Roman faith—Warrick dealt with them most cursorily in his history. But there was a breaking down of social barriers—members of all faiths for example associated with Keir Hardie in the I.L.P., children from St. John's School were invited to Coronation and other celebrations and Catholics were members of various public bodies. For some years Patrick McCormick served on the Parochial Board as later did Father O'Malley. Indeed in 1895 when fourteen candidates stood for eight seats, with only twenty-seven Catholic voters Father O'Malley got 194 votes and came in fifth. Later Father Meagher served on the School Board from 1911 till 1919. Each of these parish priests did much in his own way to earn recognition for their Church in the community. O'Malley was very popular in the town, an excellent singer of popular ballads and with the reputation of being a wit, and also reputed to use strong-arm methods to keep unruly members of his flock in order. Father Meagher was a different character, quiet and dignified, but highly esteemed by Catholic and non-Catholic alike.

Among the protestant groups there was still a strict loyalty to individual denominations. There was real religious zeal, instanced by the considerable exertions to provide new church buildings. But there was less insistence on traditional observances. In 1887 all three presbyterian congregations agreed to discontinue holding Fast Days. There was a growing willingness to co-operate for worthy purposes. There was joint participation in the annual conventicles at the old kirkyard. Members of various Protestant denominations came together in such organisations as the Ayrshire Christian Union, the Band of Hope, and the temperance movement. It is worth noting the strength of this locally in the last decades of the nineteenth century. Besides the local Total Abstinence Society, there were the Stanley and Peden Thorn Lodges of Good Templars and a juvenile branch in whose work Keir Hardie participated. At Garrallan a branch of the Lugar Temperance Society was instituted (1897) and in the early years of the twentieth century the Rechabites and Good Templars became organised at Skares.

At the beginning of the century Cumnock was fortunate in having as ministers of the three large presbyterian congregations men who had come to the town as young men and found it a good place for their entire ministry. Alexander Macdonald was ordained and inducted in the U.P. Kirk in 1871 and lived to see it come into fellowship with the Free Kirk. John Warrick came to the Free Kirk in 1883, participated in this union and just lived to see the formation of the reunited Church of Scotland in 1929. John Spence Robertson who came to the parish church in 1875 had Macdonald and Warrick as partners for the greater part of his ministry and their fellowship made the ultimate reunion of the churches locally in 1929 not only formal but real.

Obviously the churches had a continuing influence in the community even though the nature of that impact had changed.

The disciplinary control that the kirk session of the established church had once exercised over all parishioners could no longer be maintained when some belonged to other denominations and others to none. That kirk session continued to supervise the morals of the members of its own congregation till a surprisingly late date: 27th April 1898 was indeed the last occasion when persons were compeared before the session, for ' the sin of ante-nuptial fornication.'

In the nineteenth century the new secular authorities took over various duties previously performed by the kirk. The Heritors Committee on which the Session combined with the local landowners surrendered its control over poor relief in 1845 and over education in 1872. Thereafter till its final abolition in 1931 it survived only to supervise the parish graveyards and formally to approve what the established kirk decided regarding the fabric of the kirk and manse.

In 1877 the Heritors Committee performed its last significant duty in laying out the new cemetery beside New Cumnock Road. In the middle of the eighteenth century the first graveyard around the parish kirk had been closed and the Square laid out. Thereafter only the Dumfries family retained the right of burial, in the vault under the church. From 1756 onwards the new parish graveyard was on the land beside Peden's burial place up the Barrhill. After 1877 only parishioners who already owned lairs could claim the right of burial there and after a generation interments ceased. There is left behind in the Barrhill cemetery a host of memorials in stone to old Cumnockians, famed and unknown, side by side.

Chapter 7

The Modern Burgh

The year 1929 was in many ways a key date in the history of the burgh. By the Local Government (Scotland) Act of that year police burghs like Cumnock were renamed small burghs. This change involved the loss of certain powers; nevertheless in the case of Cumnock it was followed by a period of vigorous activity by the town council. The same Act extended the authority and influence of the county council, which acquired new responsibilities—major roads were taken over from the small burghs, education from the *ad hoc* county authority, poor relief and other functions from the parish councils. Indeed, parish councils were abolished and thereafter the folk in the landward part of Cumnock parish were looked after either by the county council or by the new and subordinate Cumnock District Council. These far-reaching changes in local government administration were often accompanied by new developments in the public services. In particular, 1929 marks the beginning of a new era in education. Coincidentally the same year brought the great reunion in the Scottish Church, making 1929 a turning-point in the history of all our major local institutions.

In a wider field, 1929 marked the beginning of the World Economic Crisis. To most countries it brought difficulties. Hitler came to power in Germany in 1933, leading to the second World War. In Britain in 1931 Ramsay Macdonald formed his National Government. In U.S.A. in 1933 Roosevelt became president and initiated his New Deal. In political and social outlook the thirties formed a period of difficult readjustments. But since the second World War Britain has been transformed. Successive governments, both Labour and Conservative, have contributed towards building the new Welfare State.

All these trends are echoed in the story of Cumnock since 1929.

The thirties saw Cumnock suffering distress as a result of industrial stagnation. There was mass unemployment and widespread poverty. Typically and pathetically, the Royal Jubilee of 1935 was marked by a 2/6 bonus to those on poor relief awarded by the County Council. The particular difficulties of a depressed mining area were reflected in political opinion. The parliamentary constituency of South Ayrshire which had been held for Labour from 1919 till 1929 by James Brown of Annbank was re-won in 1931 and held thereafter as a safe seat, with James Brown succeeded in 1939 by Alexander Sloan and since 1946 by Emrys Hughes. Within the burgh, the Labour Party won control of the town council in 1933, and there ensued a period of bitter partisan dispute. Despite difficulties, considerable progress was made in municipal enterprise. Foundations were being laid in these years for later developments in local industry. Wider social opportunities were becoming available. All the while daily life was punctuated by events ordinary and extraordinary. In 1931 Mrs. Cullen of Cumnock won £30,000 in a sweepstake. In 1937 William Kilpatrick, coachbuilder, Glaisnock Street, celebrated his hundredth birthday, and in 1940 died at the age of 102. There were floods in 1931, 1937, 1938, 1944, 1954, 1956, 1958, 1962, 1963, 1966; severe snowstorms in 1936, 1937, 1940, 1942, 1947, 1954, 1957, 1960, 1963, 1964, 1965; and gale damage in 1949, 1957, 1959, 1961 and 1964.

The coming of war brought a full range of problems to Cumnock. The town council reluctantly had to postpone its plans for housing and other developments. Social life became limited because of shortages, black-out, restrictions of various kinds, the absence of local men and women on war service, and the involvement of many of those left in civil defence, Home Guard and fund-raising efforts. Throughout the war the local population was augmented by evacuees from Clydeside. Cumnock also acted as host for military units during their training for active service.

By the end of the war, though British war losses were found to be fewer than in the first World War, they were still considerable. As far as Cumnock is concerned, the new war memorial unveiled in 1950 bore thirty-seven names, compared with 117 on the old memorial.

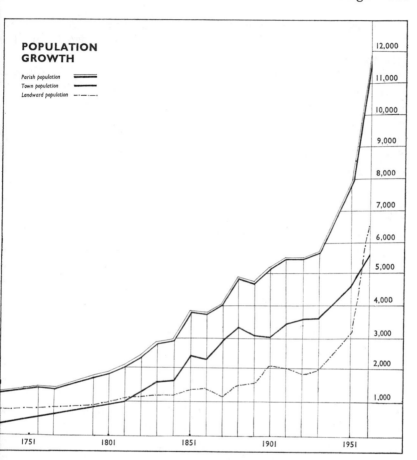

POPULATION GROWTH

Parish population
Town population
Landward population

Things were slow in getting back to normal after the war. Shortages of material, for example, delayed the Town Council's housing drive, but by the fifties speedier progress was made in various fields. Ambitious plans for the expansion of Cumnock were implemented. The burgh population of 3,653 in 1931 increased to 4,607 (1951) and 5,403 (1961). In the landward part of the parish, an even more spectacular growth occurred, from 1,984 (1931) to 3,263 (1951) and 5,926 (1961). This was the result of County Council development plans, creating three great new housing estates as suburbs of Cumnock, at Netherthird, Craigens, and Logan. To these new houses came people from old mining rows awaiting demolition, and miners and their families attracted to east Ayrshire by expansion of the local coal industry. Successful efforts were also made to diversify employment by establishing new factories. The post-war period has also been a lively time from the social point of view, with new types of recreation, and new efforts to enrich community life. Appropriately enough, on the Royal tour of Ayrshire in July 1956, Cumnock was visited by Her Majesty Queen Elizabeth and H.R.H. the Duke of Edinburgh, who were received by Provost Edgar at a ceremony in Wood Road Park. In several Honours Lists around this time distinguished local men were named: John Stevenson, M.B.E. (1951), for services to dairy farming; Robert Watson, M.B.E. (1953), for work with the Army Cadet Corps; George McTurk, O.B.E. (1953), for political services; and R. D. Hunter, M.B.E. (1960), for services to the community.

In 1966 Cumnock reached its centenary and looked forward to the future with confidence. The burgh was now the nucleus of a greater Cumnock of over 10,000 inhabitants, centre of the Cumnock County District containing another 30,000 people.

THE COUNCIL SINCE 1929

The town council of nine members in 1929 contained four veterans who had served since before the first World War— John Carruthers, 1904-1907, 1919-1934; David Smith, 1906-1932; James Neil, 1907-1910, 1911-1936; Allan McCall, 1912-1946.

Three of these four, and four of the other five more junior men ended their council careers in the hurly-burly of the thirties. By the later part of that decade it was virtually a new council, in personnel as in politics.

In November 1933 when two Moderate councillors retired, the Labour candidates were returned unopposed, to give their party a majority on Cumnock Town Council after what the *Cumnock Chronicle* described as a ' bloodless victory.' Immediately there began a period of acute and sometimes violent partisan controversy. After a year with Provost Carruthers, a Moderate, completing his three-year term of office, a crisis developed over the choice of a new provost. The senior bailie was another Moderate, schoolteacher George Bridges. But the Labour Party was determined on a provost who could enthusiastically champion their ambitious plans and Emrys Hughes was appointed. He had joined the council in 1927—five years after Bridges—and in 1932 he had been returned after topping the poll with a record vote of 932. The *Chronicle* remarked that there was ' no person in the Council, in our recollection of the past fifteen years, who has so consistently ruffled the tempers of his fellow councillors.' But it continued that ' we cannot but admire him for his solidarity, his oneness of purpose, and his unswerving directness of attack,' and praised him as ' the indefatigable protagonist of municipal idealism.'

The angry debate on the occasion of the appointment of Emrys Hughes as provost was followed in subsequent meetings by bickering over a series of quite trivial matters, with tempers frayed and several councillors involved in the Hughes-Bridges duel. The bitterness of dissension reached its peak, and standards of conduct fell to their lowest level, in May 1935 when a council meeting had to be adjourned twice. The following exchange between two councillors who shall remain nameless sufficiently indicates the spirit of the occasion:

' Have you gone wrong in the head? You are behaving like a madman. It's a crack on the gub you should get.'

' Come on and try it then. I will throw you out of the window or out of the door as quick as look at you. You would give me a crack on the gub, you rat!'

At the next meeting the provost's desk was overturned in a fracas. The verbatim reports of Town Council meetings made each issue of the *Cumnock Chronicle* at this time an eagerly-awaited event, and the doings of Cumnock Town Council were even featuring in the national Press. Older residents recalled rowdyism at town council meetings in the past, in 1910 and 1913, with the meeting in June 1910 breaking up in disorder.

In November 1936, after a year as provost, Hughes decided to resign, to face Bridges before the electorate. With a poll of over 85 per cent., Bridges won 942 votes against 887 for Hughes. At the next meeting of council, Mrs. Hughes, a councillor since 1933, was chosen as the new provost by the Labour group. This added fuel to the flames. Another council meeting had to be adjourned in disorder. But matters were suddenly resolved when Bailie Bridges was promoted to a headmastership in Kilbirnie and left Cumnock. A good deal of rancour continued however. James Neil, the pioneer socialist, remembering that in the days of a Moderate majority in the council Labour members had been given their turn as provost, had deplored and opposed the Labour group's partisan policies. In 1936 he lost his seat on the council after 28 years' service. In 1939 two Labour councillors who had become involved in another factional quarrel resigned their seats.

The Labour majority on the council, however, was confirmed at successive elections, for it was energetically managing the affairs of the burgh despite its belligerence. Under the provostship of Nan Hardie Hughes, it nourished the rebellious spirit of Keir Hardie, whose daughter she was. Appropriately, at this time the national Keir Hardie Memorial Committee commissioned Benno Schotz, R.S.A., to model a bust, to be erected in Cumnock in front of the Town Hall. It was presented by William Stewart and accepted by Provost Mrs. Hughes in August 1939—just on the eve of war. Keir Hardie had opposed the first World War and some of his rebel disciples in Cumnock Town Council lacked enthusiasm for participation in the second, even though the Labour Party nationally was firmly committed. In 1937 Councillor Bickerstaff had condemned Air Raid Precaution plans and in his capacity as Public Health Convener at the November meeting of the Town Council ceremonially threw a bundle of official

A.R.P. circulars into the Council Room fire. After the outbreak of war the Council was lukewarm in its support. When from 1940 onwards the government sponsored special savings campaigns to raise money for the purchase of war weapons the council refused to co-operate. Strong feelings were aroused, both inside Cumnock and beyond. Public opinion condemned lack of patriotism. The *Cumnock Chronicle* complained of ' the dictatorship of Lochnorris,' denounced those who opposed the war, and referred to ' rumours of subversive teaching in the class-room ' at Cumnock Academy.

Municipal elections were suspended for the duration of the war, and the pre-war council continued without change of membership. All plans for housing and other improvements had to be kept in cold storage. Local services were operated on a care-and-maintenance basis. The work of the council was reduced to routine, coping with the flood of government circulars relating to evacuation, civil defence, salvage, and the like, co-operating with voluntary local bodies in raising money for relief work and war charities, and latterly drawing up plans for post-war reconstruction.

With the coming of peace in 1945 the municipal franchise was extended from ratepayers to include all residents over the age of 21. The first local election resulted in the defeat of the two retiring Moderate councillors and Labour now held all nine seats in the council. Two years later Walter Linton, a Liberal and a popular local personality, took away one seat and held it for eleven years, in 1951 topping the poll and retiring in 1958. Thereafter, Labour recovered total control and for a number of years elections went uncontested. But once again the monopoly was challenged, and after two unsuccessful attempts, in 1965 James McHardy, a forceful Liberal schoolteacher, topped the poll. In 1966 he was joined by another Liberal. By and large Cumnock has remained satisfied with Labour control of town affairs. But there is a sizable minority of business men and others who have their reservations. With enough local people prepared to give a vote to an energetic opposition candidate, the council should not become too complacent, which is a healthy state of affairs.

The post-war period brought a new generation of Labour councillors. Allan McCall retired in 1946 after a record thirty-four years on the council. After the death in office of Provost Mrs. Hughes in July 1947 and the resignation later that year of her husband (by this time M.P. for South Ayrshire) only James Holland survived from pre-war days, till he retired in 1962. In 1963 ex-Provost Holland was signally honoured by the council with the presentation of a burgess ticket, the first and only burgess award. While a few new members served only briefly, continuity was assured by a group who served their apprenticeship, took their turn of the provostship, and continued as elder statesmen. Of the membership in 1966, John Edgar and John Weir had each twenty-one years, Keir McTurk nineteen years, and Thomas Finn fifteen years. Throughout its hundred years Cumnock Town Council has had three women members. All have been within the last quarter-century—Mrs. Hughes, elected 1934 and serving till her death in 1947; Mrs. Lindsay co-opted in 1939 and a member till 1945; and Mrs. Vallance from 1947 till 1950.

The organisation of council work continued after 1929 as before. There were eight committees—finance, water, public health, streets and lighting, town hall, cleansing and property, housing, and the dean of guild court. To these were added a parks committee in 1935 and in 1948 a civic concerts committee which became a civic attractions committee in 1954. The provost retained as always the convenership of the housing committee and until 1947 of the finance committee. In 1947 the Local Government (Scotland) Act made certain mandatory alterations including changing elections from November to May. It required the appointment of a councillor as Honorary Treasurer to be convener of the finance committee for the ensuing three years and another to be Dean of Guild. One improved procedure in the thirties after Labour obtained control was to abandon the more or less haphazard reshuffling of convenerships each year. By and large, conveners retained their appointment so long as they remained on the council, which ensured continuity and promised increased efficiency. From 1929 onwards the Town Council could appoint a burgh representative to Ayr County Council, and here too long service was the accepted arrangement— James Neil (1929-32), Emrys Hughes (1932-1946), James Holland (1946-52), John Weir (since 1952).

From time to time the town council reconsidered its own constitution and standing. In 1866 the first council had decided against dividing the burgh into wards, and this decision was confirmed in 1902. In 1948, with the prospects of further burgh growth, the council attempted, without success, to have its membership increased from nine to twelve. In 1959—on the 450th anniversary of the royal charter instituting the burgh in barony—a proper coat-of-arms for the burgh was registered by the Lord Lyon: a heraldic design based on the arms of the Dunbar family, the original superiors of the burgh; with an appropriate motto, ' Prompt in Progress.' In 1960 the title of ' Burgh of Cumnock and Holmhead' chosen in 1866 was superseded by the new official name of ' Burgh of Cumnock.'

By good fortune, the burgh benefited from long-serving officials. As Town Clerk, R. D. Hunter served for eighteen years. The second son of ex-Provost Hunter, he was noted both as solicitor and sportsman. He succeeded John Hume in 1923 and was town clerk till his death in 1941 at the age of 62. Since 1936 he had been assisted by his son, R. D. Hunter, Jr., who was appointed to succeed his father at the age of 28. When the burgh reached its centenary year R. D. Hunter had completed twenty-five years as town clerk. With his interests in music and the arts he has played a notable part in cultural developments in the town. Indeed, on the national level he has served on several Scottish committees of such bodies as the Arts Council and the B.B.C. From his father he inherited also an enthusiasm for sport, and though physical disability limited participation, he was an outstanding swimmer who in 1938 set up an unbeaten record for the annual swim across Loch Linnhe at Fort William. His long and active association with the Boy Scout movement has also brought him recognition. Other burgh officials served alongside R. D. Hunter for long periods. Robert Forbes was Burgh Surveyor and Sanitary Inspector from 1915 till 1956, forty-one years in all; and was followed by Robert Forret. When Forbes died in 1963 it was recalled that he had planned and built 1,500 of Cumnock's houses and could well be named ' the Architect of Cumnock.' In 1930 Robert Lorimer was appointed Burgh Treasurer, and also became Burgh Prosecutor in 1939 and Treasurer of the Municipal Bank in 1947. While the town clerk's post has been a part-time one, the other officials have been engaged full-time in their specialist duties, both onerous and challenging in the contribution they were called upon successfully to make towards reshaping Cumnock. Cumnock has been equally well served by its employees in a humbler capacity. Joe Handley, the burgh foreman, retired in 1942 after thirty-seven years' service. As time passed and the work of the council expanded so did its roll of employees. The burgh started in 1866 with one scavenger. In 1966 it employed, besides its three main officials, sixty-four persons in a wide variety of capacities. These included twenty-four tradesmen and eleven building trade workers; five cleansing workers and five concerned with roads, water, and parks; nine clerical and administrative staff; and ten full and part-time staff at the Swimming Pool (eight) and the Town Hall (two).

Another indication of the vastly-expanding range of council enterprise is the financial one. The first town council's annual expenditure was between £130 and £140 paid by occupiers at an assessment of 8d. in the £. By 1893 the rate had risen to 1/4½, shared from that year on between owners and occupiers. In 1926 the town council became responsible for collecting also local rates for the parish and county councils, and by 1929 this consolidated rate was 10/2 including 3/7 for the burgh assessment. After 1929 the rates continued to increase. From 10/2 (1929) they rose sharply under Labour control to 13/10 (1936). Thereafter the growth was irregular but the general trend was upwards. They rose to 14/4 (1940), 18/8 (1947), 19/8 (1956) and a dramatic increase to 27/10 (1956). This was divided between owners (11/4) and occupiers (14/10) plus a water rate (1/8). With rating reform, the levy on owners was abolished. In 1957 the occupiers' rate was fixed at 26/10 with a 1/- water rate. This dropped to 18/- for a couple of years, but in 1964 it rose again, to 21/5. In 1965 the rates were 20/10 in the £, and it was pointed out that it now cost £6,340 a week to run the town.

One reason for the increased costs to the ratepayers was obviously the heavy expense of Labour's extensive housing programme and other municipal enterprises. Moderate members of the council before 1945 complained that Cumnock's rates had become the highest in Ayrshire. But the decision of the polls confirmed that the majority of the electors felt that the money

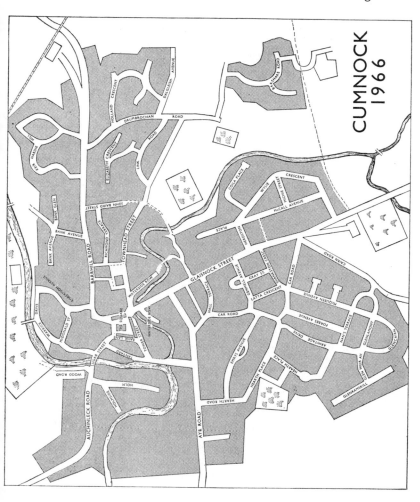

CUMNOCK 1966

was well spent. There were grumbles from some that the rates were inflated by the council pursuing a deliberate policy of low rents for council houses. But these criticisms never passed beyond outspoken opposition at the ratepayers' meetings—the sometimes packed and excited hecklers' meetings at which councillors and candidates have always presented themselves to the voters before the annual elections. In 1952 when the council increased both rates and rents there was a special ratepayers' meeting which concluded in what the *Chronicle* described as ' chaotic scenes.' In 1965 the average council house rent in Cumnock was 16/3 a week, compared with the national average of 14/2.

The expense of the town council's ambitious enterprises has however only been one factor in increasing rates. Another has been the general rise in costs—increases in wages, augmented prices of materials, and higher interest charges on loans. A third reason has been the corresponding growth of the county requisition, the annual charge by the county council for services provided within the burgh. In 1938 this had increased beyond £10,000 for one year; in 1966 it was fifteen times as great. A table in the appendix exhibits the total requirements for the financial year 1965-1966 and how the money is allocated.

Relations between Cumnock Town Council and Ayr County Council have normally been smooth. From time to time the town council has felt impelled to complain about the upkeep of the major roads in the burgh, which are the responsibility of the county council. The fact that the county council is the authority for town planning has also occasionally irritated the council in requiring to seek approval for its plans for burgh development. But friendly co-operation has been the rule. With the opening of the county council's Afton Water scheme in 1936, the town council entered into an agreement to remedy its own water shortage by purchasing a quota from the county council. In 1951 the two authorities collaborated in providing a new joint sewage undertaking to cope with new needs in the burgh and in the landward housing schemes. And the town council has always been ready to assist the county council in its efforts to extend educational provision in the burgh. More frustrating have been the town council's relations with the government departments whose control over subsidies, loans, and various features of burgh administration has not infrequently slowed down anticipated progress and caused exasperation.

Before 1929 the old Parish Council was responsible for poor relief within the burgh and ratepayers within the burgh took part in electing members. The new District Council however, was entirely concerned with the landward area, and the town council's relations with it have been consequently formal and occasional. Its headquarters have been in the burgh—since 1931 in Millbank House, which it purchased—but it has no concern with the burgh as such.

REBUILDING CUMNOCK

As a result of Cumnock Town Council's vigorous schemes for municipal redevelopment, the burgh has become virtually a new community in the course of little more than a generation. Most spectacular has been the council's housing programme. To deal with the legacy of bad housing, a start was made with a small scheme of twelve houses at Urbana Terrace as early as 1914. After the first World War further building was undertaken, mainly in an area to the west of Glaisnock Street and by 1929 the burgh had a total of 189 council houses. In 1932 Munn's field to the east of Glaisnock Street was feued and a further fifty-six houses erected, in Herdston Place. A good start had therefore been made with some 250 houses erected even before Labour took control of the council in 1933. Thereafter the Labour group set to work on an ambitious programme. It was estimated that 200 additional houses were urgently needed. One great difficulty facing the council was that of obtaining suitable land on favourable terms, and there ensued a great legal battle between the town council and Mountjoy Ltd.—the Bute estate company— with Emrys Hughes tilting at the Marquess of Bute in particular and feudal landlords in general. By compulsory purchase orders, sites were acquired east of Glaisnock Street, in the Car Road area, and up Barrhill. In six years' time over 300 houses were built, bringing the burgh total of new houses beyond the 600 mark by the outbreak of war in 1939. The scheme up Barrhill was named Keir Hardie Hill. Those adjoining Herdston Place were named McCall Avenue (after the convener of the council's housing committee), Michie Street (after the provost of Renfrew who was arbiter in the compulsory purchase enquiry), and Wylie Crescent (after a government official who was also involved). In the Car Road scheme Provost Hughes had Emrys Avenue named after him. Concurrently arrangements were made for the demolition of slum properties. In 1933 a start was made in Elbow Lane, Tower Street, Tanyard Lane, Gibb's Close (next to the Clydesdale Bank), and Manse Lane. In 1934 a clearance order listed properties to be removed in Auchinleck Road, Waterside Place, and Donaldson Brae (near the gas works). Others in 1935 included parts of Tower Street, Waterside Row, Strand, Townhead Street, Glaisnock Street, Ayr Road, New Bridge Street, Kilnholm Place, and Barrhill. Even so, sub-standard houses remained, and in 1938 the council estimated that another 180 houses required to be built to meet all needs. Plans for these had to be postponed because of war.

After 1945 further building was possible and by 1948 Cumnock had a total of 735 council houses—now 65 per cent. of all the houses in the town. But even so, here as elsewhere the housing shortage remained acute. In 1948 there were 540 applicants on the housing list, most of them young married couples living with parents or in furnished rooms. Part of the trouble was that shortages and restrictions in the immediate post-war years made progress in building much slower than desired. In 1945 Shankston Bing was acquired and twenty Swedish houses erected to form Hearth Place. Forty prefabs were erected in Hearth Place also. But a scheme of eighty-two houses in Car Road was not completed till 1951. New streets in this area were named Nan's Terrace (after the late Nan Hardie Hughes), Forbes Avenue (after the Burgh Surveyor), and McQueen Avenue and Armitage Road (after two local doctors who retired in 1947).

In the early 1950's additional houses were built in Car Road, and Emrys Avenue and Hearth Road added, all in the south-west of the town. The Glebe was purchased and a scheme of sixty houses built, with Robertson Avenue, Warrick Drive, and McDonald Street named appropriately after former local ministers. Convenient small sites were filled up: Hearth Road and Elizabeth Crescent (1953), Coila Place (1954), and the Holm (1956). But plans for the expansion of Cumnock required large-scale developments. In 1952 a start was made up Townhead at Drumbrochan with a scheme of over 200 houses. By 1954 the first phase was completed and three new streets named—Drumbrochan Road, and the other two named after former provosts, Dalgleish Avenue and Holland Crescent. Link Road was added in 1956. In 1954 the council proudly attached a commemorative plaque to its thousandth house.

Earlier schemes had been of the conventional standard types of council house. But with Barshare the council's ideas had become more ambitious. A million pound scheme of 550 houses was planned for the council by Professor Robert H. Matthew in 1957. The design of the individual houses and the layout of the scheme were novel. In 1961 the first phase of building was complete, and two years later the Saltire Society made an award, declaring Barshare the best housing design in Scotland for the year 1963. While work progressed on this major undertaking, in 1961 work began at Richmond Terrace on Barrhill with two blocks of fourteen flats of modern design, part of the council's scheme for redeveloping the old town centre. These, too, won commendation from the Saltire Society in their 1966 competition. Cumnock Town Council could congratulate itself on having an outstanding Consultant Architect in Professor Matthew, who received national recognition by a knighthood, and wider honour as chairman of the International Union of Architects.

By 1965, of the 1,741 houses in the burgh, 1,341 had been built by the town council. Of the remaining 400, just about half were owner-occupied houses, mainly in Glaisnock Street, Ayr Road, and Auchinleck Road, most of these built before 1914 but nearly all substantial and with modernised interiors. Only about 200 rented private houses, of varying quality, are found in the burgh. Two hundred and five applicants remained on the council's list for rehousing. An exact indication of how far Cumnock has progressed in housing is contained in the official Census of 1961. Of just over 1,600 dwellings in the burgh at that date there were only twenty single-ends remaining, and the average number of persons per room for the burgh had been reduced from 1.34 (1931) to 0.97 (1961). And though in 1961 overcrowding in Cumnock still remained too high (the county average in 1961 was 0.91) the general standard of housing was the best in Ayrshire. Only 140 households lacked a fixed bath (8.7 per cent. compared with 15.8 per cent. for the county); only ten lacked a water closet (0.6 per cent. compared with 0.9 per cent.); only eighty-eight lacked a hot water supply (5.5 per cent. compared with 11.3 per cent.); only four lacked a cold water supply (0.25 per cent. compared with 0.28 per cent.). Ninety per cent. of Cumnock's households had exclusive use of all of these, a higher proportion than any other Ayrshire burgh, and comparing favourably with the county average of 82 per cent. In the period since 1961, thirty-six sub-standard dwelling-houses were closed, and by the time of the burgh centenary there remained hardly any houses which could be described as unsatisfactory.

As the built-up area of Cumnock extended, so did available land within the burgh become filled up. The original area of the burgh, 268 acres, was augmented by boundary extensions. In 1937 an addition of seventy-three acres was arranged to include land for housing in the south-west and the new Woodroad Park in the north. In 1955 another 157 acres in the south was annexed. Seven years later in 1963 some additions amounting to eighty-five acres brought the total burgh area up to 583 acres.

What may be called greater Cumnock covered a wider area. County Council housing developments established the housing scheme of Skerrington just south of the burgh in the thirties. Another scheme—Glenlamont, Glencairn, Glenramskil and Glenweir Avenue—was erected in 1960 adjoining the south-west of the town. In 1948 a large-scale development was started at Logan with 307 houses, filled with people from Lugar and further afield. In 1949 a start was made at Netherthird and 434 houses erected, with a further 216 nearby at Craigens. Most of these were erected by the Scottish Special Housing Association. As part of this county council scheme of rehousing, the mining rows at Skares were demolished, and that isolated—but lively—community virtually ceased to exist.

These new housing estates were outwith the burgh, they were supplied with their own facilities, acquired their own schools and churches, formed their own societies, fostered their own loyalties. But in many ways they looked to Cumnock and became in effect outlying suburbs of the town.

Within the burgh, the council from 1929 onwards continued its work of operating and improving the various local services for which it has been responsible. While major roads became the concern of the county council in 1929, with the extension of housing schemes the total amount of road work to be done increased considerably and in 1966 the burgh had 6.64 miles of side-streets as well as the 2.42 miles of main highway. Nor did the town council abdicate all interest in the main thorough-fares. As road traffic multiplied, it co-operated with the county council, the police, and the schools with regard to road safety. It sought to relieve congestion in the Square and the Gorbals by helping to widen the Tanyard as an alternative main thorough-fare. In June 1966 with a new depot opened in the Tanyard, buses no longer need use the Square. In 1949 it opened a car park in Waterside Place and had hopes of providing others as space became available. The lighting of all streets remained the town council's responsibility. Following the introduction of electricity to the town in 1928, gas street lamps were slowly but altogether superseded. In another routine respect the town council co-operated with the county council by acting as its agent in keeping the main as well as the side streets clean. In 1946 a mechanical sweeper was purchased, abandoning the old brush and shovel method. Keeping the growing burgh tidy meant a similar extension of the scavenging service. The work of rubbish collection was still contracted out till 1934 when the council purchased a two-ton motor refuse wagon and employed a driver and loader. The disposal of refuse was another problem. Despite successive efforts to find an alternative, the council continued to dump at the Bank, despoiling the beauties of the surrounding scene, and encouraging vermin. It was described in 1933 by a country inspector as ' the worst coup in the county.' A new site was found at Garrallan but it had a limited capacity. By 1942 the refuse wagons had to go further still, to Mauchline Quarry; after 1949 to Gilmilnscroft; and then again to Mauch-line.

Water supply had always been a vexed issue. Even the new reservoir opened in the twenties could not cope with increased consumption. One particular problem recurred. The old complaints about deficient water supply up the Barrhill were renewed in the late thirties after the building of Keir Hardie Hill housing scheme. Difficulties continued till in 1947 a water-boosting plant was installed as a temporary measure, and by 1949 the Barrhill problem was finally solved by linking up directly with the county council water main. The county council in fact came to the rescue of the town in helping with its general water problem. After negotiations in 1933 the town council entered into an agreement with the county council and following the inauguration of the latter's Afton Water scheme in 1936 purchased supplies to augment the burgh's own limited resources. A growing proportion of the town supply came from this source, by 1956 half of the burgh's daily consumpt of 150,000 gallons. In 1949 a new agreement was made by which the county council agreed to meet the increasing needs of the expanding burgh. From the long-term point of view, the town council supported proposals for a regional water plan. The town council was also glad to co-operate with the county council in its sewage disposal problem. The burgh set up its own plant at Greenmill in 1929. Previously effluent had been discharged untreated into the Lugar and Glaisnock Waters. But by the forties the burgh plant was reckoned obsolete, and anglers were complaining about river pollution. In 1951 town and county councils collaborated in planning a new joint sewage purification works at Underwood, completed in 1955 and serving both the burgh and the new county housing schemes in the landward parts of the parish.

One of the earliest municipal enterprises had been the provision of a slaughterhouse, opened in 1869. After more than sixty years it was far behind modern standards and in 1934 the council decided to close it down. But this was not accomplished without complaint. There was an outcry from local butchers, who could no longer kill beasts locally. And the closures was followed by a legal dispute with the Marquess of Bute over the site. Another traditional municipal undertaking was the fire brigade. A serious fire in the Townhead in 1933 when two families lost all their possessions led to demands for something better than a barrow, hose, and group of volunteer firemen. But nothing effective was done till war brought urgency and opportunity. In 1940 the council with government backing was able to acquire a proper motor fire engine and set up a fire station in the Tanyard. After

The Square, proposed improvements:
    View to south (*above*)
    View to west (*below*)
(Robert Matthew, Johnson-Marshall and Partners, Architects)

Housing in Cumnock—
Barshare Housing Development, Phase 1, (Barshare Road)

Housing for elderly people at Richmond Terrace
(Robert Matthew, Johnson-Marshall and Partners, Architects)

Senior Citizens' Club, Cumnock
(Robert Matthew, Johnson-Marshall and Partners, Architects)

Cumnock Working Men's Club (William Nimmo, Architect)

New Bus Station, Cumnock, opened June 1966
(Robert Matthew, Johnson-Marshall and Partners, Architects)
Photograph by Henk Snoek

The last buses in the Square, June 1966
(*Cumnock Chronicle*)

the war this was taken over and the new South West Area Fire Service in 1964 opened an up-to-date fire station in New Cumnock Road, with two engines to serve the area.

Other miscellaneous responsibilities from time to time engaged the town council's attention. In 1944 and 1955 the old mercat cross—which had been classified as an ancient monument in 1935—was repaired. In 1931, following the installation of electricity, it was decided to light the church clock in the Square. The other town clock was the one projecting from over the shop in Glaisnock Street once owned by Turnbull and Allan, watchmakers, and gifted to the council in 1918 by an anonymous native of Cumnock. In 1920 it was repaired and lit. In July 1963 it was struck and knocked down by a double-decker bus, but was replaced by a new clock in 1965, on the adjacent Co-op. building.

For most of its history the town council was almost entirely concerned with the provision of environmental local services, but since the thirties it widened its activities to concern itself more and more with recreational provision and the development of community life. It enthusiastically took advantage of extended permissive powers. In the period before 1929 the only such public facility was the town hall. Built in 1885 by public subscription, the Hall continued to provide accommodation for all sorts of popular assemblies. In the twenties and thirties when ballroom dancing won a new wide appeal, the Town Hall was a favourite venue, with music purveyed by local dance bands like the Night Hawks. Saturday night dances sponsored by Cumnock Juniors were instituted and have been a feature ever since. With new types of dance becoming a craze among teenagers in the fifties and sixties, bands like the Swingers and the Merry Macs won a wide following, while Peter White and his Band acquired a reputation through broadcasts and records for Scottish country dance music. In the inter-war period the whist-drive-and-dance was the most common type of evening function organised by local societies, but thereafter its popularity waned. From time to time new crazes swept the country. In 1930 the Town Hall saw midget golf; in 1936 roller-skating. From 1957 the gambling game of bingo drew the crowds, to such an extent as to disturb the town council meeting of December 1959. At the same time the Town Hall was required for a variety of other purposes. In the thirties it was a Junior Instruction Centre for unemployed juveniles. During the war it was used by military units stationed in the town. For a few years after 1947 it had to be used by Cumnock Academy for classes because of the shortage of school accommodation. Through all this time the town hall committee was responsible for its upkeep. In 1937 an extensive modernisation was carried out. Ten years later it was redecorated and in 1949 renovated, with a new lighting and heating system. This was followed in 1950 with an improved layout on the frontage of the hall. That the Town Hall continued to offer an essential facility is indicated by the figures for 1964: during the 365 days of that year there were only fifteen in which the Hall was not in use.

One long-felt want in the town was a public park. In 1897 a proposal for a Jubilee park came to nothing. In 1907 the Marquess of Bute handed over to the care of the council Townhead Park, where football and other games had been played over a long period. Hopes of more elaborate provision were raised in 1917 with a bequest from the estate of the Misses Murray, formerly of the Dumfries Arms. But by a legal quirk the Murray Trust became the concern of the parish council and there were long delays till 1929 when the ten-acre Murray Park at Netherthird, just over the burgh boundary, was opened, with swings, playing pitches, and seats. In 1934 Townhead Park was taken over by Cumnock Juniors, when New Station Park had to be abandoned because of a cemetery extension. Early next year, when the council was considering the suggestion of Provost Hughes that a swimming pool might be provided for the town, the happy idea emerged of acquiring Woodroad land on the Templand side of the Lugar Water as a site for pool, park, and other amenities. Twenty-five acres were purchased for £500, a pool provided at a cost of £5,500 and altogether by 1939 around £9,000 had been spent on the Woodroad project. Because there was a good deal of vocal opposition to the novel idea of a municipal swimming pool, the council tested public opinion by a plebiscite in the summer of 1935 and their scheme was approved by 404 votes to 332. Provost Mrs. Hughes opened the pool in June 1936 amid a crowd of 2,500 spectators. One hundred feet long, forty-five feet wide, ranging in depth from three to ten feet, with heated filtered water, this was one of the finest open-air pools in the country, and with periodic improvements it has remained so. In the pleasant sylvan area beside the pool the council provided three tennis courts, a putting green, a cafe and pavilion, football, rugby, and cricket pitches; after the war an asphalt open-air dance floor; and in 1951 a children's play park. In 1953 a footbridge was erected across the Lugar from the Glebe to provide easier access to the park from the town centre. The admirable facilities provided in the Woodroad Park immediately commended themselves. Several local swimming clubs were formed, and the education authority each summer arranged for swimming lessons for pupils from schools in the town and throughout the area. Swimming galas brought mass audiences, and there have also been Scottish swimming and diving championships, exhibition displays, and international swimming and water polo contests. The other facilities of the park have been equally well utilised. A municipal tennis club was formed. The sports pitches were used by schools, youth clubs, and for amateur athletics. The park provided an admirable setting for carnivals and other celebrations. Near the foot of the Wood Road there was room for shows and circuses. In this corner an extension was possible when Stepends bing and adjacent land was presented to the council in 1937 by Lady Talbot. The Woodroad Park proved an attraction to people from outside the town. It was an ideal spot for Sunday School and other trips; Scout rallies and camps; West of Scotland cyclists have regularly held their annual rallies here; and it became also a popular caravan camping site.

Some minor amenities had been provided by private generosity: wayside seats in 1902 from the old Literary Society and in 1925 from Sir John Latta's gift; later bequests from Joel Slonimsky and William Sloane provided children's swings. The council in the thirties was considering various other major projects. In 1926 a proposal was mooted for a municipal cinema; in 1937 the building of a community centre was considered; and in 1939 plans were actually prepared for a gymnasium in Woodroad Park. But war forced the abandonment of such schemes. In 1945 the idea was revived of a community centre in Cairn Road, but nothing was done. Attention was directed towards the need for more extensive sports facilities, and the council sponsored from 1951 onwards a committee of interested bodies. The original choice was up Townhead in the Glaisnock valley and in 1952 a football pitch was laid out at the Flush field, but eventually the site selected was off Auchinleck Road. Thirty acres of land were acquired on Broomfield Playing Fields opened in 1962, with facilities for rugby, hockey and cricket; and plans were made for an elaborate sports pavilion. In 1961 a small play park was provided at Scott's field, off Hearth Road.

As well as providing recreational facilities, the town council took upon itself to sponsor cultural activities. In 1938 the town hall committee considered the possibility of organising concerts. During the war it co-operated with the Council for Encouragement of Music and the Arts; in 1942 they brought the Pilgrim Players; the following year a series of concerts by the Scottish Orchestra was arranged. In 1948 the council set up a civic concerts committee which sponsored various cultural activities. The BBC Scottish Orchestra came in 1948 and again in 1950. The County Council also contributed—in general through the schools, in particular by its library service. In 1937 a branch of the County Library was opened at Millbank in a new building with child welfare clinic attached. The Baird Institute with its reading room, museum and recreational facilities remained in use and was modernised in 1950.

As Cumnock expanded, so were all its facilities augmented. The number and range of shops increased. In 1950 there were over a hundred of all kinds, and in the fifties and sixties the rapidly increasing population in the burgh and the surrounding area stimulated business. Old-established firms extended their premises; several chain-stores set up branches; modern self-service supermarkets made their appearance; and travelling shops served the schemes and outlying places. The centre of Cumnock was transformed. In the inter-war years the old local fairs finally disappeared. In 1937 the *Cumnock Chronicle* noted that on the occasion of the March Fair no more than ten people gathered at the corner of Glaisnock Street and Ayr Road. The excitement of fair day, with cattle bought and sold, servants hired and farm folk enjoying a holiday in town—all this had gone. But now every day in Cumnock became as busy as a fair day, with hurrying housewives, off-shift workers gossiping at the street corners, and buses bearing their passengers out of and into the shopping centre. Besides shops, Cumnock became supplied with banks: Bank of Scotland (1838), Royal (1856), Clydesdale (1857), National Commercial (1920), as well as the Cumnock Municipal Bank (1928).

For local and passing traffic there are half a dozen garages, some of them also dealing with car sales. There are two hotels of note—the eighteenth century Dumfries Arms in Glaisnock Street and the Royal Hotel erected in the Square about 1890—both modernised, two-star establishments. The other six licensed premises near the burgh centre include the Tup Inn, Craighead Inn, Black Bull Hotel, Burns Tavern, Snug Bar and Sun Inn. To supplement these, two new public houses on the outskirts were opened in 1955, the Thistle Inn and the Logangate Arms.

Another special requirement of a modern community is the provision of adequate medical facilities. In the early part of the century town and surrounding country were served by two esteemed practitioners. Dr. J. G. Kerr and Dr. James McQueen both set up practice in 1901. The former died in 1906, but had been joined two years earlier by Dr. William Armitage. Drs. McQueen and Armitage continued to serve till their retiral in 1947. A new generation of local doctors came with Dr. A. M. Campbell (since 1929), Dr. J. R. McClure (since 1933), Dr. Alex. Mack (1946-1962), Dr. James McMillan (since 1948), Dr. R. J. I. Boyd (since 1953), and Dr. D. S. Tucker (since 1962). A modern surgery in Townhead was opened in 1959. As far as hospital facilities are concerned, for long Cumnock was fortunate in having the Bute Cottage Hospital in the town, Holmhead Hospital for infectious diseases on the outskirts, and Glenafton T.B. Sanatorium not far away by New Cumnock. With the introduction of a national hospitals service, the war-time hospital at Ballochmyle was organised to provide general facilities from a wide area of Ayrshire. Bute Hospital was thereupon closed in 1950. With decline in infectious diseases and tuberculosis Holmhead and Glenafton were converted to homes for the chronic sick and aged. One remaining cause of complaint has been the lack of maternity facilities; expectant mothers who cannot have their babies at home have to be taken to Irvine, twenty-five miles away on the other side of Ayrshire. And suggestions in the sixties to close Ballochmyle in a scheme of hospitals reorganisation brought loud and sustained protests from the Cumnock area.

In various ways, people throughout the district look to Cumnock as the natural centre. It became the centre for senior secondary schooling. Various insurance companies and other private agencies set up district offices in Cumnock. The new post office built in Cumnock in 1911 was a head post office for the area; motor vans replaced horses and traps in 1935; by 1965 a fleet of thirteen vans was based at Cumnock Post Office. In 1912 the post office took over the telephones which had since 1902 been operated by the National Telephone Company; in 1946 an automatic telephone exchange was installed. In 1938 the Cumnock exchange had 163 phones connected; in 1945, 222; by 1961, 640.

For general communications, Cumnock also became a centre. The bus services introduced by the Ayr and District Motor Services were taken over when the Western S.M.T. was formed in 1932. The original garage in Glaisnock Street continued in use till 1954 when a new depot was built in Ayr Road, with accommodation for 100 buses. Frequent regular services were provided throughout the area. Local bus services for Cumnock were introduced in 1948. Services were operated to Kilmarnock and Glasgow in the north, Ayr in the west, Muirkirk in the east, and Dumfries and Carlisle in the south. The S.M.T. and several private owners also provide facilities for hiring buses for club outings and the like. To cope with the growing number of new drivers of private cars, several local businesses were set up to provide driving instruction, and in September 1965 the Ministry of Transport set up in Cumnock a test-centre for new drivers. With the development of road traffic, the railways have declined. In 1951 passenger services on the Ayr-Muirkirk line were withdrawn, Cumnock New Station closed, and finally in 1964 the line was lifted. The Kilmarnock-Dumfries route remained important as one of the main lines to the south for passenger expresses and a heavy volume of goods traffic. But local passenger traffic dwindled. Cumnock and most other stations on the line were closed early in 1966. But this decaying railway traffic was a national phenomenon. Traffic in general increased, and with Prestwick Airport only fifteen miles away Cumnock came into closer contact with the outside world than ever before.

With Cumnock as a natural focus for traffic, it became an administrative centre. In 1929 when the county was divided into ten districts, the new District Council responsible for the large No. 5 Area set up its headquarters in Cumnock. Long before this, Cumnock had been made the centre for the division of the Ayrshire Constabulary. Superintendent Robert Cunningham (1893-1919) was followed by a series of Inspectors—John McIntosh (1919), William Meiklejohn (1925), Charles Lobban (1933), John Douglas (1937), John Paterson (1947), A. C. Jolliffe (1952), R. Borthwick (1954), and William Cook (1961), promoted to Chief Inspector in 1963, with Hugh White joining him as Inspector.

Cumnock is also a judicial centre for the area. Not only is there a burgh court—with misdemeanours committed within the town tried before the magistrates; but there is the J.P. Court which deals with cases from all other parts of the district including Mauchline, Catrine, Muirkirk, Auchinleck, Ochiltree, Drongan, New Cumnock; and there is a Juvenile Court responsible for the same area. Since a regular series of cases of breach of the peace, drunkenness and delinquencies of all kinds are tried in Cumnock and often reported in the press, outsiders too often assume that Cumnock's record is particularly blameworthy. In fact, when the Third Statistical Account investigated crime records of Ayrshire, Cumnock was found to be one of the five best-behaved burghs in Ayrshire.

One other established institution ties the district to Cumnock—the *Cumnock Chronicle*. Founded in 1901 it ousted its two predecessors, the *Express* and the *News*. An effort was made to start a new *Cumnock Express* in 1934, but this did not survive four or five issues. The reasons for the *Chronicle's* success are various. From the beginning it insisted on being a purely local paper, printed locally, locally-managed, with local interests and without party bias. When the founder, J. W. Crawford, died in 1916 it was acquired by Messrs. Ballantine and Gibb and the former took over complete control in 1931. Since James P. Ballantine's death at the age of 84 in 1947 it has been owned by Duncan McLean Ballantine, editor since 1929. As a grandson of one of Cumnock's first town councillors, he maintains the local tradition; as a past-president of the Scottish Newspaper Proprietors' Association and a member of the Press Council, he has a reputation as an able journalist. The *Cumnock Chronicle* has moved with the times, extending its premises, installing up-to-date plant, providing a full coverage in print and picture of the events of the town and district. Its circulation has grown to 8,500 with readers in town, throughout the district and overseas.

In the nineteenth century emigrants from Cumnock went far afield. In 1852 James Samson left the town for Canada, where he set up a hotel, store and post office at a spot in Ontario which became known as Cumnock. Another overseas Cumnock was founded in New South Wales by local emigrants to Australia. One version has a Cumnockian called Ross as the founder; another attributes the honour to members of the Black family who emigrated in 1882. In 1911 the school in the Australian Cumnock made contact with its partner in Old Cumnock, flags were exchanged, and a year later W. M. Hudson from Cumnock, N.S.W., paid a visit. In the twentieth century two new floods of emigration, one in the first decade, the other after 1945, took more local people overseas. The *Cumnock Chronicle* has had a close and varied association with the emigration movement. In 1885 James P. Ballantine added to his printing and stationery business that of shipping and emigration agent. In 1955 Duncan Ballantine started an Overseas Readers' Column in the *Chronicle* and with the world his parish initiated that year a *Cumnock Chronicle* Parish Reunion at Niagara Falls which became a regular annual event with sometimes as many as 500 guests with a Cumnock district connection.

THE NEW COMMUNITY

Over the period since 1929 the community life of Cumnock was sustained and enriched not only by the provisions made by the town council but by the continuing efforts of voluntary bodies.

In sport, the traditional enthusiasm for football was maintained. Here as elsewhere, radio, television and the ease of transport by bus and private car encouraged many to follow senior professional clubs furth of the area, and supporters' clubs were formed by fans of Glasgow Rangers, Glasgow Celtic, and Kilmarnock. As a result many junior and juvenile clubs found dwindling attendances at their games, but Cumnock Juniors continued to find support. After some difficulties in the early thirties, the club was reformed in 1934, moving from New Station Park to Townhead. Success brought bigger gates. In 1937, for example, the Juniors won the Western League Flag and three cups. In 1950 they had a particularly successful season. Townhead Park was extended by taking in the old bing and providing more accommodation for spectators. Nine thousand watched one cup-final match. In fact the team reached in this year the final of the Scottish Junior Cup and won a civic reception despite a disappointing defeat by Blantyre Victoria, 3-0, at Hampden Park on 20th May. In 1955 a new grandstand with accommodation for 500 spectators was provided. Things were less satisfactory for local juvenile teams. In 1950 the reformed Cumnock Thistle had to disband after one season's play. On the other hand, there was successful expansion of schools football. This developed in the inter-war years, as matches between schools became possible with the extension of bus services. An East Ayrshire Schools Football Association was set up in 1920 to organise matches. After 1945 even wider contests were organised, with county games, national cup contests, and even international games in which several Cumnock schoolboys were capped. In 1964 Cumnock Academy teams were particularly successful, one team of under-15's winning the Ayrshire Intermediate Cup, another reaching the final of the Ayrshire Cup for under-13's, and a team of older boys playing at Hampden in the final for the Scottish Secondary Shield. As a result of all this, Cumnock was recognised as a nursery for aspiring senior professional footballers. In 1938 the town council gave a civic reception to Tom Smith, who had won an international cap. This thirty-one-year-old player had graduated from the Cumnock Academy team via Townhead Thistle, to Kilmarnock, then Preston North End. The occasion was repeated for Eric Caldow in 1961. From the Academy team he had gone to Glenpark Amateurs in New Cumnock, Muirkirk Juniors at the age of 15, and two years later in 1954 was signed for Glasgow Rangers. In 1957 he won his first international cap at Wembley. In the 1960-61 season he captained both Rangers and the Scottish International team.

While football retained mass support, other sports had more fluctuating fortunes. Quoits declined in popularity, but bowls flourished. Cumnock bowlers won a number of successes, in 1937 the Scottish Rink Championship and in 1939 the Scottish Pairs Championship. Robert Cowan indeed not only won numerous successes, but became a prominent figure in the Scottish Bowling Association and in 1958 was nominated a member of the International Bowling Board. In that year the Cumnock team who played at the Empire Games was given a civic reception. Of the other old-established sports, the Ayr Road Tennis Club was disbanded after the outbreak of war, but in 1936 a municipal tennis club had been formed, playing at Woodroad. The Golf Club had to close down in 1954. Drumbrochan was taken over for housing and a plebiscite decided by 229 to 94 against a municipal course. But keen golfers could quite easily go to New Cumnock or Ballochmyle, neither very far away. Fishing became more popular and the Angling Association increased its membership from forty-three (1938) to three hundred (1950). Curling and contests for the Town Cup were necessarily intermittent, but in 1949 the Cumnock Curling Club was resuscitated, with forty members who could now enjoy regular play by travelling to indoor rinks at Ayr or Glasgow. New sports were introduced. After the opening of the pool, swimming clubs were established—Cumnock Amateur Swimming Club, Cumnock and District Miners' A.S.C., amalgamated in 1963 to form the Cumnock Dolphin A.S.C. For a time there was an amateur boxing club ; and in 1961 a Rugby Club was formed by former pupils of the Academy. For those who enjoyed horse racing, trips to races at Ayr and further afield were more convenient than ever; the Ayr Race holiday in September and the miners' holiday in May (or June in 1965 onwards) remained the main local holidays. In 1936 land was acquired for a greyhound racing track at Glengyron, but then and again in 1946 the council disapproved and refused permission.

Other recreational activities showed the same changing pattern. The Cattle Show did not survive the thirties, nor did the annual farmers' dances instituted after the first World War; but the Cumnock and District Agricultural Discussion Club formed in 1932 became well established. The Canine Club lapsed but Mr. Livingstone Hastings won successes in 1949 and 1950 at Cruft's Show with his wire-haired fox terrier ' Waterton Wendy.' The

Homing Pigeon Society was revived in 1956 after nearly twenty years dormant, and a Cage Bird Society was formed in 1949. The annual flower show flourished still and for a time there was a Cumnock and District Beekeepers' Association, with George Scott an outstanding apiarist. The long-established Rifle Club was revived in 1928 as the Kyle Rifle Club and in 1962 a Pest Extermination Club was formed. Interests of various kinds were catered for by new clubs like the Bridge Club, the Badminton Club, the Scottish Country Dancing Club, the No. 5 Area Tropical Fish Club (1956), and a Model Flying Club (1957). With the growing number of car owners a Car Club was formed (1956) organising rallies and other outings; there was also a Scooter Club (1957); and the Ramblers' Cycling Club still had its enthusiasts.

Organisations offering social activities of various kinds for their members became increasingly popular after the war. In 1948 the British Legion opened its own club. St. Barnabas Lodge and the Order of the Eastern Star of course continued, with the Masonic Temple renovated in 1949. Combining social intercourse with service, a Rotary Club was instituted in 1957, meeting every Tuesday in the Dumfries Arms. A branch of another international organisation, the Round Table, was formed in 1961, and a Ladies' Circle added in 1964. A Townswomen's Guild was formed in 1956 and a Business and Professional Women's Club in 1965. Cumnock Working Men's Club was set up and a centre in Townhead Street opened in 1965. A Cumnock Academy Former Pupils' Club was formed in 1936, with a programme of debates and reunions, revived after the war for a few years. In the sixties the dinner-dance became a popular function organised by many local groups, superseding the whist-drive-and-dance and the bus tour whose popularity had waned. Parties and outings organised by residents in the housing schemes had also become frequent, four of the major housing schemes having committees arranging outings for children and for the old folks and Keir Hardie Hill having its own little hall. Outwith the burgh, a Skerrington and Glaisnock Community Association was founded in 1945 and acquired a hall in 1948, while at Logan a Tenants' Rights Association was formed in 1949 and galas at Logan were instituted in 1950. Provisions were extended for both old and young. For the aged, an annual old folks' party organised by the Order of the Eastern Star had been instituted in 1924; it was helped by a bequest of £1,000 from Sir John Latta in 1947; and summer bus outings were also introduced in 1954. In 1951 the council organised a local committee to extend provision for old people's welfare. Various local organisations did much to help, for example in providing Christmas gifts for local people and for patients at local hospitals. The Cumnock and District Hospitals Auxiliary Association was formed in 1952 and annually raised and disbursed about £500. As a special effort, £2,400 was raised and a Sunshine verandah provided at Holmhead in June 1961. Finally, in 1965 the town council built and equipped for the older residents a Senior Club on a convenient site in Tower Street just behind the Square. Costing £6,500, it was provided with a recreation room, a lounge and reading-room, and a kitchen, and the Rotary Club donated a television set.

At the same time there had been a notable extension of facilities for young people. Youth organisations have expanded. In the late twenties and thirties the Scout movement enjoyed a period of successful growth under the leadership of W. T. H. Inglis, a local teacher (later Director of Education for Ayrshire). They met in the old parish school until in 1935 a Scout and Guide Hut was opened at Millbank. The Boys' Brigade continued under church auspices. During the war Army Cadets and an Air Training Corps were formed and the former continued into the peace. For teenagers youth clubs were formed under the auspices of the education authority, with winter meetings in schools and outdoor athletic activities in the summer. Cumnock Youth Club meeting in the Academy has attracted over a hundred members annually. The churches also formed their own youth organisations and the schools had various extra-mural societies. The town council sponsored a Boys' Club in 1962 meeting during the summer at Wood Road, in the winter in the Court Room, and with hopes eventually of supplying a modern sports centre. Enthusiastic local businessmen guaranteed contributions of £3,000, but disappointment followed, because so far the County Education Committee has found itself unable to give the necessary backing.

Many voluntary organisations have always been specifically devoted to the purposes of mutual interest or charitable help for others. The Band of Hope continued into the thirties. Most of the older friendly societies lost their erstwhile importance with the extension of National Insurance in the late forties. Similarly, in 1950 following the establishment of a national hospitals service, the Bute Cottage Hospital closed down and the local committee which had maintained it since 1920 was disbanded. But new needs constantly showed themselves. In 1947 a branch of the St. Andrew's and Red Cross Ambulance Association was formed to help provide an ambulance service for the Cumnock area. In 1953 a new depot in Car Road was opened, with three ambulances. From time to time the town council sponsored appeals for worthy causes. A Voluntary Help Committee was formed to raise funds for any worthwhile local cause. In the sixties, when the closure of Ballochmyle as a general hospital was threatened, the council played an active role in organising a campaign against this move.

Other forms of public service were performed by members of diverse organisations. The local volunteers serving in D Company of the 4/5 Royal Scots Fusiliers performed one type of public duty and a new Drill Hall was erected in 1957. Another of a quite different kind has been done by the members of the political parties. The local Labour Party for many years sponsored widely-attended Keir Hardie demonstrations in Cumnock; these lapsed, but the local branch continued active with regular meetings to keep members and supporters informed. The Unionist Association has been perhaps less active except at times of parliamentary elections. The Liberal Party and the Scottish Nationalists have also sponsored meetings from time to time. In 1961 a local branch of the Committee for Nuclear Disarmament was formed.

One special group of clubs requires separate attention—those devoted to cultural activities. First of all the Burns clubs. The Cumnock Burns Club passed its diamond jubilee in 1948 and its anniversary supper was televised in 1961. The Winsome Willie Club celebrated its centenary in 1956. Other local Burns clubs failed to maintain such a long life, but though older clubs have died they have always been succeeded by other ones and in the sixties Cumnock could actually claim a total of six local clubs. For those with an interest in drama the Cumnock Dramatic Club has produced annually full-length plays and attracted good audiences. For a small group interested in painting the Cumnock

Art Club was formed in 1963. A very active Camera Club was also formed in 1958 providing lectures, demonstrations, and exhibitions. In the realm of music renewed efforts to revive a burgh brass band failed in 1947 and 1961. But on the other hand great success attended the formation of a Cumnock Music Club in 1947 and each winter thereafter series of little concerts have been held with artistes of international calibre. And from time to time the Academy has produced performances of Gilbert and Sullivan operas which have been very popular. One older type of cultural organisation has lost favour here as elsewhere. The Literary Guild which grew out of the West Church Guild, providing a series of winter lectures, did not survive the thirties. But for those who enjoyed lectures, questions and discussion the adult education courses offered in the Academy, with lectures in literature, history, current affairs or kindred topics retained their popularity from the thirties, throughout the war and after.

The changing pattern of local societies has been influenced by the transformation of the character of social life over the last generation. Some organisations have lost their attraction because radio and television have much to offer people in their own homes and there is also the point that most homes are now much more comfortable and congenial places than they once were. Increased leisure time has also resulted in increased scope for new types of recreation locally; but on the other hand, improved facilities for travel take many away from home for evening and week-end jaunts as well as for holidays. The local cinema, for example, enjoyed great popularity in the inter-war years, especially when the 'talkies' superseded silent films in 1930. But with the introduction of television the popularity of the cinema dwindled. Reception in the area was sometimes difficult, but a private firm in 1961 introduced a piped TV relay service. Another great local occasion of 1930 was a week's flying display in October, at Loganhill Farm, with passenger flights from 5/6. A generation later flights abroad for continental holidays had become commonplace.

Despite gloomy fears that technological changes would spell the end of local community life, it is clear that local social activities, though different in character, are as lively as they ever were

That the community spirit of Cumnock remains a vital thing has been clearly vindicated by the enormous popularity of the annual carnivals which have become a highlight in the burgh's calendar. In 1946 to celebrate victory, a voluntary carnival committee was formed to arrange appropriate festivities. The occasion was such a success that this became an annual event. On a Saturday in June (originally in July) a grand procession is formed up Barrhill, with several dozen attractively decorated lorries exhibiting tableaux presented by clubs, schools and street groups. To the accompaniment of music from several bands the procession moves off through crowded decorated streets towards Woodroad Park. There the Carnival Queen is crowned. Originally this was a local beauty queen chosen at a dance; since 1960 a local schoolgirl elected by her fellow pupils. The crowning ceremony is followed by sports and festivities, and crowds come from a wide area to enjoy the great occasion. To pay for all this, the Carnival committee throughout the winter organises dances and other activities. In 1951 the town council decided to celebrate the Festival of Britain by a whole week of community activities. Festival trophies were presented by the council for swimming, bowling, tennis, angling, golf, football, and cycling. The programme ranged from a spectacular fireworks display to a concert by the B.B.C. Scottish Variety Orchestra, broadcast from the Town Hall, and featuring a special orchestral arrangement of some of the tunes of John French.

CHURCH AND COMMUNITY

The churches in mid-century smaller Scottish towns continue to occupy a place which is significant, though less central than in earlier generations. The age of great religious enthusiasms has largely died away. A large proportion of the populace has abandoned church connections save for seeking a minister's services for marriage and burial. Dogmatic controversy has gone and with it interdenominational quarrelling. This has offered opportunity for several of the groups to examine what they have in common rather than what makes them different and to come together more closely.

In 1929 the two great branches of the Scottish church reunited: the established Church of Scotland joined with the United Free Church, itself a product of the union of 1900 between the Free and United Presbyterian bodies. So in Cumnock after 1929 there were now three congregations within the Church of Scotland— Cumnock Old Parish Church, Crichton Memorial Church and Cumnock West Church. To the first of these charges John Douglas McClymont was ordained and inducted in 1927 when J. S. Robertson retired; and has been minister of the congregation ever since. In the Crichton Memorial Church after the death of John Warrick in 1931 came the ministry of Donald Budge, whose translation in 1949 provided the opportunity for a union with the West Church. There, after the short ministry of Douglas Briggs (1930-35), Hugh Lang Hall was inducted on a short-term basis and demitted the charge in 1949 to allow the two congregations to unite under a new minister. It was decided to dispose of the old West Church building (which was sold to the County Council) and the new Crichton West Church was formed in September 1949. Rev. John Hastings Millar was inducted seven months later and was followed in 1961 by Rev. George S. Young. To these two large and vital congregations of the Church of Scotland within the burgh were added church extension charges to serve the needs of the new large housing areas in the landward area. In Netherthird a congregation was formed in 1954 and a year later St. Ninian's Hall Church dedicated. Similarly in 1959 at Logan a new hall church was opened.

That sectarian spirit had not died altogether was clear in 1929 when on the occasion of the great Church reunion, a number of members of the United Free churches in Cumnock decided to remain separate in the U.F. Church continuing. Services were held first of all in the lesser town hall, seventy-six persons took communion, and in 1930 they ordained their first minister. After necessary difficulties, and a succession of short ministries, in 1939 the U.F. congregation were able to build their own church in Glaisnock Street and thereafter numbers grew very considerably. Rev. S. M. Walker, a former miner, served from 1943 till 1962 and during his ministry membership grew from forty to 400. In 1959 on its twenty-first anniversary the church was restyled St. Andrew's U.F. Church. Since 1962 the minister has been Rev.

Robert Brown. The older separate bodies remained with much smaller congregations. The Congregational Church passed its centenary in 1938, and as pastors had J. C. Drife (1934-1950), W. McGill Thomson (1951-1955) followed by Matthew Sullivan, the first to be ordained to the local congregation. The Baptists continued their witness under a series of ministers. J. Stewart, who had served from 1919, was succeeded in 1933 by Austin Stirling, by James Malcolm (1933), William Barry (1947), Thomas Lannigan (1956), James Martin (1963).

Despite differences in points of doctrine, all these congregations collaborated from time to time in Christian work; in 1965, for example, together protesting at the town council's proposal to allow Sunday-night dancing in the town hall. Each congregation had its own activities, social as well as spiritual, and its own range of organisations. Each shared in the work with youth—organising activities for teenagers, participating in a church football league, and their ministers taking religious instruction in Cumnock Academy. The other Protestant sects which emphasised their separateness remained small. There were two assemblies of Open Brethren and a small assembly of Exclusive Brethren. For a time in the thirties there was a small Apostolic Church. The local corps of the Salvation Army, though it built its own headquarters in Townhead Street in 1925, retained limited support. The following figures compiled in the early sixties reveal the relative strength of all the religious bodies in the burgh:

Denomination	Estimated Membership	Estimated Average Attendance	Estimated Attendance at Communion
Church of Scotland (Old Parish)	700	250	400
Church of Scotland (Crichton West)	550	150	330
United Free Church	300	100	200
Congregational Church	250	150	85
Baptist Church	100	80	70
Open Brethren	40	30	—
Open Brethren	60	—	40
Close Brethren	20	—	15
Salvation Army	75	40	—
Roman Catholic Church (St. John's)	1,100	800	800

Separate from all the congregations already considered is the Roman Catholic Church. Though that Church has in the past remained aloof from association with Protestant bodies, there are signs of closer communion. The basis has been laid in Cumnock by participation of Catholic priests and parishioners in public bodies and various community activities. Traditional anti-Catholic feeling has virtually disappeared. The Loyal Order of Orangemen continued in existence—in 1939 the Orange Walk was held in Cumnock and 30,000 came; and in 1955 a new Lodge was opened—but local influence is limited. The local Catholic congregation has grown steadily under the care of a series of widely-respected parish priests. From 1906 till 1936 the incumbent was Father Martin Meagher who served the wide area of St. John's parish, on foot, by horse and trap and latterly by motor car. For his good work, he was elevated to the Chapter of Galloway and became a canon. But worn out by his exertions, visiting his parishioners in all weathers, Canon Meagher was transferred in 1936 to a less demanding charge in Irvine, where he died two years later. He served on the Cumnock School Board, later on the Area School Management Committee, and was a member of the Parish Council from 1914 till 1925, topping the poll at one election—all this a measure of the wide esteem in which he was held. He was succeeded by Father Martin Doyle (1936-1938), Father Hugh Mimnagh (1938-1950), Father George McCafferty (1950-1965), and Father Nicholas Murphy.

While the impact of religion on the community is less direct than it once was, its continuing force should not be minimised. Approximately 3,700 people over the age of 16 reside in the burgh. The several Protestant congregations in the town have a total of 2,100 adult members, though this includes some hundred from the landward area. The Catholics, numbering 1,100, are of all ages and include probably a higher proportion from outwith the burgh. While an exact calculation would be difficult, one may conclude that the proportion of church members in the burgh of Cumnock is well above the national Scottish average. Church attendance is also high—though Sabbath observance is almost a thing of the past and most church members after attending morning service indulge in a wide variety of recreations. Christian liberality is also above average. Money is generously donated not only to charitable causes, but for all the works of the Church. In the Church of Scotland, the local congregations often have the distinction of topping the list in the Presbytery of Ayr for financial contributions. And the Old Parish Church, which celebrates a hundred years in its present building in the centenary year of the burgh, commemorates the occasion by renovating the interior and completely scouring the exterior stonework, emphasising the dignity and importance of the Church in the Square, set in the very heart of Cumnock.

THE EXPANSION OF EDUCATION

Since the County Council Education Committee took over in 1929 from the *ad hoc* Ayrshire Education Authority, a tremendous expansion has taken place in the provisions for education. With the growth of the town, and the raising of the statutory school-leaving age in 1947 from 14 to 15, the numbers of children in the burgh have risen from 697 between five and fourteen at the 1931 Census to 1,022 between five and fifteen thirty years later. In addition, more children are staying on at school beyond the age of fifteen, and an increasing number have been brought into Cumnock for their secondary education. Besides the provision of extra places for all the additional scholars, the Education Committee has extended the range of courses available, introduced new facilities, and the character of education has been widened. In 1873 the School Board levied an assessment of £250 on the parish; by the 1920's the Education Authority was spending over £5,000 a year on Cumnock; by 1965 the annual County requisition on Cumnock burgh included £116,000 for education. But despite the vastly increased expenditure, the expansion of education was not achieved without difficulties, and while progress was made there were often aggravating delays.

It will be recalled that Cumnock Public School, opened in 1876, was in a few years' time overcrowded, and successive extensions failed to keep pace with the growing school population. When Hillside House was taken over in 1911 to provide secondary accommodation this too was soon found inadequate, and a new secondary building had to be provided in 1926. In the forty years since, this cycle has continued to recur, and, despite all that has been done, achievement remains unfulfilled. It is a sad commentary that the old parish school, built in 1847 and abandoned in 1875, has had to be reopened again and again, and remains in use in 1966.

The newly-named Cumnock Academy had a roll of 919 in 1927. By 1935 it had increased to 1,040—630 primary and 410 secondary—and work was soon after commenced on an extension. Hillside House was demolished and in September 1939 the new annexe was completed, with nine classrooms, two domestic science rooms, two technical rooms, two art rooms, one sewing room, one music room, and a dining hall. This was just in time to cope with a wartime influx of pupils. The official evacuation scheme of September 1939 brought 200 pupils from Glasgow and after the Clydeside air-raids evacuee numbers rose to more than 350, giving a total school roll of 1,334 at Easter 1941. This temporary overcrowding was eased as the evacuees went back home in the later years of the war, but after 1945 a period of intensified difficulties commenced. With the raising of the school-leaving age in 1947 and more pupils staying on at school beyond that, the secondary roll swelled. Five hundred and forty-two in 1946, it reached 665 (1948), 762 (1953), and 866 (1958).

With the 'bulge' of extra babies born just after the war reaching school, the primary department was also taxed and the total school roll increased from 1,165 (1946) to 1,443 (1948), making Cumnock Academy the largest school in the county. The various buildings were filled to capacity—the primary building, the infants' building, the old wing of the secondary school, the new annexe and of course the old parish school. From 1947 it was necessary to hire the Town Hall and the West Church Hall for use as classrooms and in 1952 infants who could not be taken in had to be transported for schooling at Cronberry.

Plans were made to deal with the crisis, accentuated by the building of the new housing schemes at Netherthird, Craigens and Logan. In 1952 the foundations of a new primary school were laid at Greenmill down the Ayr Road, and another primary school started at Netherthird. With the opening of these schools in 1954 and 1959, pressure was relieved at the Academy. In 1959 all the primary children were transferred to the two new schools.

From August 1959 Cumnock Academy became a purely secondary school. But the departure of its primary pupils failed to relieve its overcrowding problem. With the influx of additional secondary pupils from the new housing schemes the roll of secondary pupils jumped from 866 in 1958 to 1,027 in 1959, reached 1,223 in 1961 and became settled around 1,100 in succeeding years. Four additional classrooms in huts built in the playground have done little to relieve the congestion. Even the dining hall must be used for classes. The old parish building remains in use, and in 1965 the Church Mission Hall had to be utilised again. Some of the accommodation is far from satisfactory. Originally designed for primary pupils of other days, it is unfitted for modern secondary needs. Nineteenth-century buildings, ill-lit and ill-ventilated, have become dilapidated and disreputable. The primary building was in 1936 described by the Director of Education: ' In appearance an imposing structure built of red sandstone and marked by certain attractive architectural features, it is so marred by internal defects that it can no longer be regarded as a suitable school building, and opinion is unanimous that only after drastic remodelling can its period of usefulness be extended.' The outbreak of war prevented the suggested renovation. The primary building remained unimproved, thirty years later, and the authorities have been loathe to spend money repairing a building fit only for demolition. To add to dissatisfaction, pupils and teachers have to cross and recross the busy Barrhill Road several times daily, in all weathers. Fortunately hopes were sustained by anticipation of better things. It was hoped to begin building a new Academy in 1961, ready for 1963. Ultimately plans for a school costing three quarters of a million pounds were approved in 1965. Late that year a start was made with this new establishment, adjoining and including Greenmill School, whose pupils will be transferred to a new school at the Barrhill created out of the more modern parts of the old Academy.

Eventually Cumnock will be equipped with a splendid new Academy with accommodation for 1,800 pupils, adequate to provide for the raising of the school-leaving age to 16, and for the additional numbers of secondary pupils who will be brought in to obtain comprehensive secondary schooling. For younger pupils sufficient provision is offered by the primary school within the burgh, the other primary school at Netherthird and the third new primary school opened at Logan in 1963 to replace the old school at Lugar. In the remoter part of the parish at the old Skares-Garrallan school, W. D. Jardine succeeded R. Walker as headmaster in 1939. He was followed by R. Watson (1945-1954). Thereafter Garrallan was adapted as an occupational centre for mentally-handicapped children of the Cumnock area. Skares continued as a one-teacher school till 1966, when it was closed.

Separate provision is made by the Education Committee for Roman Catholic children. St. John's School, opened in 1886 and rebuilt in 1907, also proved a problem, as the Catholic population increased and secondary education was extended. By 1955 three classes had to be sent to Cronberry School because of overcrowding. In 1961 a new school for secondary pupils was built at Broomfield on the Auchinleck Road. St. John's School continued with primary pupils. The new St. Conval's Secondary School takes pupils up to the age of 15. Those wishing a senior secondary course have had to travel to Ayr or Kilmarnock. But soon St. Conval's may offer facilities.

The following are the rolls of the local schools in September 1965, at the beginning of the 1965-66 session:

Greenmill Primary School	632
Netherthird Primary School	376
Logan Primary School	209
Skares Primary School	7
St. John's R.C. Primary School	230
Cumnock Academy	1,124
Glaisnock Rural Secondary School	135
St. Conval's R.C. Secondary School	98
Garrallan Special School	13

Despite difficulties of accommodation, standards of education have risen. For primary pupils, aged five to twelve, the old tradition of effective teaching was transferred to the new schools, where there was scope to develop modern methods and attempt experiments in bright classrooms equipped with up-to-date facilities. Already in the thirties the primary pupils at Cumnock Academy had sampled school radios and educational films. New aids came into more general use after the war. The primary school curriculum, while still retaining the three Rs as its core, was extended in various directions. Progress was limited by the post-war shortage of teachers. In 1951 the Academy log book records regretfully the employment for the first time of an ' unqualified person.' In succeeding years in both primary and secondary classes more vacancies had thus to be filled. Nevertheless, steady advances were made. In the primary schools classwork was supplemented with extra-scholastic activities, teachers co-operating to provide for their pupils outwith the nine-to-four school-day such things as Christmas parties, school concerts, primary schools football, class outings, as well as taking parties of older primary children for fortnights at West Linton residential camp as organised by the Education Committee.

Secondary education showed the same pattern of change, with particular attention to new types of courses for pupils without academic aspirations. This was true both of Cumnock Academy and of St. Conval's and a special example of the trend was the opening in 1952 of Glaisnock Rural Junior Secondary School. In 1949 the County Council Education Committee purchased Glaisnock mansion house and the surrounding policies of 140 acres with the idea of providing a residential school for boys going into farming work. It opened with a roll of eighty-nine pupils, twenty-six boarders and the rest travelling daily by bus from accessible parts of central Ayrshire, and under the headmastership of John Weir has combined the usual school subjects with vocationally-centred studies, involving plant culture, the raising of stock, and work with farm machinery.

For most pupils secondary education has meant Cumnock Academy: all pupils from the burgh and the surrounding housing areas from the age of twelve till school-leaving; pupils for academic courses from Auchinleck, Catrine, Sorn, and Mauchline in the north, Muirkirk in the east, New Cumnock in the south and Ochiltree and Drongan in the west; and taking all pupils from the whole Cumnock District who stay on for senior courses. The scope and standard of education offered at the Academy has commended it to parents. Hardly ever does anyone, however well-off, choose the alternative of sending his child to a fee-paying school.

In 1931 a new chapter in the Academy's history opened with the appointment of Andrew Martin as rector. His predecessor had served for over thirty years and had been appointed in 1899 by the old School Board. The new appointment was outwith local hands, being made by the Education Committee in Ayr. This, plus the fact that the new headmaster did not make his home in Cumnock, caused some local feeling. But with the enthusiasm and energy of a man of 37, selected from applicants from all parts of Scotland, he assumed effective control of this large and growing school and superintended developments both in primary and secondary classwork and in the corporate life of the Academy. After twenty-eight years' good service he retired. Thereafter, with the departure of the primary pupils, the Academy became a purely secondary school under the new rector, John Edgar. An Ayrshire man, with experience of teaching both here and in Canada, he had come to Cumnock Academy in 1940, been promoted principal teacher of English in 1947 and made a place for himself in the community as councillor from 1945 and provost from 1954 till 1957. Under his rectorship since 1959 the Academy continued to thrive despite the difficult physical conditions prevailing.

When Andrew Martin became rector in 1930, the secondary courses were based on the traditional academic subjects—English, Mathematics, Classics, French, and Science; the others were in the nature of poor relations—Art, Music, Domestic and Technical Subjects, and Physical Education. Only a handful of pupils continued beyond school-leaving age. In the late-thirties about twenty pupils each year were presented for the Scottish Leaving Certificate, in half-a-dozen subjects. In 1964 239 candidates were presented in thirty-one subjects. A transformation had taken place not only in the school, but in the teaching of all the individual subjects.

The English department not only expanded, but the character of its work altered and under its aegis an Academy Magazine was instituted (1937), a Literary and Debating Society formed (1938), and dramatic activities were fostered. These continued after the war. The Debating Society held inter-debates with other schools and instituted an annual Burns Supper. The magazine in 1964 won the recently-instituted award of the *Kilmarnock Standard* shield for the best Ayrshire school magazine. In 1961 a special booklet of play-rhymes collected by the pupils was published, with the title *Bluebells My Cockle Shells;* and in 1965 a sequel entitled *Those Dusty Bluebells* won widespread acclaim with national Press and TV notices. Originally the English department was also responsible for the teaching of History and Geography. In due course separate departments were formed with their own principal teachers, History (1954), and Geography (1965), and developed under specialist teachers. Similarly the rapidly-progressing subjects of Science blossomed into separate departments of Physics and Chemistry (1963) with a new minor department of Biology (1965). The Mathematics department introduced new courses and advanced work. Modern Languages in the early thirties meant French, with a handful of pupils taking up the recently-introduced German. Both subjects were offered to a wider range of pupils, and in 1963 Russian became an additional choice. Classics remained an important department, but naturally with fewer alterations; the ablest pupils had Latin and sometimes one or two pupils took Greek. Some completely new departments were established. A pre-nursing class was instituted in 1946. Courses in commercial subjects were introduced in 1945 and a principal teacher appointed in 1959. The various departments collaborated in providing courses in additional subjects like Modern Studies, Botany, Anatomy, Italian, and Spanish. Religious Instruction was established on a more satisfactory footing when arrangements were made from 1959 onwards for several of the local ministers to become part-time teachers of this subject and take over responsibility for regular lessons to all classes. Special Christmas and Easter services in the Old Parish Church also became a feature of the school year.

Even more spectacular have been advances in the subjects which in the early thirties were still widely regarded as of minor educational importance. With the opening of the new annexe in 1939, reasonable facilities were for the first time available for the teaching of Technical and Domestic subjects. Since the war limitations of space have prevented development to the fullest desirable extent, but nevertheless the scope and importance of Technical and Homecraft subjects have increased, both for the majority of pupils who leave at fifteen and for those who can now follow certificate courses in woodwork, metalwork, technical drawing, applied mechanics, home management, dress and design. Similarly widening opportunities have become available in Art. Since the twenties the Academy Art department specialised in craftwork—described in the H.M.I. report of 1930 as ' worthy of the highest praise.' Regular art displays have been held, there has been frequent co-operation with other departments in various projects such as magazine production, pupils have won numerous successes in national art competitions, and a large number have gone forward to become students in Colleges of Art. Of Music much the same can be said. In 1932 annual School Concerts in the Town Hall were instituted, with school choirs featuring prominently in the programmes. In 1938 the H.M.I. report noted as ' an interesting innovation ' that the Academy had an orchestra. In 1950 when the BBC Orchestra visited Cumnock, pupils at the Academy had the opportunity of attending a special performance, and from time to time celebrities performing at Cumnock Music Club have given afternoon shows for school pupils. At the same time the Academy became more ambitious. In 1958 the Town Hall was taken over for a week and a full-scale production of *The Pirates of Penzance* was presented. Such was its success that every other year it has been repeated with various Gilbert and Sullivan operas.

Extensive developments also resulted in Physical Education. Despite limited facilities—there was only one gymnasium till 1939 when two classrooms in the old primary building were converted to provide another—athletics and sports flourished. An annual Academy sports was instituted in 1927 and after the opening of the Woodroad Park better opportunities were available. The new swimming pool there was utilised to advantage. The small pool in the Academy was of limited use and was abandoned. Now all classes could have regular swimming instruction in the summer term at the Woodroad Pool; annual Academy swimming galas were held; and some expert swimmers were produced. In the realm of other sports, rugby was intro-duced and regular games arranged with other senior secondary schools. For a time as a consequence, association football went into eclipse, but with increasing numbers of secondary boys it became possible to offer both soccer and rugby and in the post-war years the Academy soccer teams did particularly well. In the summer term cricket was also played. Girls had both netball and hockey and equalled the boys in their athletic prowess. In 1962 a Cappercauld Cup for gymnastics was donated by a former pupil, Dr. Ian Cappercauld.

It is obvious that in many departments activities extended into the extra-mural field. A wide range of school societies was formed, and during and after school hours many outings were arranged for pupils. Trips to Glasgow theatres became frequent; parties made visits to works and institutions; for a time class picnics in the summer term were popular. In 1935 a special outing for the children of unemployed parents was provided. In later years annual school outings by bus or train to places of interest in the south of Scotland attracted large numbers. Holiday trips for smaller groups became more ambitious. In 1932, 102 pupils and twelve teachers went off to London and this was repeated in 1935. After the war an excursion to Stratford-on-Avon was arranged in 1959. From 1954 onwards trips to the Continent at Easter and in the summer became regular. Smaller groups went off youth-hostelling. And from 1963 parties from the Academy joined others on cruises in term-time organised by the Education Committee.

The general picture is of an Academy making remarkable advances despite difficulties. In the thirties the curriculum expanded, extra-mural activities were extended, prefects were introduced and school colours (navy blue and white) adopted. From 1931 the Academy held a prize-giving ceremony each June in the Town Hall.

Generous donations of prizes were made by public-spirited persons. In 1930 Sir John Latta donated an annual Dux Medal. The Dick, Brown, and Martin prizes were financed by relatives of former headmasters; while Stevenson and Ballantine prizes were gifted by local firms. During the war certain activities had to be curtailed, but an Air Training Corps was formed, a school garden cultivated, £500 raised for war charities, and over £14,000 collected in school savings. The new dining hall provided 300 meals daily, rising after the war to 390 meals served in three sittings by 1947. To assist in administering the growing school, a secretary was appointed in 1930, with an assistant since the war. To help the girl pupils a woman adviser was appointed in 1946, and while one of the principal teachers had always acted as depute rector, this became an official appointment in 1965, with Robert Laughlin taking office.

The post-war expansion of education at the Academy can be summarised by listing some statistics of the Scottish Certificate of Education examinations. In 1964 the number of candidates was 239; in 1965 it was 281. Papers in thirty-two subjects were taken. In another sphere of school activities, by 1965 the range of extra-mural societies was as follows: Literary, Social and Dramatic Society; Technical Society; Scientific Society; Scripture Union; Chess Club; Stamp Club; Magazine; Athletic Club; Rugby Club (four teams); Football Club (four teams); Hockey Club (four teams); Netball Club (five teams); Cricket Club (four teams); Tennis Club; Swimming Club; Badminton Club; Golf Club; and various choirs.

With education managed on a county basis, many features of school life have tended to become standardised. Holidays, for example, became fixed by the Area Education Sub-committee in association with the parent committee in Ayr. The long summer holiday of approximately eight weeks was supplemented by an Easter holiday of some ten days and a similar spell at Christmas and New Year time. The experiment of 1934, repeated in 1935 and 1939 of having a single-day Christmas holiday and the extended holiday at New Year did not become permanent. During wartime, a special harvest holiday in October was a temporary arrangement. From time to time, special holidays were decreed—for royal weddings in 1935, 1947 and 1960; for the funeral of George V in 1936; and for coronations in 1937 (one day) and 1953 (three days); for the capitulation of Italy in 1943; two days to celebrate victory in 1945; and a half-day for the Walter Scott centenary in 1932. Long week-ends at local holidays in early summer and September remained the rule, but closing of schools for special local occasions almost ceased. There were holidays for skating in 1929 and 1930, but not thereafter. Bad weather became the only excuse for emergency closure of schools.

Under the direction of the Education Committee one special branch of education widely extended its facilities—continuation classes held in the evening for those who had left school. The Further Education centre at Cumnock Academy became a flourishing institution. In the 1964-65 session, there were over 600 enrolments for over thirty classes. There were thirteen commercial classes, five classes in English and Arithmetic and three specialised vocational classes, with a total of over 350 enrolments. There were also ten classes with 250 persons choosing from a variety of recreational interests: dressmaking, keep-fit, country-dancing, woodwork, motor car maintenance, fly-tying, first-aid, art, archaeology, and Russian language. There were also 130 members of the Cumnock Youth Club meeting here.

Education has obviously become one of the major features of local life. Apart from the growing numbers of pupils, the increases in staff has been considerable. By 1965 Cumnock Academy itself had a staff of sixty-four teachers plus another eight part-time. In the seven schools in and around the town the total number of teachers came to about 120. A considerable number travel in from Ayr and Kilmarnock, but sufficient reside in and near the town to make a considerable contribution to the life of the local community. It is worth noting that of the Academy staff, almost a score are actually former pupils who have chosen to return to their old school to teach. Another feature is the long periods of local service given by various teachers. In 1960 Miss J. Jack (Domestic Science) retired after forty years' service in the Academy; Mr. G. Swan (Modern Languages) after thirty-five years; in 1961, Mr. C. Sturrock (Mathematics) after twenty-five years; in 1962 Miss E. Jarvie (Art) after thirty-seven years, and ex-Provost H. E. Turner (Science) after eighteen years retired to go into the ministry; in 1963 J. R. McLure (Physical Education) went off to Ayr after twenty-seven years; in 1964 Miss M. Cairns retired after thirty-nine years, eighteen of them as the woman adviser. The contribution local teachers have made to community life outwith their scholastic duties has been considerable.

A hundred years ago the parish schoolmaster played a prominent part in the first town council. In 1966, three of the council's nine members were teachers, two of them with long service as councillors—John Edgar, rector of Cumnock Academy; Thomas Finn, headmaster of St. Conval's R.C. Secondary School. Also in wider educational affairs local teachers take an active part, particularly in the work of the Educational Institute of Scotland. For a number of years John McInnes, headmaster of Nether-third, John Weir, headmaster of Glaisnock, and James T. Cree, headmaster of Greenmill, have been office-bearers of the Ayrshire E.I.S. When Ayrshire teachers elected two teachers to the County Council Education Committee for the first time in 1964 they chose two of these Cumnock headmasters, Messrs. Weir and Cree. Nationally, John Weir was vice-president of the E.I.S. in the session 1964-65. In 1965 James Cree was elected national president of the E.I.S., president also of the international teachers' organisation, and for this signal achievement the Council honoured him with a civic reception early in 1966.

ECONOMIC GROWTH

Over the last generation Cumnock has seen a cheering revival of her economic fortunes. The 1930's were accompanied by scenes of depression and decay, with few apparent prospects of recovery. But since the war the picture has completely changed. A new vitality has been brought to the Cumnock area. The staple industry of coal-mining has been reorganised and developed along hopeful lines. New businesses have been developed to widen the basis of the local economy. A measure of the industrial health of the burgh and its environs is the growth of the parish population from 5,637 (1931) to 7,870 (1951) and 11,329 (1961).

In the early thirties the only pits still operating in Cumnock parish—and doing so intermittently—were those at Whitehill and Garrallan. The first had been sunk by William Baird & Co. Ltd., the biggest coalmasters in Ayrshire, who in 1931 combined with their main competitors to form Baird and Dalmellington Ltd. General economic conditions limited demands for coal and ration-alisation meant shortage of work. Fortunately for local miners, as the thirties advanced and trade picked up, there were more jobs available at the Barony pit which Baird and Dalmellington were opening up.

With the nationalisation of the coal industry after the war all major units were taken over by the National Coal Board. In

January 1947 the N.C.B. flag was unfurled at Whitehill by James Finn, the oldest worker. The policy of the Coal Board was to rationalise and modernise the industry, concentrating production in new large pits and closing down small and uneconomic units. In east Ayrshire this meant the further development of Barony Colliery in Auchinleck parish, and the opening of the new Killoch pit in nearby Ochiltree. Cumnock was thus to enjoy expansion as the residential centre of a growing mining area. But it meant the eventual extinction of mining operations in Cumnock parish itself. The small private pit at Garrallan continued under private ownership. In 1950 with seventy-three workers it produced 100 tons daily, but in 1960 it closed down. Whitehill continued for a time, employing 300 workers and producing 76,000 tons of coal a year. Open-cast mining also was carried on at Whitesmuir, to exploit a patch of easily accessible coal, and Hindsward 3/4 was opened up for a few years till 1958. But thereafter Whitehill was the only pit working in the parish and flooding in 1965 resulted in a closure which otherwise would not have been long delayed. Thus ended more than 200 years of mining operations in Cumnock parish.

Cumnock has thus become a kind of dormitory town for miners travelling out to work in the large modern pits in the neighbourhood. Conditions of work have vastly improved. Pit-head baths for example had been available at Whitehill since 1934. In 1947 a five-day week was introduced. Improved bus services ended the isolation of the mining community. The rehousing of miners in the new housing schemes of Cumnock and around it was accompanied by the demolition of the old remote miners' rows. The village of Skares though a lively place, with shops, school, a hall, and annual Skares Reunions for a number of years in the thirties, virtually ceased to exist. Most of the houses were far below modern standards, it was ill-provided with services— electricity only reached it in 1956—and the people had restricted opportunities for social life. From 1949 onwards families from Skares were rehoused in the new houses on the outskirts of Cumnock and the old village almost totally demolished.

In 1948 a Cumnock girl—Dorothy Stevenson—was chosen as Scotland's Coal Queen. This was just at a time when plans were afoot to attract to the area mining families from Lanarkshire and other areas where pits were closing down. Developments at the Barony Pit in Auchinleck offered new jobs, and in 1953 a start was made with the new modern large-scale Killoch Pit near Ochiltree. The importance of the district in plans for the expansion of the coal industry was confirmed when in 1962 the East Ayrshire offices of the Coal Board at Lugar were extended to become the headquarters for the whole of the Ayr and Sanquhar area, with a staff of about four hundred. The various plans for development were not accomplished without difficulties. In 1951 disaster at Knockshinnoch Colliery, New Cumnock, and another at Kames, Muirkirk, in 1957 were grim reminders of always-present dangers. In 1962 the collapse of a shaft at Barony Pit threatened the livelihood of 1,600 miners and resulted in an exodus south of the border. The new pit at Killoch was slow in getting into production. But by 1965 Killoch was in full operation, with a record annual output of one million tons. After a new shaft was sunk, the Barony was back up to former standards. It was clear that with these two large units and a group of smaller productive pits the coal industry in the Cumnock area was on a sound basis and able to look forward to the future with confidence.

In the thirties one of Cumnock's basic troubles was that coal was virtually the only industry. All the other local trades had decayed. Even the long-established McCartney's engineering works closed down in 1933. But after the war a remarkable transformation was effected. An impressive start was made when John Foster & Sons Ltd., the Yorkshire woollen firm, set up the Bankend Mill in Ayr Road, employing 200 women and girls weaving pile fabrics. The new factory was opened in August 1948, to the music of the firm's famed Black Dyke Mills Band, and the factory did so well that an extension to employ another eighty workers was undertaken in 1959. In June 1960 a second textile undertaking commenced manufacture. In another new factory off Ayr Road, Cumnock Knitwear Ltd. began making children's and ladies' knitted outwear. Here too growth was rapid and after five years 135 workers were employed, working three shifts night and day, and looking forward to further expansion. Just outside the burgh boundary, in 1964, the Bata Shoe Company set up a factory. By 1966 a staff of 110 women and 70 men were

Cumnock Centenary Festival, Dedication Service,
Cumnock Old Parish Church, 5th June 1966   (*Cumnock Chronicle*)

From one Festival to another. The Lord Provost of Edinburgh with
the Provost of Cumnock at BBC Scottish Orchestra Concert, Centenary
Week, 1966   (*Cumnock Chronicle*)

Cumnock Centenary Festival, Industrial Exhibition, June 1966.
Mr. J. R. Outram, Director, John Foster & Sons Ltd., in conversation
with Town Clerk Mr. R. D. Hunter and Mrs. Hunter.
Lord David Crichton Stuart is on the right.   (*Cumnock Chronicle*)

Centenary Festival Week, Black Dyke Mills Band in the Square
(*Cumnock Chronicle*)

Part of the extensive factory of the British Bata Shoe Co. Ltd.,
Cumnock

John Foster & Sons Ltd., Bankend Mill, Cumnock

Saturday morning in Cumnock, 1966
(*Cumnock Chronicle*)

Glaisnock Street shops, 1966
(*Cumnock Chronicle*)

producing six thousand pairs of shoes weekly, and this international company was so satisfied with local labour as to decide on expansion to a total of 400 workers. The traditional trades of textiles and shoemaking were thus once more represented in Cumnock. The town council also laid aside an area of 45 acres in the south-west of the burgh for future industrial development. In April 1966, Chemstrand, the big American synthetic fibre corporation, announced plans for a factory at Cumnock; and the town council had hopes that the centenary year would see further major undertakings.

These post-war manufacturing undertakings have provided welcome openings for female labour. Many more jobs are available for women and girls who are prepared to travel to the cotton works at Catrine, the optical factory at Mauchline, or to Kilmarnock and Ayr. These two large centres also attract girls looking for office and shop jobs, for openings locally are limited, though growing in numbers. Several other types of work, in hospitals, for example, are available, for there are excellent services of regular and special buses. The buses themselves require a large staff of conductresses. There is thus no general exodus of girls from the area of the kind which still leaves many mining communities with a predominantly male population. Similarly, the development of other businesses, the growth of Cumnock as a district centre, and the ease of travel to works outside the area have meant that boys have now a wider choice of careers.

Outwith the town, agriculture of course retains its traditional importance, though employing fewer than ever before. Farming, like other enterprises, experienced difficulties in the thirties, but here too better prospects opened up. In the twenties with the breakup of the estates, most of the local farms had passed into the hands of the farmers, and this gave them an incentive for initiating improvements. The establishment of the Scottish Milk Marketing Board in 1932 gave them a more assured sale for their milk. Thirteen of the farms in Cumnock parish were still making cheese in 1934, but this was soon given up altogether and the production of liquid milk in increasing quantities for sale through the Board became general. Great importance was given to improving the stock by selective breeding, and the sale of pedigree Ayrshire cattle became on some farms as important as milk production.

By milk-recording and improved feeding the milk yields were increased. It was thus possible to maintain bigger herds on more limited areas. The total farmland in the parish declined from 9,371 acres (1927) to 8,984 (1937), 8,156 (1947), and 7,934 acres (1957). Over the same period the cattle herds grew from 3,191 to 3,573, 3,903 and 4,376. Of these 4,298 were dairy cattle, 1,484 of them in milk. Of the farmland, more was devoted to crops. During the war, through necessity and government direction, the acreage cropped was doubled, but afterwards farmers found it worthwhile to grow more fodder than they had done pre-war. The making of silage, for example, became common, and the problems of hay-harvesting in a wet climate became a thing of the past. Improved and labour-saving techniques were introduced. Tractors came into general use—and the number of horses declined from 183 in 1937 to thirty-two twenty years later. Milking machines became standard.

Though the dairy was the principal concern, the farmers often developed other sidelines. The keeping of pigs had declined as cheesemaking went out and in 1937 there were only 112 in the parish, but after the war pig-fattening revived and numbers by 1957 were up to 269. And while poultry keeping was given up by some farmers, many still found it a profitable proposition. In the twenty years between 1937 and 1957 the total parish population of poultry declined from 17,737 to 11,149. Ducks in particular went out of favour—236 down to fifty; but turkeys rose in numbers from eighty-three to 109. The main type of poultry remained fowls.

The total area of farmland actually declined as patches were allowed to revert to rough pasture—this increased steadily throughout the century from 1,049 acres (1907) to 1,959 (1927) and 2,781 (1957). This land was of course devoted to sheep and they recovered their popularity, increasing in numbers from 2,756 (1907) to 4,417 (1937) and 5,550 (1957). One outstanding local farmer who combined sheep and dairy farming was Jacob Murray of Dalgig, who retired in 1946. He held 2,500 acres at Dalgig and elsewhere and maintained sixty-two score sheep. On his 200 acres of arable he raised a noted herd of Ayrshires at 800 feet above sea level and won successes both at Ayr and at the London Dairy Show.

Another local enterprise requiring special mention is that of Stevensons of Changue. In 1867 John Stevenson, formerly factor of Sorn Castle, took a lease of Changue farm from the Boswells of Garrallan and set up a herd of Ayrshire cattle. His son and successor, David Stevenson, purchased Changue and several adjacent farms. After his death in 1932 the farms were inherited by a third generation of three brothers—John, James and William Stevenson—who set about with vigour building up a dairy marketing business. Stevenson's Dairy Farms was established, with 800 acres maintaining ninety pedigree cows producing 200 gallons a day, handling another 200 gallons, and employing forty men and women at the Model Farm, at the milk bar and tea room they set up in Cumnock in 1936, and in retail distribution. After the war they extended their activities. More farmland was acquired, the model farm modernised in 1950, the Hotel Royal in Cumnock was taken over in 1956, a bakery shop in the old tea rooms opened in 1964, and the retail trade widely extended. In 1953 they had fourteen vans and supplied milk to 5,000 customers and twenty-five schools. By 1957 eighteen vans dealt with 1,600 gallons daily. By 1966 over a hundred workers were employed. Sixty full-time and eight part-time employees were engaged in seventeen retail and one wholesale milk rounds, delivering 2,000 gallons daily to homes, schools, and hospitals throughout the Cumnock area from New Cumnock and Muirkirk to Mauchline, and extending to include Ayr (after 1962) and Dalmellington and Patna (after 1965). At the dairy farms of Changue, Bankhead, and Crofthead, and the upland farm of Newfield, twelve full-time workers were employed. In Cumnock itself the Royal Hotel has nineteen full-time and six part-time workers, the Bakery has a staff of seven bakers and five shop assistants.

Despite some difficulties and doubts about future government policies, dairy-farming has advanced immeasurably in the course of a generation. There is an air of prosperity about the modern farms. Standards of domestic comfort have progressed at the same time as agricultural plant has been modernised. Productivity has increased, compensating for the decline in actual numbers involved in the industry. In the thirties in Old Cumnock parish around 170 were engaged in farming.

During the war when labour was in short supply numbers were augmented by girls of the Women's Land Army, who had a hostel at Clockclownie, and by Prisoners of War. Since the war, with improved equipment, output has been increased with fewer persons employed in farm work. Full-time male workers numbered eighty-six in 1957 as compared with 118 in 1937; female workers were only twenty-nine as compared with forty-nine. There were more casual and part-time workers, but farmers' wives and children were less tied than they used to be. Altogether in 1957 the total numbers engaged in farming were 149, somewhere about 2 per cent. of all employed persons in Cumnock burgh and parish.

The social life of the countryside was transformed with the breakup of the estate in the twenties. At Garrallan, P. C. D. Boswell had died in 1892; his widow died in 1914, and their daughters went to live in Ayr. The lands were sold off and the mansion house passed into the hands of Stevenson's Dairy Farms. Glaisnock passed through several hands and in 1952 began a new life as a residential school. Logan's fate was demolition, to make way for new housing developments. The great estate around Dumfries House alone survived. Many farms were sold off, but the extensive wooded policies remained and the mansion house continued in its architectural glory, a rare example of a great house continuing in private hands. John, fourth Marquess of Bute, had succeeded in 1900 at the age of 18. To cope with the fiscal pressures that troubled landowners, the Mountjoy Company was formed in 1922 to take over administration of the Bute estates, and in 1938 the great Cardiff properties were sold off. The fourth Marquess like his father was interested in social and philanthropic work, and in Scottish historical buildings. He was a president of the Scottish History Society, and author of *The Arms of the Baronial and Police Burghs of Scotland* (1903), a copy of which he presented to Cumnock Town Council. Relations between the council and the Marquess were cordial—in 1930 he entertained the councillors at Dumfries House—until after 1933 difficulties over purchase of land for house-building led to litigation. The fourth Marquess died in 1947 and the Dowager Marchioness's death came three weeks after her husband. John, fifth Marquess of Bute, succeeded at the age of forty. From his father and grandfather he inherited an interest in antiquarian subjects and added a special enthusiasm for ornithology, in which he was a recognised authority. He served during the second World War, and making his home at Mount Stuart was a member of Rothesay Town Council and Bute County Council of which he was latterly the convener. He died suddenly in 1956 at the age of forty-nine. John, sixth Marquess of Bute, was born in 1933. When he married in 1955 Cumnock Town Council in association with several local organisations presented him as Earl of Dumfries with a wedding gift, a replica in silver of Cumnock mercat cross. Three years later, two years after he succeeded as Marquess, a son and heir was born, John Colum Crichton-Stuart, the new Earl of Dumfries.

Over the last two centuries how great a change there has been. Then the Dumfries estate comprised most the parish. Its owner dominated the life of the community, economically, politically and socially. Economic growth has transformed the way of life. In the middle of the eighteenth century most of the people lived on the land, with a handful of craftsfolk in the village of Cumnock. In the latter part of that century industrial developments began and the village grew into a town, as manufactures of various kinds developed. From the 1850's a further growth began with the exploitation of the local coal resources and as other trades declined this became the basis of the economy. In two hundred years the parish population has grown from 1,305 (1765) to 11,329 (1961) and its central community from a village of 580 to a burgh of 5,403. In the second half of the twentieth century Cumnock looks forward to further progress.

THE TOWN COUNCIL AND THE FUTURE

In the late 1940's when plans were afoot for the redevelopment of the Ayrshire coal industry, detailed schemes were prepared by Ayr County Council and by St. Andrew's House in Edinburgh for the creation of a new town in east Ayrshire and plans were made for the extension of the burgh of Cumnock into a large centre with a population of 21,000. This grandiose project did not materialise and the blueprints for vast new housing developments, community services, and a completely new town centre near Netherthird were all pigeon-holed. But expansion did take place, on a more modest yet significant scale. County Council housing schemes on the outskirts of the burgh brought in families from outlying villages and from further afield adding a suburban population of five thousand to a burgh population which had itself grown to a similar figure. In the circumstances, the town council accepted responsibility to provide many of the central facilities required by this greater Cumnock of some ten thousand people.

The burgh itself was extended in 1955 by 157 acres and in 1963 another eighty-five acres were added to give a total burgh area of 583 acres. This provided land for continuing the burgh's great programme of rehousing the existing population and providing accommodation for incomers. In 1959 an overspill agreement was signed to provide houses for families coming from Glasgow and from time to time houses were made available for key-workers coming into the town. To attract new industry to the town, the town council published its first Industrial Brochure in 1959 and for a number of years retained C. A. Oakley as an Industrial Consultant. Sites were allocated for potential employers and those who did in fact take advantage found themselves well satisfied with the facilities provided by the council and by the standard of labour which they employed.

The town council also directed its attention to redesigning the old and cramped town centre to make it a worthy focus for the new and greater Cumnock. Though town planning is the responsibility of the county council the town council took the initiative in urging schemes for central redevelopment. Plans were made for new wide thoroughfares which would take the heavy traffic through the town and avoid the congestion at the Square. The first and major step in this direction was the opening up of the Tanyard. The old Dubb Bridge was replaced by a new one in 1964 and a broad roadway opened through to Lugar Street in 1966. At the same time the clearance of old properties in the Townhead was continued, with plans for a new shopping centre in this area to supplement the new shops already opened in Glaisnock Street and to extend the excellent shopping facilities in this central area. A scheme for the complete redevelopment of the central seventeen acres was initiated. The Square will be redesigned as a pedestrian precinct, with wheeled traffic segregated from this area. In the surrounding area will be adequate car parks, open spaces, the new bus station in the Tanyard, while the Senior Citizens' Club will be joined by a group of other new social and recreational facilities.

The town council of Cumnock in its century of voluntary endeavour has rebuilt the town, developed its public services, and provided a wide range of recreational facilities. It has given a lead to the local people in sponsoring and encouraging social and cultural facilities. It has gone beyond the provision of immediate needs to estimate the future requirements of a growing town. At a time when plans are afoot for local government reorganisation and suggestions have been made that town councils might be swept away in a process of regionalisation, it is appropriate to conclude this historical survey with a reminder of the vitality and effectiveness of Cumnock Town Council and the significant contribution it continues to make to the life of this thriving community.

Appendices

THE COUNCIL, 1866-1867

Members of Council

Police Magistrates

Senior:	WILLIAM DALGLIESH, woollen manufacturer
Junior:	DANIEL KING, woollen manufacturer
	WILLIAM McGAVIN, miller

Police Commissioners: DAVID LAWSON SCOTT, schoolmaster

WILLIAM McLETCHIE, wright and builder

THOMAS BARROWMAN, contractor

JOHN DRUMMOND, engineer

JOHN McCOWAN, innkeeper

DUNCAN BALLANTINE, printer

Officials

Clerk and Collector:	ANDREW WHITE
Burgh Treasurer:	THOMAS SHIELDS
Inspector of Nuisances:	DAVID SMITH

THE COUNCIL, 1966-1967

Members of Council

Provost:	THOMAS FINN, M.A., headmaster, St. Conval's School
Senior Bailie:	DAVID B. LORIMER, administrative assistant, Ballochmyle Hospital
Junior Bailie:	JOHN KING, engineer
Police Judge:	JOHN A. WEIR, J.P., retired
Police Judge:	JAMES K. H. MCTURK, J.P., civil servant
Hon. Treasurer:	THOMAS GUTHRIE, sales representative
Dean of Guild:	JOHN EDGAR, J.P., M.A., Rector, Cumnock Academy
Councillor:	JAMES W. MCHARDY, M.A., teacher
Councillor:	DONALD MACRAE, electrical contractor

Officials

Town Clerk:	ROBERT DALGLISH HUNTER, M.B.E., solicitor
Burgh Treasurer:	ROBERT B. LORIMER
Burgh Surveyor:	ROBERT FORRET, M.I.Mun.E.

ROLL OF PROVOSTS, 1866-1966

Senior Police Magistrate was the official designation from 1866 till 1892 and Provost thereafter.

1866-1878	WILLIAM DALGLIESH, woollen manufacturer
1878-1881	JOHN McCOWAN, innkeeper, auctioneer
1881-1887	GEORGE T. SAMSON, cheese merchant
1887-1890	WILLIAM McLETCHIE, wright, builder
1890-1893	JOHN BANNATYNE, draper
1893-1896	THOMAS HUNTER, seed merchant
1896-1899	JAMES RICHMOND, mason, builder
1899-1902	JOHN ANDREW, chemist
1902-1905	THOMAS McCAUGHIE, barber
1905-1908	JAMES RICHMOND (*second term*)
1908-1911	WILLIAM HILL, draper
1911-1917	JAMES RICHMOND (*third term*)
1917-1919	DAVID SMITH, retired policeman
1919-1922	ANDREW MILLER, photographer
1922-1925	CHARLES TAYLOR, engineer
1925-1928	ALLAN McCALL, miner, fruit merchant
1928-1931	JAMES NEIL, commercial traveller
1931-1934	JOHN CARRUTHERS, shoemaker
1934-1935	EMRYS HUGHES, journalist
1935-1947	NAN HARDIE HUGHES, housewife
1947-1954	JAMES HOLLAND, miner
1954-1957	JOHN EDGAR, teacher
1957-1960	JOHN WEIR, bus driver, security officer
1960-1963	HARRY E. TURNER, teacher
1963-1966	JAMES KEIR HARDIE McTURK, civil servant
1966-	THOMAS FINN, teacher

ROLL OF COUNCILLORS, 1866-1966

William Dalgliesh	1866-1878	David Robert Dunsmor	1896-1899
David Lawson Scott	1866-1872	Robert Craig	1896-1899
,,	1873-1879	,,	1901
William McLetchie	1866-1877	William Alfred Shand	1897-1900
,,	1879-1890	James Moodie	1898-1900
Thomas Barrowman	1866-1874	John Andrew Bingham	1899-1902
,,	1875-1880	,,	1905-1908
Daniel King	1866-1875	,,	1913-1918
William McGavin	1866-1868	George Brown Cree	1899-1902
John Drummond	1866-1873	John Wilson	1900-1906
John McCowan	1866-1881	John Templeton	1900
Duncan Ballantine	1866-1877	Robert Stoddart	1901
Robert Anderson	1868-1871	Samuel Galbraith	1901-1904
,,	1872-1878	William Hill	1901-1911
George T. Samson	1871-1887	Robert Hyslop	1902-1904
John Baird	1874-1877	Hugh Brown McCulley	1902-1904
John Bannatyne	1877-1893	James Moodie	1902-1903
James Gray	1877-1885	David Murray	1903-1904
George Mackervail	1877-1879	George Scott	1903-1905
John Ballantine	1878-1890	Thomas Pollock	1903-1905
,,	1887-1890	,,	1908-1913
Thomas Hunter	1878-1895	,,	1918-1919
Robert Brown	1879-1885	John Reid	1903-1906
William McGeachin	1880-1889	John Carruthers	1904-1907
William Kay	1881-1901	,,	1919-1934
James McGavin Nicol	1881-1886	David Smith	1906-1932
Adam Drummond	1885-1888	Charles Taylor	1906-1909
James Richmond	1885-1901	,,	1910-1925
,,	1905-1917	James Neil	1907-1910
Hugh Climie	1885	,,	1911-1936
John Milligan	1888-1890	John Miller	1907-1913
William Smith	1890-1892	Andrew Miller	1907-1922
David White	1890-1892	Allan McCall	1912-1946
William White	1890-1895	Alexander Gilchrist	1913-1920
William Kilpatrick	1891-1897	Hunter Bowie	1917
Charles Allan	1892-1895	Livingstone Russell	1917-1919
John Andrew	1892-1902	William W. Lorimer	1918-1919
,,	1905-1917	George Scott	1919-1927
Edward Martin	1893-1898	Andrew Cairney	1919-1922
Thomas McCaughie	1895-1905	William Daniel Geddes	1920-1923
John Walters Crawford	1895-1901	John Wilson	1922-1930

George Milne	1922-1927	John Edgar	1945-
George Bridges	1923-1936	John Alexander Weir	1945-
George McTurk	1925-1928	Harry E. Turner	1946-1963
Emrys Hughes	1927-1947	Robert Graham	1946-1951
Alexander F. Borland	1927-1933	J. K. H. McTurk	1947-
William Scott	1928-1934	Elizabeth M. Vallance	1947-1950
William Miller Reid	1930-1933	Walter Linton	1947-1958
James Holland	1932-1935	William C. G. Pearson	1949-1961
,,	1937-1962	Richard Gilmour	1950-1955
Archibald Douglas	1933-1936	Thomas Finn	1951-
,,	1945-1947	Robert McTurk	1955-1964
Nan Hardie Hughes	1933-1947	Andrew Duncan	1958-1965
William Meiklejohn	1934-1937	Thomas Guthrie	1961-
Hugh Scoular	1934-1946	Joseph Cockburn	1962-1965
Robert Cowan	1935-1937	,,	1965-1966
,,	1939-1945	David Lorimer	1963-
Donald Stalker	1936-1949	John King	1965-
Andrew Bickerstaff	1936-1939	James McHardy	1965-
William Smith	1937-1939	Donald Macrae	1966-
Joan Ross Lindsay	1939-1945		

POPULATION GROWTH

			Parish	Town	Landward
1755	.	.	1,336 *a*		
1765	.	.	1,305 *b*	580 *b*	725 *b*
1791	.	.	1,632 *b*	787 *b*	854 *b*
1801	.	.	1,798		
1811	.	.	1,991	950 *c*	1,041 *c*
1821	.	.	2,343		
1831	.	.	2,763	1,600 *d*	1,163 *d*
1841	.	.	2,836	1,650 *x*	1,200 *x*
1851	.	.	3,777	2,395 *e*	1,382 *e*
1861	.	.	3,721	2,316 *e*	1,405 *e*
1871	.	.	4,041	2,903	1,138
1881	.	.	4,861	3,345	1,516
1891	.	.	4,712	3,104	1,608
1901	.	.	5,144	3,088	2,056
1911	.	.	5,465	3,417	2,048
1921	.	.	5,491	3,541	1,950
1931	.	.	5,637	3,653	1,984
1941	.	.	—	—	—
1951	.	.	7,870	4,607	3,263
1961	.	.	11,329	5,403	5,926

SOURCES: *a—Webster*   *d—N.S.A.*
          b—O.S.A.   *e—Ord. Gazetteer*
          c—Aiton   *x*—Estimated

All other figures from *Census Reports*

COMPOSITION OF THE BURGH
POPULATION, 1961

Age last Birthday	MALES			FEMALES		
	Total	Single	Married	Total	Single	Married
Total .	2,630	1,243	1,308	2,773	1,202	1,325
Widowed	78			236		
Divorced	1			10		
0-4 .	238	238		197	197	
5-9 .	238	238		222	222	
10-14 .	289	289		273	273	
15-19 .	199	198	1	226	219	7
20-24 .	155	120	35	175	94	81
25-29 .	138	31	107	150	19	129
30-34 .	192	33	159	207	20	181
35-39 .	180	17	162	194	21	166
40-44 .	186	14	170	191	10	174
45-49 .	181	15	166	202	11	170
50-54 .	200	13	182	188	20	155
55-59 .	142	10	126	152	18	107
60-64 .	126	11	101	131	16	78
65-69 .	64	7	49	97	18	42
70-74 .	46	2	30	73	20	19
75-79 .	26	3	11	58	14	14
80-84 .	22	3	9	26	8	2
85-89 .	5	1		10	2	
90-94 .	3			1		
95 & over	0			0		

SOURCE: *Census* 1961: *County of Ayr*

FARM STATISTICS, 1867-1957

Year	Oats	Potatoes	Turnips	Other Crops	Total Crops	Total Grass & Hay	Total Crops and Grass	Rough Grazing	Cattle	Sheep	Pigs	Horses
1867 :	1251	81	141	25	1598	7476	9074	—	2115	6088	414	—
1877 :	1403	81	161	22	1667	7689	9356	—	2571	6062	473	187
1887 :	1281	63	110	11	1465	7924	9389	—	2745	4071	467	186
1897 :	1166	45	105	15	1331	8298	9539	1049	3008	2676	387	206
1907 :	1193	36	119	17	1365	8197	9562	1049	2998	2756	400	223
1917 :	1233	48	112	12	1405	7849	9254	1255	3347	3065	545	267
1927 :	836	32	110	40	1018	8353	9371	1959	3191	2991	331	182
1937 :	894	24	109	23	1050	7934	8984	2470	3573	4417	112	183
1947 :	1719	37	183	121	2060	6090	8150	2766	3903	2577	22	167
1957 :	988	14	133	89	1224	6710	7934	2781	4376	5550	269	32

SOURCE: Land use acreages and livestock numbers from annual 'June Returns' for Parish of Old Cumnock—Agricultural Census: Parish Summaries (Scottish Record Office)

PUBLIC EXPENDITURE, 1965-1966

I   CUMNOCK TOWN COUNCIL ESTIMATES

	Expenditure	*Income*	*Cost to Rates*
Water . .	£6,725	£925	£5,800
Lighting . .	4,360	300	4,060
Cleansing . .	10,050	400	9,650
Roads . .	3,050	—	3,050
Sewers . .	13,350	300	13,050
Cemeteries . .	1,175	—	1,175
Housing . .	112,650	92,850	19,800
Parks . .	6,400	800	5,600
Swimming Pool .	4,475	1,875	2,600
Cumnock Senior Club	1,350	—	1,350
Town Hall . .	4,000	1,810	2,190
Miscellaneous . .	6,235	770	5,465
(including town development, public health, administration, burgh court)			
Total . .	£173,820	£100,030	£73,790

II   AYR COUNTY COUNCIL ESTIMATES

Apportionment to Cumnock Burgh

	Cost to Rates
Services provided within Burgh by County Council:	
Education	£116,204
Main Roads	6,640
Health	9,143
Welfare	2,577
Children	3,072
Police	7,726
Fire Service	3,878
Miscellaneous	6,601
(including town planning, courts, weights and measures, valuation, etc.)	
Total	£155,841

III ASSESSMENT OF RATES FOR 1965-1966

by Cumnock Town Council

Town Council's estimated expenditure . .	£173,820
Deduct estimated income . . .	100,030
Estimated deficit	73,790
Deduct surplus from 1964-1965 . .	3,600
Required for 1965-1966 . . .	70,190
County Council Requisition to be added . .	155,841
Total sum required for 1965-1966 . .	236,031
Government Grants to the Town Council . .	136,130
Amount required to be raised by assessment. .	89,901
Rateable value of properties in burgh . .	£92,853

Assessment of 20/10 per £, being a consolidated rate
of 19/4 plus 1/6 domestic water rate.

Sources and Notes

The history of Cumnock is dealt with in the following works, each containing original material, but usually also borrowing much from its predecessors. These works are later referred to by the short titles indicated:

O.S.A. – *The Statistical Account of Scotland*, ed. Sir John Sinclair, Vol. VI (1793), pp. 407-416, 'The Parish of Old Cumnock,' by Rev. Thomas Miller, D.D.

Chalmers – *Caledonia*, by George Chalmers, 3 vols. (1810-1824), also new edition in 8 vols. (1887-1902). Vol. VI of the new edition, pp. 521-522, deals with Old Cumnock parish.

N.S.A. – *The New Statistical Account of Scotland*, Vol. V (1845), pp. 475-508, 'The Parish of Old Cumnock,' by Rev. Ninian Bannatyne (written 1837).

Paterson – *History of the County of Ayr*, by James Paterson, 2 vols. (1847-1852), also new edition in 5 vols. (1863-1866). The second book of this new edition, Vol. I, Part II, pp. 301-360, deals with Cumnock.

Warrick – *The History of Old Cumnock*, by Rev. John Warrick (1899).

Steven – *The Cumnocks, Old and New*, by Helen J. Steven (1899).

Ballantine – *Illustrated Guide to Cumnock*, published by J. P. Ballantine (1915).

3rd Stat. Acct. – *The Third Statistical Account of Scotland: Ayrshire*, by John Strawhorn and William Boyd (1951).

The present book supplements these with new material from the following sources:

T. C. Minutes – Minute Books of the Burgh of Cumnock (1866-   ); Town Clerk's Office, Cumnock.

Heritors' Minutes – Minutes of the Heritors of Cumnock (1803-1931); Scottish Record Office, Edinburgh.

Parish Minutes – Minutes of the Parochial Board (1845-1895) and of the Parish Council of Old Cumnock (1895-1931); District Council Office, Cumnock.

Kirk Session Records – Old Cumnock Parish Church Minute Books
(1704-1815) and Cash Books (1746-1799); Scottish Record Office,
Edinburgh. Minute Books (1815-   ) and other documents; Kirk
Session, Cumnock.

S.B. Minutes – Minutes of the School Board for the Parish of Old
Cumnock (1873-1919); Library Basement, County Buildings, Ayr.

Log Books – Log Books (1872-   ) of Cumnock Public School, Ayr
Road Public School, Cumnock H. G. School, Cumnock Academy;
Rector, Cumnock Academy.

Dumfries House Papers – Access to the extensive MS. collection in
Dumfries House was granted by gracious permission of the Marquess
of Bute; relevant material was extracted and generous assistance
given by Miss Catherine Armet, archivist.

C. Chron. – *Cumnock Chronicle* (1901-   ), Files in *Chronicle* Office,
Cumnock. Efforts to trace the files of the defunct *Cumnock News*
(Ardrossan) and *Cumnock Express* (Ayr) have been unsuccessful.

Ayrshire Collections – *Collections of the Ayrshire Archaeological and Natural
History Society*, 7 vols. (1950-   ).

Scottish gazetteers containing short articles on Cumnock supply some
items of contemporary interest not available elsewhere:

Gazetteer of Scotland (Dundee 1803).
Topographical Dictionary of Scotland, by N. Carlisle, 2 vols. (1813).
Gazetteer of Scotland, by Robert Chambers (1832).
Topographical Gazetteer of Scotland, by A. Fullerton, 2 vols. (1845).
Topographical Dictionary of Scotland, by Samuel Lewis (1846).
Abridged Statistical History of Scotland, by J. H. Dawson (1853).
Ordnance Gazetteer of Scotland, by F. H. Groome, 6 vols. (1882-1885)
also later editions in 1, 3 and 6 vols.

Information from all these sources, and from other specialised works
as detailed later, was used as indicated in the subsequent notes on
individual chapters:

CHAPTER 1—THE BACKGROUND

EARLY TIMES

Information from John Smith, *Prehistoric Man in Ayrshire* (1895) is
supplemented by material from Mr. T. A. Hendry. For finds at
Boreland, N.S.A., V, 482; Steven, 102; *Proceedings of the Society of
Antiquaries of Scotland* (1892, 1921, 1939). The Roman road is discussed
in *Transactions of the Dumfries and Galloway Natural History and Antiquarian
Society*, XXXVII (1960), and *Ayrshire Collections*, VI (1961) superseding

Warrick, 17-19. *A Corner of Old Strathclyde* (1952), by Hugh Lorimer, offers an original study of the Dark Ages in the Cumnock area. Mr. Lorimer, a Fellow of the Society of Antiquaries of Scotland, through a study of place-names, claimed for this part of Ayrshire the location of the ancient kingdom of Manau, whose situation has long been a matter of controversy among students of Welsh bardic poetry. The career of Conval is examined by Warrick, 71-80.

THE MIDDLE AGES

William Dillon, formerly of Cumnock, has written 'The Origins of Feudal Ayrshire' in *Ayrshire Collections*, III (1955) and *Catholic Ayrshire* (Catholic Truth Society pamphlet, 1958). Also for various medieval topics—Cumnock Castle : Paterson, 311; Warrick, 38. Boreland Castle: N.S.A., V, 482; Paterson, 308; Warrick, 23. Mote Hill: O.S.A., IV, 415 n; Warrick, 44; Steven, 8, 9; P.S.A.S. (1892). The Dunbars: Paterson, 316 ff.; Warrick, Ch. II; Dumfries House Papers. Boreland lairds: Paterson, 313-316; Warrick, 23, 24; Steven, 102, 103. Leifnoreis: Paterson, 326-331; Warrick, 19-21. Terrinzean: O.S.A., IV, 415 n; Paterson, 307, 357-359; McGibbon and Ross (1892), 352-353; Warrick, 21-22; Steven, 100-103. Boreland Chapel: O.S.A., VI, 415 n; N.S.A., V, 479, 482; Paterson, 308; Steven, 73, 74, 102. Wallace, Bruce and their local connections: Warrick, Ch. III; G. W. S. Barrow, *Robert the Bruce* (1965).

CHAPTER 2—THE ORIGINS OF CUMNOCK

CHARTER OF JAMES IV

The charter is in *Registrum Magni Sigilli*, II, 722, no. 3376; and Warrick 51-53, gives a translation. Burghs in barony are considered in 'The Burghs of Ayrshire' by G. S. Pryde in *Ayrshire Collections*, IV (1958).

SIXTEENTH CENTURY—REFORMATION TROUBLES

William Robertson, *Ayrshire: Its History and Historic Families*, 2 vols. (1908), gives a popular account of the Reformation in Ayrshire. Some documentary details are added from Pitcairn's 'Ayrshire Criminal Trials' in William Robertson's *Historic Ayrshire*, 2 vols. (1891,1894); and from Warrick, 34, 48-50. Gordon Donaldson, *The Scottish Reformation* (1960) gives a modern interpretation, which incidentally clears up Warrick, 81-83, in his confusion about the position of the parish priest after 1560.

For early parish ministers see *Fasti Ecclesiae Scoticanae*, as well as Warrick, Ch. VI, and Steven, Ch. III. For the school in Cumnock see Paterson, 339; J. J. Fowler, 'The Presbytery of Ayr—Its Schools and Schoolmasters, 1642-1746' in *Ayrshire Collections*, VI (1961); and William Boyd, *Education in Ayrshire Through Seven Centuries* (1961).

SEVENTEENTH CENTURY—COVENANTING TROUBLES

For the Crichton family, information is from Chalmers, V, 393; Paterson, 330 ff.; Warrick, 39-41; *Scots Peerage*; and Dumfries House Papers. For other local lairds see Paterson: viz. Glaisnock (338), Skerrington (352), Garrallan (335), Logan (343), Terrinzean (314), Schankston (351).

Details of local Covenanters are from Warrick, Chas. VI, VIII; Steven, Ch. VII; Ballantine, 45-54. See also *Cumnock Chronicle*, 14.10.60, 28.10.60, 25.11.60, 2.12.60, 1.1.61. For the Blue Tower see Steven, 11.

THE TOWN BEFORE 1750

A few details of early Cumnock are given in N.S.A., V, 480; and Warrick, 47, 50, 176.

From the Dumfries House Papers the following have been extracted— Documents (1733-1738) relating to the Countess of Dumfries and Col. Hon. William Dalrymple, Cause against Sir Thomas Wallace; Miscellaneous documents (1699-1738) relating to several lands in and around the town of Cumnock.

CHAPTER 3—CUMNOCK BEGINS TO GROW

EIGHTEENTH CENTURY LAIRDS

Information about the Earls of Dumfries comes from Paterson, 333-334; *Scots Peerage*; and Dumfries House Papers. The improvements made by the 5th Earl are described by Andrew Wight, *Present State of Husbandry in Scotland*, Vol. III, Part I (1784), 265-270; O.S.A., VI, 408, 409, 412, 414, 415; N.S.A., V, 477; Warrick, 256; Steven, Ch. XIV. Paterson deals with Garrallan (337), Logan (346-347), Glaisnock (341), Skerrington (356), Avisyard (312), Whitehill (359) and Boreland (314-315). See also John Strawhorn, *Ayrshire at the Time of Burns* (1959). J. D. Carrick, *The Laird of Logan: or Anecdotes and Tales Illustrative of the Wit and Humour of Scotland* (1854), gives a biography, from which a passage is quoted; see also N.S.A., V, 481; Paterson, 346; Warrick, 284-288, for references to Hugh Logan.

THE TOWN, 1750-1800

For economic developments see John Strawhorn's 'Industry and Commerce in eighteenth century Ayrshire' in *Ayrshire Collections*, IV (1958). This section is based largely on O.S.A., supplemented by Warrick, 224-225; 302-303, 321-323. For mineral workings, material was obtained from the Dumfries House Papers. It is sometimes stated that William Murdoch in 1798 returned to Cumnock, set up a foundry, and lit it with gas—the first instance of gas lighting. There is no real evidence for this unlikely story.

Three maps are useful—*General William Roy's Military Survey*, drawn about 1750 (MS maps in British Museum); *A. & M. Armstrong's Map of Ayrshire*, 1775 (reprinted by Ayrshire Archaeological Society, 1959); James McDermont & Sons, *Maps of the Turnpike Parish Roads in the District in Ayr*, 1852 (copies in Carnegie Library, Ayr).

Eighteenth century population figures must be accepted with caution—1755, Rev. Alexander Webster's Enumeration, quoted in O.S.A.; 1757, Rev. George Muir's enumeration, quoted in Warrick, 118, 119; 1765 and 1792, Rev. Thomas Miller's figures in O.S.A., the former presumably an estimate, the latter probably reasonably accurate.

EIGHTEENTH CENTURY SOCIAL LIFE

Information about the parish kirk from Kirk Session Records; Warrick Ch. IX; Steven, Ch. IV; and *Fasti*. For the Secession, O.S.A., VI, 413; Warrick, Ch. VII; Steven, Ch. VI; Robert Small, *History of the Congregations of the U.P. Church*, 2 vols. (1904); John Kirkwood, *The United Presbyterians in Ayrshire* (1900); Hugh M. Agnew, *U.F. Church West, Cumnock*, 1773-1923 (1923); List of Schoolmasters from Warrick, 267; corrected by *Ayrshire Collections*, VI, 116; Kirk Session Records; Dumfries House Papers. John French's life is told by Warrick, 288-290; see also *Cumnock Chronicle*, 11.8.61, 1.9.61. For Burns associates see Warrick, Ch. XI; and Strawhorn, *Ayrshire at the Time of Burns*.

CHAPTER 4—EARLY NINETEENTH CENTURY

Parish population figures from 1801, and burgh figures from 1871, are from the official *Census Reports*, decennially from 1801 (except 1941); other figures are from O.S.A. and N.S.A.

ECONOMIC DEVELOPMENTS

Cotton industry: W. Aiton, *General View of the Agriculture of the County of Ayr* (1811), esp. 717; N.S.A. V, 474, 475; Warrick, 251-258;

Cumnock Chronicle, 5.8.32; Margaret Swain, 'Ayrshire Needlework' in *Ayrshire Collections*, III (1955), and *The Flowerers* (1955). Snuff-boxes: Chambers (1832) and later Gazetteers; N.S.A., V, 485-487; Warrick, 240-251; *Cumnock Chronicle*, 2.5.02. George McCartney and engineering: N.S.A., V, 487; Warrick, 293-295, 356; Ballantine, 42-44; *C. Chronicle*, 7.2.02, 16.2.12, 18.3.27. James Taylor and the pottery: Dumfries House Papers; William McCarter, *Ayrshire* (1830,1832); N.S.A. V, 480, 481, 487; Warrick, 290-292, 356; Ballantine, 44. Coal: N.S.A., V, 477, 478, 491. The Dumfries House Papers (boxes 10, 19, 23) contain a mass of material on mineral workings, including details of James Taylor's activities. Road transport: William McCarter, *Ayrshire* (1830, 1832) and other directories; N.S.A., V, 488; Warrick, 321-323, 356; Steven, 13, 14; for Murdoch's bicycle, Warrick, 340-342; Kirkpatrick MacMillan's life is the subject of Gordon Irving's *The Devil on Wheels* (Dumfries 1946). Railways: *Ayrshire Collections*, IV (1958), 199-200; W. McIlwraith, *Glasgow and South Western Railway* (1880); *The Glasgow and South Western Railway*, 1850-1923 (Stephenson Society, 1950).

SOCIAL CHANGES

Smallpox and cholera; O.S.A., VI, 407; Warrick, 334; Parish Minutes, 26.1.49, 5.2.49, 19.2.49. Poverty and poor relief: Heritors' Minutes, 23.4.40, 2.1.45, 26.6.45, 8.1.46; Parish Minutes, 19.2.49, 24.11.49; N.S.A., V, 490, 491; Dawson (1853); J. E. Handley, *The Irish in Scotland* (1943), 201. Vagrants: Parish Minutes, 9.7.51; Steven, 75-78. Bequests, etc.: Heritors' Minutes, passim.; N.S.A., V, 490, 491; Warrick, 216-218. Electors: *Ayrshire at the Time of Burns*, 100-113; William McCarter, *Ayrshire* (1832). Political agitation: H. W. Meikle, *Scotland and the French Revolution* (1912); A. Murdoch, *Ochiltree* (1921), 160-164; Steven, 148, 183-187; Tom Johnston, *History of the Working Classes in Scotland* (4th edition 1946), 341; Warrick, 337-338; Alexander Wilson, 'John Taylor, the Ayrshire Chartist' in *Ayrshire Collections*, I (1950); L. C. Wright, *Scottish Chartism* (1953). Parish church: Kirk session records; Dawson (1853); Warrick, 127-134; Steven, 32. Seceders' Church: Warrick, 147-151; Steven, 44; Ballantine, 20; Small, Kirkwood and Agnew, op.cit. Free Church: Warrick, 131-135; Steven, 32-33, 35; Ballantine, 22. Congregational Church: Minute Books of Cumnock Congregational Church (1838-   ); Warrick, 152-154; Steven, 45, 46; Ballantine, 22-24. Roman Catholic Church: *St. John's Magazine* (1895); Ballantine, 24-26; J. E. Shaw, *Ayrshire* (1953), 96-112. Schools: Heritors' Minutes; N.S.A., V, 489, 490; Warrick, 228, 267-272; Ballantine, 32. Schoolmasters: *C. Chronicle*, for John McKinnel (16.2.06 quoted, 3.11.33); D. L. Scott (15.11.01); Moses Inglis (14.2.02, 16.2.06, 19.8.30); other adventure schools (15.11.01, 26.9.02, 24.4.14). Changes in life and manners: Warrick, Ch. XV quoted. Temperance: N.S.A., V, 491; Dawson (1853); Warrick, 314-316; *C. Chronicle*, 12.12.13. Athenaeum Library: A library was proposed for the new school (Heritors' Minutes, 27.2.04) but it is doubtful if it was built; N.S.A., V, 490, mentioned two libraries; Ord. Gazetteer gives 1792 as foundation date of the Athenaeum; an alternative date (1859) is given in *C. Chronicle*, 4.5.23. Bands: *C. Chronicle*, 21.8.03, 25.9.03, 28.2.08. Yeomanry: W. Steel Brownlie, *The Proud Trooper* (1964).

TOWN AND COUNTRY IN MID-CENTURY
N.S.A., V; Ordnance Survey Map, 6 inches to mile, Ayrshire Sheet XXXV (1860); supplemented by details from Warrick, Steven, Ballantine and *C. Chronicle*. In particular—Fairs and markets: O.S.A., VI, 414; Carlisle (1813) and later gazetteers; William McCarter, *Ayrshire* (1830,1832); N.S.A., V, 487, 491; Warrick, 304-308 quoted; Steven, 72-74; Ballantine, 38-39. Agriculture: N.S.A., V, 482; individual estates from Paterson—Glaisnock (341); Logan (346, 347); Garallan (337); Skerrington (356, 357); Avisyard (312, 313); Boreland (316). Marquesses of Bute: Paterson, 333-335; *Scots Peerage*; W. Robertson, *Ayrshire*, Vol. 2 (1908), 213-218; Dumfries House Papers; Burke's *Peerage*. *Ayrshire Directory* 1851-1852 is extensively quoted in *C. Chronicle*, 1.8.52 and subsequent issues.

CHAPTER 5—THE POLICE BURGH, 1866-1929

Local government developments are outlined by G. S. Pryde in 'The Burghs of Ayrshire,' *Ayrshire Collections*, IV (1958).

THE FORMATION OF THE BURGH
T.C. Minutes; with details from Warrick, 350, 351; Steven, 116-118; Ballantine, 11.

PROGRESS IN PUBLIC SERVICES
T. C. Minutes; with *C. Chronicle* references after 1901. Details of housing from decennial *Census Reports;* verses from *A Selection of the Poems of Alexander Barrowman* (n.d.); Warrick, Ch. XVI; Ballantine, 11-15.

THE COUNCIL AT WORK
T.C. Minutes; *C. Chronicle*. Biographical details of the first five provosts and other early councillors and officials are few, depending on stray references; but after 1901 all public figures are fully dealt with in *Cumnock Chronical* reports, often with photographs, at times of appointment, resignation and death.

CHAPTER 6—KEIR HARDIE'S CUMNOCK

Details about Hardie's life are mainly from the biographies by William Stewart (1921), G. D. H. Cole (Fabian Society pamphlet, 1941) and Emrys Hughes (1956). Reports of his speeches, letters to the editor and reminiscences by those who knew him appeared in the *Cumnock Chronicle*. For reminiscences see *C. Chronicle*, 1.10.15, 26.4.18, 11.7.24, 24.10.24, 20.11.36, 27.11.36, 4.12.36, 25.8.39, 17.8.56. Hardie is mentioned in the following local records: T.C. Minutes—Nov. 1886 election, 30.2.93, 10.9.00, 11.5.03, 12.2.12; S.B. Minutes—10.6.82, 19.10.82, 8.2.83, 7.6.83, 7.6.88; Auchinleck S.B. Minutes—26.3.85 till 20.10.87 passim.; Minute Book of Cumnock Congregational Church—1882 till 1885 ·passim. Certain points were illuminated through correspondence with Mr. Fred Reid, Oxford research student, who is writing a thesis on Hardie's political ideas.

THE AGE OF COAL
Information about mines was supplied by the N.C.B., Lugar, especially from their Catalogue of Abandoned Mine Plans. Details about social conditions from a variety of sources and the account of the strike is quoted from William Stewart's biography of Keir Hardie. Farm statistics come from the Agricultural Census, Parish Summaries (annually since 1866) in the Scottish Record Office, Edinburgh. Details of estates are given in *Scotland: Owners of Lands and Heritages*, 1872-3 (1874). References to other local trades appear in Warrick, Steven, Ballantine and *C. Chronicle*.

'THE GOOD OLD DAYS'
C. Chron. provides not only information about the period after 1901, but a store of facts about the 19th century from reminiscences, speeches at reunions, old folks' parties and obituaries. Series of articles on aspects of local history appeared in 1910 (Cumnock 50 Years Ago); 1916 (reminiscences by John Hodge); 1926-7 (James Neil on burgh development); 1930 (reprint of J. W. Crawford's articles in old

Cumnock News); 1932-3 (more by John Hodge); 1942 and after (articles by Hugh Lorimer); 1945 (articles on old beggars); 1959 (commemorating the 450th anniversary of the burgh in barony); 1961 (on Banks and Bankers); 1961 (J. M. Hill on Cumnock Shops and Shopkeepers). *C. Chron.*, 9.1.48, reprinted extracts from a *Cumnock Register and Almanac for* 1869, originally published by D. Ballantine. The Jubilee issues of the *Chronicle*, 9.11.51, 16.11.51, provide an invaluable survey of the period after 1901. Other specially useful issues deal with such topics as: Cumnock Burns Club (30.1.48); Lugar Boswell and early football teams (26.10.51); early buses (5.2.54); the Dumfries Arms (25.3.17, 7.4.33, 27.7.34, 26.8.38); precentors (2.6.33); the Post Office (12.2.04, 26.3.09, 1.12.11, 5.1.17, 14.9.17); the first car (27.9.40); John French (31.5.12); Annie Rankin (31.1.02, 19.3.15, 12.1.51).

EDUCATION, 1872-1929

Information derived almost entirely from S.B. Mins., Log Books and *C. Chron.*

THE CHURCHES, 1843-1929

Warrick, Steven, Ballantine and works mentioned in notes for Chapter 4; plus *C. Chron.* references after 1901. For the old church bell see *Ayrshire Collections*, I (1950); Warrick, 345-346; *C. Chron.*, 5.9.02.

CHAPTER 7—THE MODERN BURGH

For THE COUNCIL SINCE 1929, REBUILDING CUMNOCK, and THE NEW COMMUNITY: information from T.C. Minutes and *C. Chron.*

For THE CHURCHES AND THE COMMUNITY, THE EXPANSION OF EDUCATION, and ECONOMIC GROWTH, sources as in notes for Chapter 6, plus references in 3rd Stat. Acct.

For this chapter in particular, the author is indebted to many persons for supplying additional information not otherwise accessible.

In the preparation of the book for publication, certain contributions require special note: R. D. Hunter, the Town Clerk, for his enthusiastic co-operation; Tom Kirkwood for preparing the line diagrams;

the pupils of Cumnock Academy who helped with the index; and Ronald Bell for his skilful supervision of the production.

To all who supplied information or helped in the preparation of this history, councillors, officials and others, too numerous to mention individually, the author acknowledges his grateful indebtedness.

Index

Centenary Programme

Message from Provost Thomas Finn, M.A.

(Joint Chairman of Festival Committee).

This week's activities are a fine example of a well integrated community in action. Clubs and organisations from the district, as well as from the burgh, have enthusiastically co-operated to produce a nicely balanced programme of entertainment and interest to suit, surely, all tastes.

May I, on behalf of the people of Cumnock, offer sincere thanks to all who have contributed and are contributing to the joy and festivity of these centenary celebrations — with a special word of thanks to the Marquess of Bute and the Dowager Marchioness of Bute for their kindness in permitting the use of Dumfries House for the purposes of the Festival.

Our thanks are also due to the Town Clerk, Mr R. D. Hunter, who so willingly accepted the burden of directing and co-ordinating the whole programme.

It is the earnest wish of the Council that all citizens enter fully into the spirit of the occasion so that this week may be a worthy tribute to our historic past and, we hope, a herald of an even greater future.

THOMAS FINN (Provost).

Joint Chairman:

Ex-Provost
J. K. H. M'TURK, J.P.

Artistic Director:

R. D. HUNTER, M.B.E.

The Festival Officials.

Treasurer:
R. B. LORIMER.

Master of Works:
ROBERT FORRET.

Secretary:
DAVID GIBSON.

Production Manager:
KEIR M'CALL.

Festival Council.

Cumnock Town Council:
Bailie D. Lorimer.
Bailie John King.
Police-Judge John A. Weir, J.P.
Hon. Treasurer Thomas Guthrie.
Dean of Guild John Edgar, J.P., M.A.
Councillor James W. M'Hardy, M.A.
Councillor Donald Macrae.

Churches:
Rev. J. D. M'Clymont, B.D., Old
Cumnock Old (Religious Services
Convener).
Rev. G. S. Young, Crichton West.
Rev. M. Sullivan, B.A., Congregational.
Rev. Robt. Brown, B.Sc., St. Andrew's
United Free.
Rev. James Martin, Baptist.
George Gowans Congregational.
John Devine, B.Sc., St. John's R.C.

Cumnock Art Club:
William Cooper, D.A. (Art Exhibition
Convener).
John M. Turner.

Cumnock Dolphin A.S.C.
T. Lennox (Swimming Gala Convener).

Cumnock Carnival Committee:
Andrew M'Knight (Carnival Con-
vener).
William Mackay.
R. F. Faulds.
George Mackay.
Mrs A. M'Knight.

Cumnock Dramatic Club:
Ian Macdonald.
Kenneth R. Smith.

Cumnock Juniors F.C.:
William Twist (Football Convener).
James Shirkie.

Cumnock Horticultural Society:
John Hamilton.
M. B. Smith.

Cumnock Bowling Club:
S. K. M. Burns (Bowling Compe-
tition Convener).
William M'Cubbin.

Cumnock Merchants' Association:
William M'Donald.
Ronald G. Robertson.

Cumnock & District Camera Club:
Major William Porter, M.B.E. (Photo-
graphic Exhibition Convener).
William Dickie.
John Napier.
John Ronald.

" Cumnock Chronicle ":
D. M. Ballantine (Programme Editor)

Cumnock & District Round Table:
Dr. David S. Tucker (Field Day Con-
vener).
George S. Rillie.

Cumnock Townswomen's Guild:
Mrs Violet H. B. Connell (Joint Con-
vener Arts & Crafts Exhibition).
Mrs Agnes Murray (Joint Convener
Arts & Crafts Exhibition).
Mrs Elizabeth Cook.
Mrs Mary Clive.
Mrs Jane Trousdale.

Cumnock Angling Association:
James Wardrop (Angling Competition Convener).

Cumnock Picture House:
D. S. G. Ward (Old Folk's Film
Entertainment Convener).

John Baird Institute:
James Livingstone.

East Ayrshire Car Club:
Robert Smith (Car Rally Convener).

Area Youth Organiser:
Alex. M'Lachlan (Youth Sports Convener).

Kyle Youth Panel:
John Turner.

Hospitals' Auxiliary Committee:
Owen Finn (First Aid Convener).

National Coal Board:
A. H. Torrance.
H. F. Watson.
R. Blair.
W. A. J. Devine.

Scottish Gas Board:
George Hannah.
A. Blue.

South of Scotland Electricity Board:
J. E. Price.
M. M'Kenzie, Barony Gen. Station.

Messrs John Foster & Son, Ltd.:
J. R. Outram.

The British Bata Shoe Co. Ltd.:
A. Taylor.
M. O'Connor.

Cumnock Knitwear Co. Ltd.
D. Kelso.
Denis E. Riddell.

Messrs Stevensons' Dairy Farms:
Robert M. M. Clark.

Messrs Hollybush Knitwear Ltd.:
T. Murdoch.

James Finlay & Co. Ltd.:
R. Meikle.
Miss B. F. Paul.

Mrs J. W. M'Hardy.
Walter Linton, J.P.

EXHIBITIONS and ENTERTAINMENTS

Open Monday 6th - Friday 10th.

LESSER TOWN HALL,
2.30 - 9 p.m.

Exhibition of Water Colours and Drawings

by Contemporary Scottish Artists

(From the Collection of the Scottish Committee of the Arts Council).

Artistes include—ANNE REDPATH, ROBIN PHILIPSON, JOHN MAXWELL, JOHN HOUSTON, W. G. GILLIES, JOAN EARDLEY, R. HENDERSON BLYTH, ELIZABETH V. BLACKADDER and W. BARNS-GRAHAM.

*

COUNCIL CHAMBERS,
TOWN HALL.

Exhibition of Local Photographs, Paintings and Drawings.

Artists include:

CAMERA CLUB—William Dickie, Gilbert Ingham, John Napier, John Pearson, William Porter, John Ronald, George Smith, Archibald Stewart, John Stirling.

ART CLUB—William Cooper, James Kilpatrick, Robert Morrison, Joseph Robinson, John Turner, Duncan Ballantine.

Convener—Major WM. PORTER, M.B.E.

*

CUMNOCK ACADEMY.

"A Century of Cumnock."

Exhibition, staged by junior pupils, includes models of Cumnock a hundred years ago and to-day, and a reconstruction of a 'single-end' house of 1866.

Open to the public on the afternoons of Centenary Week; at other times by arrangement with the Rector.

PARISH CHURCH HALL,
2.30 - 9 p.m.

Industrial Exhibition.

Exhibits by — BRITISH BATA SHOE CO., LTD. :
CUMNOCK KNITWEAR CO. LTD. : JAS. FINLAY &
CO. LTD., Cotton Works, Catrine : Messrs JOHN FOSTER
& SONS, LTD. : HOLLYBUSH KNITWEAR CO. LTD. :
THE MINISTRY OF LABOUR : NATIONAL COAL
BOARD : SOUTH OF SCOTLAND ELECTRICITY
BOARD : SCOTTISH GAS BOARD (Western Group) :
Messrs STEVENSONS' DAIRY FARMS.

Convener—R. D. HUNTER.

*

CRICHTON WEST CHURCH HALL,
2.30 - 9 p.m.

Arts and Crafts Exhibition

Organised by Cumnock Townswomen's Guild.

Joint Conveners—Mrs V. CONNELL & Mrs. K. MURRAY.

*

JOHN BAIRD INSTITUTE.

Short Wave Radio Transmitting

to the World by Amateur Operator, Daniel M'Lean.

*

THE SHOWGROUND, WOODROAD PARK.

The Centuries Old " Cumnock Fair."

Lawrence's Amusements.

OPEN: Friday, 3rd June—6 p.m. - 11 p.m. Saturday,
4th—2 p.m. - Midnight. Monday, 6th—6 p.m. - 10
p.m. Friday, 10th—7 p.m. - 1 a.m. Saturday,
11th—3 p.m. - Midnight.

DAY BY DAY EVENTS.

SATURDAY, 4th JUNE.

IN THE SQUARE,
11 a.m. - Noon.

Popular Music Programme

by the SILVER BAND of the 279th (CITY OF GLASGOW & AYRSHIRE) REGIMENT.

*

BROOMFIELD SPORTS GROUND.
2 p.m. - 6 p.m.

" Field Day "

Organised by Cumnock & District Round Table.
Programme includes:

1—5-A-SIDE SOCCER TOURNAMENT.
2—7-A-SIDE RUGBY TOURNAMENT.
3—AMERICAN SOFT BALL.
4—GO-KARTS.
5—T.A. DRILL COMPETITION and MOCK ATTACK.
6—AYR MAJORETTES.
7—PRAM RACE and PROCESSION.
8—FOLK SONG GROUPS.
9—SILVER BAND.
10—CAKE & CANDY and SOFT GOODS STALLS.
11—NUMEROUS SIDE STALLS and EXHIBITIONS.
12—PONY and TRACTOR RIDES.

Fund-Raising Convener—Dr. DAVID S. TUCKER.

*

AT DUMFRIES HOUSE,
6 p.m.

The Marquess and Dowager Marchioness of Bute entertain guests, including members and officials of the Town Council and their wives, to cocktails.

SATURDAY, 4th JUNE (Continued).

ROYAL HOTEL,
8 p.m.

Civic Reception for Homecoming Visitors.

*

TOWN HALL,
7.45 - 11 p.m.

Dancing to the Merry Macs.

*

IN THE SQUARE,
8 to 11 p.m.

Open-Air Dancing to Bert Hall and his Band.

POP COMPETITION.

SUNDAY, 5th JUNE.

CUMNOCK OLD CHURCH,
10.30 a.m.

B.B.C. T.V. Live Transmission.

Morning Service

to mark the Centenary of the Burgh of Cumnock and the Tenth Centenary of the Parish.

Conducted by the Minister,
The Rev. J. DOUGLAS M'CLYMONT.

Lessons read by
MARQUESS OF BUTE.
Provost T. FINN.
Ex-Provost J. K. H. M'TURK.

Organist—PETER WHITE.

Presented for Television by
STANLEY PRITCHARD.

Rev. J. Douglas M'Clymont, B.D.

LUGAR WATER.
6 a.m. - 10 p.m.

Angling Competition

Staged by Cumnock & District Angling Club.
Convener—Mr J. WARDROP.

*

AT THE SWIMMING POOL,
3.30 - 5 p.m.

Concert by S.C.W.S. Band.

Popular Programme.

*

AT BARSHARE ROAD,
6 to 7.30 p.m.

Concert by S.C.W.S. Band.

Popular Programme.

*

CUMNOCK OLD CHURCH,
8.15 p.m.

"Songs of Praise"

B.B.C. T.V. Recording (for future transmission)

With Church Choirs from the Parish and Cumnock Academy Senior Choir, conducted by JOHN HARVEY and ROBERT T. DUNSMORE.

Organist—PETER WHITE.

Prayer and Blessing by The Rev. J. DOUGLAS M'CLYMONT.

Introduced by MURDOCH M'PHERSON.

Producer—The Rev. Dr. RONALD FALCONER.

" Ye gates lift up your heads on high " (Tune: St. George's, Edinburgh).
" The Lord's My Shepherd " (Tune: Orlington).
" Brightly beams our Father's mercy" (Tune: Lower Lights).
" Who would true valour see " (Tune: Monk's Gate).
" Our Lord Christ hath risen " (Tune: Kirn).
" The Love of God " (Tune: St. Clairsville).
" Thou art coming, O my Saviour " (Tune: Beverley).
" Glory now to Thee be given," from " Sleepers, Wake " from J. S. Bach (Cantata No. 140).
" Beneath the Cross of Jesus " (Tune: St. Christopher).
" I'm not ashamed to own my Lord " (Tune: Jackson).
" Now the day is over " (Tune: Lyndhurst).

TOWN HALL,
6.30 & 8.40 p.m.

The B.B.C. T.V.

White
Heather
Club
Show

Starring

James Urquhart.

ROBIN HALL and JIMMIE MACGREGOR
and
JIMMY SHAND AND HIS BAND

and featuring

MOIRA ANDERSON,

JAMES URQUHART,

DIXIE INGRAM,

HARRY CARMICHAEL,

BRIAN SIEVEWRIGHT,

JOHN MERRY,

ISOBEL JAMES,

and THE WHITE HEATHER DANCERS.

Produced by IAIN MACFADYEN.

John Merry.

*

ROYAL HOTEL,
10 p.m. to 2 a.m.

Night Club Supper and Floor Show
by Stars of the B.B.C. T.V. " White Heather Club."

Dancing
to the Music of the HARRY CARMICHAEL TRIO.

TUESDAY, 7th JUNE.

TOWN HALL,
7.30 p.m.

**The Graham Players
of London**

Present

"Fresh Fields"

A COMEDY by

IVOR NOVELLO.

Cast:

Victor Graham.

MISS SWAINE .... MARGARET DUNLOP.
LUDLOW .... COLIN BEAN.
LADY LILIAN BEDWORTHY ... SUZANNE JEFFERIES.
LADY MARY CRABBE .... ANNE LEE.
TIM CRABBE .... CHRISTOPHER ROBINS.
MRS. PIDGEON .... BERNADETTE HUGHSON.
UNA PIDGEON .... KATHERINE SCOTT.
TOM LARCOMB .... VICTOR GRAHAM.
LADY STRAWHOLME .... ANNE MILROY.

Suzanne Jefferies.

The play directed by SUZANNE
  JEFFERIES.

Setting by EDWARD ROBINS.

Stage Management—
  MARGARET DUNLOP.
  JANE JENNER.

SYNOPSIS OF SCENES — The
  action of the play takes place
  in the morning-room of a
  house in Belgravia.

ACT I—April.

ACT II—Scene 1—A month later.
    Scene 2—Ten days later.

ACT III—Late June.

IN DUMFRIES HOUSE,
7.30 p.m.

Recital

by the

Jean Harvey
Trio.

JEAN HARVEY (Violin)

MARIE DARE ('Cello)

JULIAN DAWSON
(Piano)

Jean Harvey.

PROGRAMME:

Trio in B flat .... Mozart
(Allegro : Larghetto : Allegretto).

Trio in D .... Beethoven
(Allegro vivace : Largo : Presto).

INTERVAL.

Rondo in D .... Beethoven

Fantasy Pieces .... Schubert
(Romance : Humoresque : Duet : Finale).

(Organised by " Cumnock Music Club " — Promoter:
R. D. HUNTER).

WEDNESDAY, 8th JUNE.

TOWN HALL,
7.30 p.m.

THE GRAHAM PLAYERS OF LONDON
Present IVOR NOVELLO'S COMEDY,

" Fresh Fields."

For details see Tuesday evening's programme.

*

CUMNOCK BOWLING GREEN,
5 p.m.

Bowling Competition

Organised by Cumnock Bowling Club.
Convener—Mr S. K. M. BURNS.

*

BROOMFIELD SPORTS GROUND,
7 p.m.

" Youth Athletics Meeting "

Organised by the Kyle Youth Panel.
COUNTY INTER-AREA FIELD & TRACK EVENTS.

*

DUMFRIES ARMS HOTEL,
10 p.m. to 2 a.m.

Night Club Supper and Floor Show

Featuring Jack Milroy from Ayr Gaiety Theatre.

Dancing

to PETER WHITE AND HIS BAND.

THURSDAY, 9th JUNE.

TOWN HALL,
7.30 p.m.

Piano & Violin Concerto
Programme.

B.B.C. Scottish Orchestra.

Leader—
TOM ROWLETTE.

Conductor—
GRAHAM TREACHER.

With
JEAN HARVEY
Pianist and Violinist.

Graham Treacher.

PROGRAMME:

The National Anthem.

1—" Lieutenant Kije " .... Prokofiev

2—Piano Concerto in A. Minor .... Greig
(Allegro Molto Moderato : Adagio : Allegro Moderato
Molto e Marcato).

INTERVAL.

3—" Nutcracker Suite " .... Tchaikovsky

4—Violin Concerto in E. Minor ...... Mendelssohn
(Allegro Molto Appassionato : Andante :
Allegretto Non Troppo).

AS THE FIRST HALF OF THIS CONCERT IS BEING BROADCAST
BY THE B.B.C., THE AUDIENCE MUST BE SEATED BY 7.25 P.M.

*

5 p.m.

Bowling Competition

Continues at Cumnock Green.

*

CUMNOCK PICTURE HOUSE,
7 p.m.

Film Entertainment for Old Folks.

Programmed by Cumnock Picture House, Ltd.
Managing Director—Mr D. S. G. WARD.

TOWNHEAD PARK,
7 p.m.

Football Match.

Organised by Cumnock Juniors F.C.
Convener—Mr W. TWIST.

*

DUMFRIES ARMS HOTEL,
10 p.m.

Civic Reception for Musicians of the Orchestra.

(The Public will be admitted by Ticket — Late Licence)

FRIDAY, 10th JUNE.

WOODROAD PARK,
6 p.m.

Pony Rides.

*

AT THE SWIMMING POOL,
7 p.m.

Swimming Gala.

Organised by Cumnock Dolphin Amateur Swimming Club.
SWIMMING : DIVING : NOVEL EVENTS.
Convener—Mr T. LENNOX.

*

THE SQUARE,
8 to 11 p.m.

Open-Air Dancing to the Music of The Merry Macs.

POP CONTEST FINALS.

TOWN HALL,
7.30 p.m.

CONCERT by

Black Dyke Mills Band

(By kind permission of the Directors, John Foster & Son. Ltd.)

with BILL M'CUE.

Conductor—
ROY NEWSOME,
F.R.C.O., A.R.C.M.

Compere—
PETER M'NAB.

Roy Newsome.

Programme:

1—MARCH: " Queensbury," .... Kaye.

2—OVERTURE: " Fingal's Cave " (The Hebrides)
Mendelssohn (arr. G. Thompson).

3—BILL M'CUE.
" Non Piu Andrai " (Figaro) .... Mozart.
" Isis and Osiris " (Magic Flute) .... Mozart.
(Accompanied by the Band).

4—PATROL: " Swing o' the Kilt," .... Ewing.

5—CORNET SOLO: " Cleopatra," .... Damare.
(Soloist—Jim Shepherd).

6—OVERTURE: " Le Roi d'Ys " (The King of Ys)
Lalo, arr. F. Wright.
(Testpiece, Yorkshire Championships, 1966).

INTERVAL.

7—SELECTION: " Mary Poppins," Sherman, arr. D. Wright.

Bill M'Cue.

8—SCOTTISH BALLAD:
" The Skye Boat Song,"
arr. W. Rimmer.

9—EUPHONIUM SOLO—
" Carnival of Venice "
arr. Mannings.
(Soloist—John Clough).

10—HARLEM NOCTURNE
Earle Hagen.

11—BILL M'CUE.
" The Holy City "
Stephen Adams.
" The Trumpeter."
(Accompanied by the Band).

12—FINALE: " Life Divine,"
Cyril Jenkins.

NATIONAL ANTHEM.

(Programme subject to slight alteration).

DUMFRIES ARMS HOTEL,
7.30 p.m.

" Eve of Rally Ball "

Organised by East Ayrshire Car Club.

Convener—Mr R. SMITH.

*

AT THE SWIMMING POOL,
10 till 11.45 p.m.

Night Bathing.

*

AT WOODROAD PARK,
11.30 p.m.

POPULAR MUSIC by

Black Dyke Mills Band

followed by a

" Fireworks Display "

about Midnight.

*

TOWN HALL,
12 Midnight till 4 a.m.

Dancing to The Merry Macs.

Organised by Cumnock Carnival Committee.

Convener—Mr ANDREW M'KNIGHT.

Late Buses after Dance.

SATURDAY, 11th JUNE.

THE SQUARE,
11 a.m. till noon.

Programme by Black Dyke Mills Band

*

1.15 - 4.00 p.m.

The Carnival Parade.

Convener—A. M'KNIGHT.

Programme:

1.15 p.m.—PARADE OF MASSED BANDS from Town Hall to Cumnock Academy. Bands taking part: Black Dyke Mills Band.
Coalburn Silver Band, Dalmellington Silver Band, Girvan British Legion Pipe Band, Killoch Pipe Band, Boys' Brigade Pipe Band.

1.30 p.m.—FANCY DRESS PARADE AND PAGEANT assembles at Cumnock Academy. Lorries at Academy. Judging 1.30.

1.30 p.m.—DISTRIBUTION of BAGS and LEMONADE to Children, who must queue up as directed by Stewards. Tickets must be surrendered.

2.00 p.m.—MARCH OFF. Route of Parade—Square, Glaisnock Street, Shankston Crescent, Car Road, Ayr Road, Glaisnock Street, Square, Lugar Street to Woodroad Park.

3.00 p.m.—At Swimming Pool—OPEN BABY SHOW. Age Limit 18 Months. Classes for under 6 months; 6-12 months; 12-18 months; Twins; and Best Baby. Prize for Baby born on Carnival Day. Prizes will be presented by Mrs Tom Finn.

3.00 p.m.—BAND MUSIC. Introductory remarks by Provost T. Finn.

3.00 p.m.—CROWNING OF QUEEN by Mrs A. M'Kechnie, Barshare (Carnival Queen 1948).
QUEEN ELECT—Miss Eleanor Harkness, 34 Boswell Crescent, Logan, Cumnock.
LADIES-IN-WAITING — Miss Teresa Martin, 10 Craigens Road, Netherthird, Cumnock, and Miss Helen Burns, 47 Craigens Road, Netherthird, Cumnock.

3.30 p.m.—HIGHLAND DANCING COMPETITION.

4.00 p.m.—TUG-O'-WAR.

4.15 p.m.—PRESENTATION OF PRIZES by QUEEN.

4.30 p.m.—SHEEP DOG DISPLAY.

*

TOWN HALL,
7.45 - 11 p.m.

Dancing to The Merry Macs.

THE SQUARE,
8 to 11 p.m.

Open-Air Dancing to Bert Hall and his Band.

*

THE SQUARE,
10 p.m.

Start of All-Night Rally.
Organised by East Ayrshire Car Club.
Convener—Mr R. SMITH.

*

AT THE SWIMMING POOL,
10 p.m. till Midnight.

Night Bathing.

*

IN DUMFRIES HOUSE.
6.30 p.m.

Distinguished Guests

will be received by Provost Thos. Finn and Mrs Finn and by the Marquess of Bute and the Dowager Marchioness of Bute.

Marquess of Bute.

*

7 p.m.

Champagne Buffet
in the Dining Room, Dumfries House.

DUMFRIES HOUSE,
8 pm.

Song Recital

by

Jacqueline Delman

Soprano,

Accompanied by
JULIAN DAWSON
at the Piano

in the Tapestry Room.

Jacqueline Delman.

PROGRAMME:

"Allelujah" (Exultate Jubilate) .... Mozart.
"Die Forelle"
"Ave Maria" .... Schubert.
"On Wings of Song"
"And'res Maienlied" .... Mendelssohn.
"Morgen"
"Schlechtes Wetter" .... R. Strauss.

INTERVAL.

ENGLISH SONGS:

1—"Young Love Lies Sleeping" .... Arthur Somervell.
2—"The Singer" .... Michael Head.
3—"O to be in England" .... Michael Head.
4—"Spring" .... Ivor Gurney.

SCOTTISH SONGS:

1—"Winter it is past."
2—"Tam Glen."
3—"Ca' the Yowes."
4—"O Whistle an' I'll come to ye."

POPULAR OPERATIC ARIAS.

FAVOURITE SONGS FROM OPERETTA
(Gilbert & Sullivan, J. Strauss and Franz Lehar).

(Organised by "Cumnock Music Club." Promoter—R. D. HUNTER).

The important musical items in the foregoing programme are being presented with the support of the Arts Council of Great Britain.